The Tragedy of King Richard II
Part One

An Acting Edition
with Notes and
A Short History of the Text

Michael Egan

Westshore Press
770 IH 35 North
Suite 117
New Braunfels
Texas 78130
USA

© Michael Egan 2017
drmichaelegan@yahoo.com

ISBN-13: 978-1523987771
ISBN-10: 1523987774

The Tragedy of King Richard II, Part One

Contents

Introduction 7

The Tragedy of King Richard II, Part One 8

Notes 158

A Short History of the Text 180

Introduction

The Tragedy of King Richard the Second, Part One, also known as *Woodstock* or *Thomas of Woodstock*, is an anonymous, untitled and incomplete historical drama of some 51 pages and 2989 lines.

The MS is missing a front cover, title and author, a list of *dramatis personae* and part of the final scene. There are no act or scene divisions nor, with one exception, scene locations. It is written in a faded chicken-scrawl with major and minor edits, corrections, deletions and interventions by several hands in a variety of inks.

The battered manuscript is owned by the British Library, London, fols. 161-185 in a hand-bound anthology of 349 pages catalogued as Egerton 1994. It appears to be a Jacobean copy of a popular Elizabethan touring play written ca. 1592.

Thirteen editions of uneven quality have appeared since the MS's discovery and original publication in 1870. The one in this volume is the first to employ digital technologies to accurately transcribe the text while examining it for clues concerning its composition, stage history and possible authorship.

At some point the MS's last page was removed, most likely because it depicted Richard II's 1387 deposition, the climax of the action. I have thus included an extended 'conjectural emendation' winding up the story, in the hopes that completion may lead to performance and thus acceptance of this unjustly neglected masterpiece.

For permissions, please contact drmichaelegan@yahoo.com

Michael Egan
February, 2017

The Tragedy of King Richard the Second, *Part One*

Dramatis Personae

KING RICHARD THE SECOND *Grandson of Edward III and son of Edward, the Black Prince*
QUEEN ANNE *Anne a' Beame (Anne of Bohemia) wife of Richard II*

THE GHOST OF KING EDWARD III *Richard II's grandfather*
THE GHOST OF EDWARD, THE BLACK PRINCE *Richard II's father*

THOMAS OF WOODSTOCK *Duke of Gloucester, Richard II's uncle and Lord Protector of England*
JOHN OF GAUNT *Duke of Lancaster, Richard II's uncle*
EDMUND OF LANGLEY *Duke of York, Richard II's uncle*

DUCHESS OF GLOUCESTER *Wife of Thomas of Woodstock*
DUCHESS OF IRELAND *Widow of Robert de Vere, Duke of Ireland*

EARL OF ARUNDEL *Lord Admiral of England*
EARL OF SURREY *Councilor to Richard II*
SIR THOMAS CHENEY *Steward to Thomas of Woodstock*
SIR PIERCE OF EXTON *Assistant to Thomas of Woodstock*

SIR ROBERT TRESILIAN *Lord Chief Justice of England*
NIMBLE *Assistant to Tresilian*

SIR WILLIAM LAPOOLE *Governor of the English fortress at Calais*
SIR HENRY GREEN
SIR THOMAS SCROOP
SIR EDWARD BAGOT
SIR WILLIAM BUSHY

A SPRUCE COURTIER
THE SPRUCE COURTIER'S HORSE

CROSBY *A law officer*
FLEMING *A law officer*
MASTER SIMON IGNORANCE *Bailiff of Dunstable*

COWTAIL *A rich grazier of Dunstable*
A BUTCHER
A FARMER
A SCHOOLMASTER
THE SCHOOLMASTER'S SERVANT
A MAN WHO WHISTLES TREASON

CYNTHIA *Truchman of the masque*

THE LORD MAYOR OF LONDON
THE SHRIEVE OF KENT
THE SHRIEVE OF NORTHUMBERLAND

FIRST MURDERER
SECOND MURDERER

A MAID-IN-WAITING
A GENTLEMAN MESSENGER
A GUARD

A Guard of Archers, Knights for the Masque, Soldiers, Officers, Courtiers and Citizens

Scene: ENGLAND, 1387

The Tragedy of King Richard II, Part One

Act I Scene I

[A noble house near London]

Alarum. Enter hastily at several doors the Dukes of Lancaster and York, the Earls of Arundel and Surrey, with napkins on their arms and knives in their hands, and Sir Thomas Cheney with others bearing torches and some with cloaks and rapiers

ALL
Lights, lights! Bring torches, knaves! 1

LANCASTER
Shut to the gates!
Let no man out until the house be search'd!

YORK
Call for our coaches, let's away, good brother!
Now by th' bless'd saints, I fear we are poison'd all! 5

ARUNDEL
Poison'd, my lord?

LANCASTER
Ay, ay, good Arundel, 'tis high time begone!
May heaven be bless'd for this prevention.

YORK
God for thy mercy! Would our cousin king
So cozen us, to poison us in our meat? 10

LANCASTER
Has no man here some helping antidote
For fear already we have ta'en some dram?
What thinkest thou, Cheney?
Thou first brought'st the tidings.
Are we not poison'd, thinkest thou? 15

The Tragedy of King Richard II, Part One

RICHARD II, PART ONE, I.1

CHENEY
Fear not, my lords,
That mischievous potion was as yet unserv'd.
It was a liquid bane dissolv'd in wine,
Which after supper should have been carous'd
To young King Richard's health.   20

LANCASTER
Good, i' faith! Are his uncles' deaths become
Health to King Richard? How came it out?
Sir Thomas Cheney, pray resolve this doubt.

CHENEY
A Carmelite friar, my lord, reveal'd the plot,
And should have acted it, but touch'd in conscience   25
He came to your good brother, the Lord Protector,
And so disclos'd it; who straight sent me to you.

YORK
The Lord protect him for it, ay, and our cousin king.
High heaven be judge, we wish all good to him!

LANCASTER
A heavy charge, good Woodstock, hast thou had,   30
To be Protector to so wild a prince,
So far degenerate from his noble father,
Whom the trembling French the Black Prince call'd,
Not of a swart and melancholy brow,
For sweet and lovely was his countenance,   35
But that he made so many funeral days
In mournful France. The warlike battles won
At Crécy Field, Poitiers, Artoise and Maine
Made all France groan under his conquering arm.
But heaven forestall'd his diadem on earth   40
To place him with a royal crown in heaven.
Rise may his dust to glory! Ere he'd 'a done
A deed so base unto his enemy,

RICHARD II, PART ONE, I.1

Much less unto the brothers of his father,
He'd first have lost his royal blood in drops,   45
Dissolv'd the strings of his humanity,
And lost that livelihood that was preserv'd
To make his unlike son a wanton king!

YORK
Forbear, good John of Gaunt. Believe me, brother,
We may do wrong unto our cousin king: 50
I fear his flattering minions more than him.

LANCASTER
By the bless'd Virgin, noble Edmund York,
I'm past all patience! Poison his subjects,
His royal uncles? Why, the proud Castilian,
Where John of Gaunt writes King and Sovereign,   55
Would not throw off their vile and servile yoke
By treachery so base. Patience, gracious Heaven!

ARUNDEL
A good invoke, right princely Lancaster!
Calm thy high spleen. Sir Thomas Cheney here
Can tell the circumstance, pray give him leave.   60

LANCASTER
Well, let him speak.

CHENEY
'Tis certainly made known, my reverend lords,
To your lov'd brother and the good Protector,
That not King Richard but his flatterers—
Sir Henry Green join'd with Sir Edward Bagot   65
And that sly machiavel, Tresilian,
Whom now the King elects for Lord Chief Justice—
Had all great hands in this conspiracy.

The Tragedy of King Richard II, Part One

RICHARD II, PART ONE, I.1

LANCASTER
By blessed Mary, I'll confound them all!

YORK
Your spleen confounds yourself.   70

LANCASTER
By kingly Edward's soul, my royal father,
I'll be reveng'd at full on all their lives!

YORK
Nay, if your rage break to such high extremes
You will prevent yourself, and lose revenge.

LANCASTER
Why, Edmund, can'st thou give a reason yet   75
Though we, so near in blood, his hapless uncles,
(His grandsire Edward's sons, his father's brothers!)
Should thus be made away? Why might it be
That Arundel and Surrey here should die?

SURREY
Some friend of theirs wanted my earldom sore.   80

ARUNDEL
Perhaps my office of the Admiralty!
If a better and more fortunate hand could govern it,
I would 'twere none of mine!
Yet this much can I say—and make my praise
No more than merit!—a wealthier prize   85
Did never yet take harbor in our roads
Than I to England brought! You all can tell!
Full three-score sail of tall and lusty ships,
And six great carracks, fraught with oil and wines,
I brought King Richard in abundance home!—   90
So much, that plenty hath so stal'd our palates
As that a tun of high-pric'd wines of France

The Tragedy of King Richard II, Part One

RICHARD II, PART ONE, I.I

Is hardly worth a mark of English money.
If service such as this done to my country
Merit my heart to bleed, let it bleed freely.   95

LANCASTER
We'll bleed together, warlike Arundel!
Cousin of Surrey, princely Edmund York,
Let's think on some revenge. If we must die,
Ten thousand souls shall keep us company!

YORK
Patience, good Lancaster. Tell me, kind Cheney,   100
How does thy master, our good brother Woodstock,
Plain Thomas?—for by th' rood, so all men call him,
For his plain dealing and his simple clothing.
'Let others jet in silk and gold,' says he,
'A coat of English frieze best pleaseth me!'   105
How thinks his unsophisticated plainness
Of these bitter compounds? Fears he no drug
Put in his broth? Shall his healths be secure?

CHENEY
Faith, my lord, his mind suits with his habit:
Homely and plain, both free from pride and envy,   110
And therein will admit distrust to none.

*Enter The Duke of Gloucester, Thomas of Woodstock,
in frieze, the Mace carried before him, the Lord
Mayor of London with Sir Pierce of Exton and others
with lights afore them*

And see, his Grace himself is come to greet you.
By your leave there, room for my Lord Protector's
Grace!

YORK AND LANCASTER
Health to your Grace!   115

The Tragedy of King Richard II, Part One

RICHARD II, PART ONE, I.i

WOODSTOCK
I salute your healths, good brothers. Pray pardon me,
I'll speak with you anon. Hie thee, good Exton!

Exit Sir Pierce of Exton

Good Lord Mayor, I do beseech ye, prosecute
With your best care a means for all our safeties.
Mischief hath often double practices: 120
Treachery wants not his second stratagem.
Who knows, but steel may hit though poison fail.
Alack the day, the night is made a veil
To shadow mischief! Set, I beseech thee,
Strong guard and careful to attend the city.   125
Our Lady help, we know not who are friends,
Our foes are grown so mighty. Pray, be careful!

LORD MAYOR
Your friends are great in London, good my lord.
I'll front all dangers, trust it on my word.

WOODSTOCK
Thanks from my heart. [*Exit Lord Mayor*] I swear   130
afore my God,
I know not which way to bestow myself,
The time's so busy and so dangerous too.
Why, how now, brothers? How fares good John o'
Gaunt?   135
Thou'rt vex'd, I know. Thou griev'st, kind Edmund
York.
Arundel and Surrey, noble kinsmen,
I know ye all are discontented much,
But be not so. Afore my God, I swear   140
King Richard loves you all, and credit me,
The princely gentleman is innocent
Of this black deed and base conspiracy.
Speak, speak, how is't with princely Lancaster?

15

RICHARD II, PART ONE, I.I

LANCASTER
Sick, Gloucester, sick! We all are weary, 145
And fain we would lie down to rest ourselves,
But that so many serpents lurk i' the grass
We dare not sleep.

WOODSTOCK
Enough, enough.
Good brother, I have found out the disease: 150
When the head aches, the body is not healthful.
King Richard's wounded with a wanton humor,
Lull'd and secur'd by flattering sycophants.
But 'tis not deadly yet, it may be cur'd.
Some vein let blood where the corruption lies, 155
And all shall heal again.

YORK
Then lose no time, lest it grow ulcerous!
The false Tresilian, Green and Bagot,
Run naught but poison, brother. Spill them all!

LANCASTER
They guide the nonage king, 'tis they protect him! 160
Ye wear the title of Protectorship,
But like an under-officer, as though
Yours were deriv'd from theirs. Faith, you're too plain!

WOODSTOCK
In my apparel, you'll say. 165

LANCASTER
Good faith, in all!
The commons murmur 'gainst the dissolute king:
Treason is whisper'd at each common table
As customary as their thanks to heaven.
Men need not gaze up to the sky to see 170

The Tragedy of King Richard II, Part One

RICHARD II, PART ONE, I.1

Whether the sun shine clear or no. 'Tis found
By the small light should beautify the ground.
Conceit you me? A blind man thus much sees.
He wants his eyes to whom we bend our knees.

ARUNDEL
You all are princes of the royal blood, 175
Yet like great oaks ye let the ivy grow
To eat your hearts out with his false embraces.
Ye understand, my lord?

WOODSTOCK
Ay, ay, good coz, as if ye plainly said,
'Destroy those flatterers and tell King Richard 180
He does abase himself to countenance them.'
Soft, soft!
Fruit that grows high is not securely pluck'd.
We must use ladders, and by steps ascend,
Till by degrees we reach the altitude. 185
You conceit me too? Pray, be smooth awhile.
Tomorrow is the solemn nuptial day
Betwixt the King and virtuous Anne a' Beame,
The Emperor's daughter, a right gracious lady
That's come to England for King Richard's love. 190
Then, as you love his Grace, and hate his flatterers,
Discountenance not the day with the least frown.
Be ignorant of what ye know. Afore my God,
I have good hope this happy marriage, brothers,
Of this so noble and religious princess, 195
Will mildly calm his headstrong youth to see
And shun those stains that blurs his majesty.
If not, by good King Edward's bones, our royal father,
I will remove those hinderers of his health,
Though't cost my head. 200

YORK AND LANCASTER
On these conditions, brother, we agree!

The Tragedy of King Richard II, Part One

RICHARD II, PART ONE, I.I

ARUNDEL
And I.

SURREY
And I.

LANCASTER
To hide our hate is soundest policy.

YORK
And, brother Gloucester, since it is your pleasure 205
To have us smooth our sullen brows with smiles,
We'd have you suit your outside to your heart,
And like a courtier cast this country habit
For which the coarse and vulgar call your Grace
By the title of Plain Thomas. Yet we doubt not 210
Tomorrow we shall have good hope to see
Your high Protectorship in bravery.

WOODSTOCK
No, no, good York, this is as fair a sight,
My heart in this plain frieze sits true and right.
In this I'll serve my King as true and bold 215
As if my outside were all trapp'd in gold.

LANCASTER
By Mary, but you shall not, brother Woodstock!
What, the marriage-day to Richard and his Queen,
And will ye so disgrace the state and realm?
We'll have you brave, i'faith! 220

WOODSTOCK
Well, well,
For your sakes, brothers, and this solemn day,
For once I'll sumpter a gaudy wardrobe, but 'tis more
Than I have done, I vow, these twenty years!
Afore my God, the King could not have entreated me 225

To leave this habit, but your wills be done.
Let's hie to court, you all your wishes have.
One weary day Plain Thomas will be brave.

Exeunt omnes

Act I Scene II

[A house near London]

Enter Sir Henry Green, Sir Edward Bagot and Sir Robert Tresilian, in rage.

TRESILIAN
Nay, good Sir Henry, King Richard calls for you! 1

BAGOT
Prithee, sweet Green,
Visit his Highness and forsake these passions.

GREEN
'Sblood, I am vex'd, Tresilian, mad me not!
Thyself and I and all are now undone. 5
The lords at London are secur'd from harm,
The plot's reveal'd. Black curses seize the traitor!

BAGOT
Eternal torments whip that Carmelite!

TRESILIAN
A deeper hell than *Limbo Patrum* hold him,
The fainting villain! Confusion crush his soul! 10

BAGOT
Could the false slave recoil and swore their deaths?

The Tragedy of King Richard II, Part One

RICHARD II, PART ONE, I.II

GREEN
Mischief devour him! Had it but ta'en effect
On Lancaster and Edmund, Duke of York,
Those headstrong uncles to the gentle King,
The third brother, Plain Thomas, the Protector,   15
Had quickly been remov'd. But since 'tis thus,
Our safeties must be car'd for, and 'tis best
To keep us near the person of the King.
Had they been dead, we had rul'd the realm and him.

BAGOT
So shall we still, so long as Richard lives.   20
I know he cannot brook his stubborn uncles.
Come, think not on't. Cheer thee, Tresilian,
Here's better news for thee: we have so wrought
With kingly Richard that by his consent
You are already mounted on your footcloth   25
(Your scarlet or your purple, which ye please)
And shortly are to underprop the name—
Mark me, Tresilian—of Lord Chief Justice of
England!

TRESILIAN
[*Aside*] Hum, hum, hum, *legit* or *non legit*? Methinks   30
already I sit upon the bench with dreadful frowns,
frighting the lousy rascals! And when the jury once
cries 'Guilty!' could pronounce 'Lord have mercy
on thee!' with a brow as rough and stern as surly
Rhadamanth! Or when a fellow talks, cry 'Take him,   35
jailor, clap bolts of iron on his heels and hands!'
[*To Green and Bagot*] Chief Justice, my lords! Hum,
hum, hum, I will wear the office in his true ornament!

GREEN
But good your Honor, as 'twill shortly be,
You must observe and fashion to the time   40
The habit of your laws. The King is young,

The Tragedy of King Richard II, Part One

RICHARD II, PART ONE, I.II

Ay, and a little wanton. So perhaps are we!
Your laws must not be beadles, then, Tresilian,
To punish your benefactors. Look to that.

TRESILIAN
How, sir, to punish you, the minions to the King,   45
The jewels of his heart, his dearest loves?
'Zounds, I will screw and wind the stubborn law
To any fashion that shall like you best!
It shall be law what I shall say is law,
And what's most suitable to all your pleasures.   50

BAGOT
Thanks to your Lordship, which is yet to come!

GREEN
Farewell, Tresilian, still be near the court,
Anon King Richard shall confirm thy state.
We must attend his Grace to Westminster,
To the high nuptials of fair Anne a' Beame   55
That must be now his wife and England's queen.

Exeunt Green and Bagot

TRESILIAN
So, let them pass. Tresilian, now bethink thee.
Hum, Lord Chief Justice! Methinks already
I am swell'd more plump than erst I was.
Authority's a dish that feeds men fat,   60
An excellent delicate! Yet best be wise:
No state's secure—without some enemies!
The dukes will frown; why, I can look as grim
As John of Gaunt, and all that frown with him.
But yet until mine office be put on   65
By kingly Richard, I'll conceal myself,
Framing such subtle laws that Janus-like
May with a double face salute them both.

RICHARD II, PART ONE, I.II

I'll search my brain and turn the leaves of law:
Wit makes us great, greatness keeps fools in awe. 70
My man there, ho! Where's Nimble?

Enter Nimble

NIMBLE
As nimble as an eel, sir! Did ye call, sir?

TRESILIAN
Sir!—Look out some better phrase! Salute again.

NIMBLE
I know no other, sir, unless you'll be Frenchified and
let me lay the Monsieur to your charge, or Sweet   75
Signior.

TRESILIAN
Neither, 'tis higher yet! Nimble, thou buckram scribe,
think once again.

NIMBLE
[*Aside*] Neither Sir, nor Monsieur, nor Signior! What
should I call him? Trow, he's monstrously translated   80
suddenly! At first, when we were schoolfellows, then
I call'd him Sirrah, but since he became my master
I par'd away the Ah and serv'd him with the Sir.
What title he has got now, I know not, but I'll try
further. [*To Tresilian*] Has your Worship any   85
employment for me?

TRESILIAN
Thou gross uncaput, no! Thou speakest not yet!

NIMBLE
[*Aside*] My mouth was open, I'm sure!—If your
Honor would please to hear me—

RICHARD II, PART ONE, I.II

TRESILIAN
Ha, Honor, say'st thou? Ay, now thou hittest it,   90
Nimble!

NIMBLE
[*Aside*] I knew I should wind about ye till I had your
Honor.

TRESILIAN
Nimble, bend thy knee,
The Lord Chief Justice of England speaks to thee!   95

NIMBLE
The Lord be prais'd! We shall have a flourishing
commonwealth, sir.

TRESILIAN
Peace, let me speak to thee.

NIMBLE
Yes, anything, so your Honor pray not for me, I care
not. For now you're Lord Chief Justice, if ever ye cry   100
'Lord have mercy' upon me, I shall hang for't, sure!

TRESILIAN
No, those fearful words shall not be pronounc'd
'gainst thee, Nimble.

NIMBLE
Thank ye, my lord! Nay, and you'll stand between me
and the gallows, I'll be an arrant thief, sure. If I cannot   105
pick up my crumbs by the law quickly, I'll cast away
my buckram bags and be a highway lawyer now,
certainly.

TRESILIAN
Can'st thou remember, Nimble, how by degrees I

RICHARD II, PART ONE, I.II

rose, since first thou knew'st me? I was first a 110
schoolboy—

NIMBLE
Ay, saving your Honor's speech, your worshipful tail
was whipp'd for stealing my dinner out of my satchel.
You were ever so crafty in your childhood that I knew
your Worship would prove a good lawyer. 115

TRESILIAN
Interrupt me not! Those days thou knew'st, I say,
From whence I did become a plodding clerk,
From which I bounc'd, as thou dost now, in buckram,
To be a pleading lawyer. And there I stay'd,
Till by the King I was Chief Justice made. 120
Nimble, I read this discipline to thee
To stir thy mind up still to industry.

NIMBLE
Thank your good Lordship.

TRESILIAN
Go to thy mistress, Lady you now must call her,
Bid her remove her household up to London. 125
Tell her our fortunes, and with how much peril
We have attain'd this place of eminence.
Go and remove her.

NIMBLE
With a *Habeas Corpus* or *Surssararis*, I assure ye.
And so I leave your lordship, always hoping of your 130
wonted favor, that when I have pass'd the London.
Bridge of Affliction I may arrive with you at the
Westminster Hall of Promotion. And then I care not!

TRESILIAN
Thou shalt. Thou hast an executing look,

And I will put the ax into thy hand. 135
I rule the law, thou by the law shalt stand.

NIMBLE
I thank your Lordship, and a fig for the rope, then!

Exeunt

Act I Scene III

[London, the royal court]

Sound a sennet. Enter in great state King Richard and Queen Anne, crowned, with Green and Bagot. Enter also Woodstock, very brave, with the Duchesses of Gloucester and Ireland, and Lancaster, York, Arundel and Surrey

KING
Bagot and Green, next to the fair Queen Anne 1
Take your high places by King Richard's side,
And give fair welcome to our queen and bride!
Uncles of Woodstock, York, and Lancaster,
Make full our wishes, and salute our queen: 5
Give all your welcomes to fair Anne a' Beame.

LANCASTER
I hope, sweet prince, her Grace mistakes us not
To make our hearts the worser part of us;
Our tongues have, in our English eloquence,
Harsh though it is, pronounc'd her welcomes many 10
By oaths and loyal protestations,
To which we add a thousand infinites.
But in a word, fair queen, forever welcome!

The Tragedy of King Richard II, Part One

RICHARD II, PART ONE, I.III

WOODSTOCK
Let me prevent the rest, for mercy's sake!
If all their welcomes be as long as thine 15
This health will not go round this week, by th' Mass!
Sweet queen and cousin—now I'll call you so
In plain and honest phrase—welcome to England!
Think they speak all in me and you have seen
All England cry with joy, 'God bless the Queen!' 20
And so, afore my God, I know they wish it,
Only—I fear my duty be not misconstrued—

King moves to silence Woodstock

Nay, nay, King Richard, 'fore God I'll speak the truth!
Sweet Queen, you've found a young and wanton
choice, 25
A wild-head, yet a kingly gentleman,
A youth unsettled, yet he's princely bred,
Descended from the royal'st bloods in Europe,
The kingly stocks of England and of France.
Yet he's a harebrain, a very wag, i'faith! 30
But you must bear, madam, 'las, he's but a blossom.
But his maturity, I hope you'll find,
True English-bred, a loving king and kind.

KING
I thank ye for your double praise, good uncle.

WOODSTOCK
Ay, ay, good coz, I'm Plain Thomas. By th' rood, 35
I'll speak the truth.

QUEEN
My sovereign lord, and you true English peers,
Your all-accomplish'd honors have so tied
My senses by a magical restraint
In the sweet spells of these, your fair demeanors, 40

The Tragedy of King Richard II, Part One

RICHARD II, PART ONE, I.III

That I am bound and charm'd from what I was.
My native country I no more remember
But as a tale told in my infancy,
The greatest part forgot; and that which is,
Appears to England's fair Elysium   45
Like brambles to the cedars, coarse to fine,
Or like the wild grape to the fruitful vine.
And having left the earth where I was bred,
And English made, let me be Englished.
They best shall please me shall me English call.   50
My heart, great King, to you; my love to all!

KING
Gramercy, Nan, thou highly honor'st me.

YORK
And bless'd is England in this sweet accord.

WOODSTOCK
Afore my God, sweet Queen, our English ladies,
And all the women that this isle contains,   55
Shall sing in praise of this your memory,
And keep records of virtuous Anne a' Beame,
Whose discipline hath taught them womanhood:
What erst seemed well by custom, now looks rude.
Our women, till your coming, fairest cousin,   60
Did use like men to straddle when they ride,
But you have taught them now to sit aside.
Yet, by your leave, young practice often reels;
I have seen some of your scholars kick up both
their heels!   65

DUCHESS OF GLOUCESTER
What have you seen, my lord?

WOODSTOCK
Nay, nay, nothing, wife,

RICHARD II, PART ONE, I.III

I see little without spectacles, thou know'st.

KING
Trust him not, aunt, for now he's grown so brave,
He will be courting, ay, and kissing too! 70
Nay, uncle, now I'll do as much for you,
And lay your faults all open to the world.

WOODSTOCK
Ay, ay, do, do.

KING
I'm glad you're grown so careless. Now, by my
crown, 75
I swear, good uncles York and Lancaster,
When you this morning came to visit me,
I did not know him in this strange attire!
How comes this golden metamorphosis
From homespun huswifery? Speak, good uncle! 80
I never saw you hatch'd and gilded thus.

WOODSTOCK
I am no Stoic, my dear sovereign cousin,
To make my plainness seem canonical,
But to allow myself such ornaments
As might be fitting for your nuptial day 85
And coronation of your virtuous queen.
But were the eye of day once clos'd again,
Upon this back they never more should come.

KING
You have much grac'd the day. But, noble uncle,
I did observe what I have wonder'd at: 90
As we today rode on to Westminster,
Methought your horse, that's wont to tread the ground
And pace as if he kick'd it scornfully,

RICHARD II, PART ONE, I.III

Mount and curvet like strong Bucephalus, 95
Today he trod as slow and melancholy
As if his legs had fail'd to bear his load.

WOODSTOCK
And can ye blame the beast? Afore my God,
He was not wont to bear such loads. Indeed,
A hundred oaks upon these shoulders hang 100
To make me brave upon your wedding-day.
And more than that, to make my horse more tire,
Ten acres of good land are stitch'd up here.
You know, good coz, this was not wont to be.

KING
In your t'other hose, uncle? 105

GREEN
No, nor his frieze coat, neither!

WOODSTOCK
Ay, ay, mock on! My t'other hose, say ye?
There's honest, plain dealing in my t'other hose!
Should this fashion last, I must raise new rents,
Undo my poor tenants, turn away my servants, 110
And guard myself with lace; nay, sell more land
And lordships too, by th' rood! Hear me, King Richard:
If thus I jet in pride, I still shall lose,
But I'll build castles in my t'other hose. 115

QUEEN
The King but jests, my lord, and you grow angry.

WOODSTOCK
T'other hose! Did some here wear that fashion
They would not tax and pill the commons so!

The Tragedy of King Richard II, Part One

RICHARD II, PART ONE, I.III

YORK
'Sfoot, he forewarn'd us, and will break out himself.

LANCASTER
No matter, we'll back him, though it grows to blows.   120

WOODSTOCK
Scoff ye my plainness? I'll talk no riddles,
Plain Thomas will speak plainly! There's Bagot there,
And Green—

GREEN AND BAGOT
And what of them, my lord?

WOODSTOCK
Upstarts, come down, you have no places there!   125
Here's better men to grace King Richard's chair,
If't please'd him grace them so.

KING
Uncle, forbear.

WOODSTOCK
These cuts the columns that should prop thy house!
They tax the poor, and I am scandal'd for it   130
That, by my fault, those late oppressions rose
To set the commons in a mutiny
That London even itself was sack'd by them!
And who did all these rank commotions point at?
Even at these two, Bagot here, and Green,   135
With false Tresilian, whom your Grace, we hear,
Hath made Chief Justice! Well, well, be it so,
Mischief on mischief sure will shortly flow.
Pardon my speech, my lord—since now we're all so
brave   140
To grace Queen Anne, this day we'll spend in sport;
But in my t'other hose, I'll tickle them for't.

RICHARD II, PART ONE, I.III

GREEN
Come, come, ye dote, my lord.

LANCASTER
Dote, sir? Know ye to whom ye speak?

KING
No more, good uncles! [*Aside*] Come, sweet Green,   145
ha' done. I'll wring them all for this, by England's
crown! [*To Woodstock*] Why is our Lord Protector
so outrageous?

WOODSTOCK
Because thy subjects have such outrage shown them
By these, thy flatterers! Let the sun dry up   150
What th' unwholesome fog hath chok'd the ground
with.
Here's Arundel, thy ocean's Admiral,
Hath brought thee home a rich and wealthy prize,
Ta'en three-score sail of ships and six great carracks,   155
All richly laden. Let those goods be sold
To satisfy those borrowed sums of coin
Their pride hath forced from the needy commons.
To salve which inconvenience I beseech your Grace
You would vouchsafe to let me have the sale   160
And distribution of those goods.

KING
Our word, good uncle, is already pass'd,
Which cannot, with our honor, be recall'd.
Those wealthy prizes already are bestow'd
On these our friends.   165

ALL LORDS
On them, my lord?

RICHARD II, PART ONE, I.III

KING
Yes! Who storms at it?

WOODSTOCK
Shall cankers eat the fruit
That planting and good husbandry hath nourish'd?

GREEN AND BAGOT
Cankers? 170

YORK AND ARUNDEL
Ay, cankers! Caterpillars!

LANCASTER
Worse than consuming fires
That eats up all their furies falls upon!

KING
Once more, be still!
Who is't that dares encounter with our will? 175
We did bestow them! Hear me, kind uncles:
We shall ere long be past protectorship,
Then will we rule ourself. And even till then
We let ye know those gifts are given to them.
We did it, Woodstock! 180

WOODSTOCK
Ye have done ill, then.

KING
Ha, dare ye say so?

WOODSTOCK
Dare I? Afore my God, I'll speak, King Richard,
Were I assur'd this day my head should off!
I tell ye, sir, my allegiance stands excus'd 185
In justice of the cause. Ye have done ill!

RICHARD II, PART ONE, I.III

The sun of mercy never shine on me
But I speak truth! When warlike Arundel,
Beset at sea, fought for those wealthy prizes,
He did with fame advance the English cross, 190
Still crying, 'Courage, in King Richard's name!'
For thee he won them, and do thou enjoy them,
He'll fetch more honors home. But had he known
That kites should have enjoy'd the eagle's prize,
The fraught had swum unto thine enemies! 195

KING
So, sir. We'll soothe your vexed spleen, good uncle,
And mend what is amiss. To those slight gifts,
Not worth acceptance, thus much more we add:
Young Henry Green shall be Lord Chancellor,
Bagot, Lord Keeper of our Privy Seal, 200
Tresilian, learned in our kingdom's laws,
Shall be Chief Justice. By them and their directions
King Richard will uphold his government.

GREEN
Change no more words, my lord, ye do deject
Your kingly majesty to speak to such 205
Whose homespun judgments, like their frosty beards,
Would blast the blooming hopes of all your kingdom.
Were I as you, my lord—

QUEEN
Oh, gentle Green, throw no more fuel on,
But rather seek to mitigate this heat. 210
Be patient, kingly Richard, quench this ire.
Would I had tears of force to stint this fire!

KING
Beshrew the churls that makes my queen so sad,
But by my grandsire Edward's kingly bones,
My princely father's tomb, King Richard swears 215

The Tragedy of King Richard II, Part One

RICHARD II, PART ONE, I.III

We'll make them weep these wrongs in bloody tears!
Come, fair Queen Anne a' Beame. Bagot and Green,
Keep by King Richard's side. [*To the uncles*] But as for you,
We'll shortly make your stiff obedience bow! 220

Exeunt King, Queen and attendants

BAGOT
Remember this, my lords:
We keep the Seal. Our strength you all shall know.

Exit Bagot

GREEN
And we are Chancellor. We love you well, think so.

Exit Green

YORK
God for His mercy! Shall we brook these braves?
Disgrac'd and threaten'd thus by fawning knaves? 225

LANCASTER
Shall we, that were great Edward's princely sons,
Be thus outbrav'd by flattering sycophants?

WOODSTOCK
Afore my God and holy saints, I swear,
But that my tongue hath liberty to show
The inly passions boiling in my breast, 230
I think my overburden'd heart would break!
What then may we conjecture? What's the cause
Of this remiss and inconsiderate dealing
Urg'd by the King and his confederates,
But hate to virtue, and a mind corrupt 235
With all preposterous rude misgovernment?

RICHARD II, PART ONE, I.III

LANCASTER
These prizes ta'en by warlike Arundel
Before his face are given those flatterers!

SURREY
It is his custom to be prodigal
To any but to those do best deserve. 240

ARUNDEL
Because he knew you would bestow them well,
He gave it such as for their private gain
Neglect both honor and their country's good.

Wind horns within

LANCASTER
How now, what noise is this?

YORK
Some posts, it seems. Pray heaven the news be good! 245

WOODSTOCK
Amen, I pray for England's happiness.

Enter Cheney bearing posts

Speak, speak, what tidings, Cheney?

CHENEY
Of war, my lord, and civil dissension!
The men of Kent and Essex do rebel!

WOODSTOCK
I thought no less and always fear'd as much. 250

CHENEY
The shrieves in post have sent unto your Grace

RICHARD II, PART ONE, I.III

That order may be ta'en to stay the Commons
For fear rebellion rise in open arms.

WOODSTOCK
Now, headstrong Richard, shalt thou reap the fruit
Thy lewd, licentious willfulness hath sown!   255
I know not which way to bestow myself!

YORK
There is no standing on delay, my lords.
These hot eruptions must have some redress
Or else in time they'll grow incurable.

WOODSTOCK
The commons, they rebel, and the King, all careless,   260
Heaps wrong on wrong, to stir more mutiny.
Afore my God, I know not what to do!

LANCASTER
Take open arms! Join with the vexed commons,
And hale his minions from his wanton side!
Their heads cut off, the people's satisfied.   265

WOODSTOCK
Not so, not so! Alack the day, good brother,
We may not so affright the tender prince.
We'll bear us nobly, for the kingdom's safety
And the King's honor. Therefore, list to me.
You, brother Gaunt, and noble Arundel,   270
Shall undertake by threats or fair entreaty
To pacify the murmuring Commons' rage;
And whiles you there employ your service hours,
We presently will call a parliament
And have their deeds examin'd thoroughly,   275
Where, if by fair means we can win no favor,
Nor make King Richard leave their companies,
We'll thus resolve for our dear country's good

To right her wrongs, or for it spend our blood!

LANCASTER
About it, then: we for the Commons, you for the court. 280

WOODSTOCK
Ay, ay, good Lancaster, I pray be careful.
Come, brother York, we soon shall right all wrong
Or send some headless from the court ere long!

Exeunt omnes

Act II Scene I

[London, the royal court]

Trumpets sound. Enter King Richard, Green, Bagot, Bushy, Scroop, Tresilian, and others

KING
Thus shall King Richard suit his princely train 1
Despite his uncles' pride. Embrace us, gentlemen!
Sir Edward Bagot, Bushy, Green, and Scroop,
Your youths are fitting to our tender years,
And such shall beautify our princely throne. 5
Fear not my uncles nor their proudest strength,
For I will buckler ye against them all.

GREEN
Thanks, dearest lord. Let me have Richard's love,
And like a rock unmov'd my state shall stand,
Scorning the proudest peer that rules the land. 10

BUSHY
Your uncles seeks to overturn your state,

The Tragedy of King Richard II, Part One

RICHARD II, PART ONE, II.1

To awe ye like a child, that they alone
May at their pleasures thrust you from the throne.

SCROOP
As if the sun were forced to decline
Before his dated time of darkness comes.   15

BAGOT
Sweet King, set courage to authority,
And let them know the power of majesty!

GREEN
May not the lion roar because he's young?
What are your uncles but as elephants
That set their aged bodies to the oak?   20
You are the oak against whose stock they lean:
Fall from them once, and then destroy them ever!
Be thou no stay, King Richard, to their strength
But as a tyrant unto tyranny,
And so confound them all eternally!   25

TRESILIAN
Law must extend unto severity
When subjects dare to brave their sovereign!

KING
Tresilian, thou art Lord Chief Justice now,
Who should be learned in the laws but thee?
Resolve us therefore what thou think'st of them   30
That under title of Protectorship
Seek to subvert their king and sovereign?

TRESILIAN
As of the King's rebellious enemies,
As underminers of his sacred state,
Which in the greatest prince or mightiest peer   35
That is a subject to your Majesty

RICHARD II, PART ONE, II.I

Is nothing less than treason capital,
And he a traitor that endeavors it!

KING
Attaint them then, arrest them and condemn them!

GREEN
Hale them to th' block and cut off all their heads,   40
And then, King Richard, claim the government!

KING
See it be done, Tresilian, speedily.

TRESILIAN
That course is all too rash, my gracious lord.

ALL
Too rash? For what?

TRESILIAN
It must be done with greater policy,   45
For fear the people rise in mutiny.

KING
Ay, there's the fear—the commons love them well,
And all applaud the wily Lancaster,
The counterfeit, relenting Duke of York,
Together with our fretful uncle Woodstock,   50
With greater reverence than King Richard's self.
But time shall come when we shall yoke their necks
And make them bend to our obedience!

Bushy reads a book

How now, what read'st thou, Bushy?

The Tragedy of King Richard II, Part One

RICHARD II, PART ONE, II.1

BUSHY
The Moniment of English Chronicles, my lord, 55
Containing acts and memorable deeds
Of all your famous predecessor kings.

KING
What find'st thou of them?

BUSHY
Examples strange and wonderful, my lord!
The end of treason even in mighty persons, 60
For here 'tis said your royal grandfather,
Although but young and under government,
Took the Protector then, proud Mortimer,
And on a gallows fifty-foot in height
He hung him for his pride and treachery. 65

KING
Why should our proud Protector then presume,
And we not punish him, whose treason's viler far
Than ever was rebellious Mortimer's?
Prithee, read on: examples such as these
Will bring us to our kingly grandsire's spirit. 70
What's next?

BUSHY
The battle, full of dread and doubtful fear,
Was fought betwixt your father and the French.

KING
Read on, we'll hear it.

BUSHY
[*Reading*] 'Then the Black Prince, encouraging his 75
soldiers, being in number but 7,750, gave the onset to
the French king's puissant army, which were
number'd to 68,000, and in one hour got the victory,

slew 6,000 of the French soldiers, took prisoners of
dukes, earls, knights and gentlemen to the number   80
1,700 and of the common sort, 10,000; so the
prisoners that were taken were twice so many as the
Englishmen in number. Besides, the thrice-
renowned prince took with his own hand King John
of France and his son prisoners.' This was call'd the   85
Battle of Poitiers, and was fought on Monday, the
nineteenth of September, 1363, my lord.

KING
A victory most strange and admirable!
Never was conquest got with such great odds!
Oh, princely Edward, had thy son such hap,   90
Such fortune and success to follow him,
His daring uncles and rebellious peers
Durst not control and govern as they do.
But these bright shining trophies shall awake me,
And, as we are his body's counterfeit,   95
So will we be the image of his mind,
And die but we'll attain his virtuous deeds!
What next ensues? Good Bushy, read the rest.

BUSHY
Here is set down, my princely sovereign,
The certain time and day when you were born.   100

KING
Our birthday, say'st thou? Is that noted there?

BUSHY
It is, my lord.

KING
Prithee, let me hear't,
For thereby hangs a secret mystery
Which yet our uncles strangely keeps from us.   105

RICHARD II, PART ONE, II.1

On, Bushy.

BUSHY
[*Reading*] 'Upon the third of April, 1365, was Lord Richard, son to the Black Prince, born at Bordeaux.'

KING
Stay, let me think awhile. Read it again.

BUSHY
'Upon the third of April, 1365, was Lord Richard, son to the Black Prince, born at Bordeaux.' 110

KING
Thirteen sixty-five! And what year then is this?

GREEN
'Tis now, my lord, 1387!

KING
[*Angrily*] By that account, the third of April next 115
Our age is number'd two-and-twenty years!
Oh, treacherous men that have deluded us,
We might have claim'd our right a twelve-month since!
Shut up thy book, good Bushy. Bagot, Green, 120
King Richard in his throne will now be seen.

A knock within. Bagot to the door

This day I'll claim my right, my kingdom's due.
Our uncles well shall know they but intrude,
For which we'll smite their base ingratitude.

BAGOT
Edmund of Langley, Duke of York, my lord, 125

RICHARD II, PART ONE, II.I

Sent from the Lord Protector and the peers,
Doth crave admittance to your royal presence.

KING
Our uncle Edmund? So. Were it not he,
We would not speak with him. But go, admit him.
Woodstock and Gaunt are stern and troublesome, 130
But York is gentle, mild and generous,
And therefore we admit his conference.

BAGOT
He comes, my lord.

Enter York, who kneels

KING
Methinks 'tis strange, my good and reverend uncle,
You and the rest should thus malign against us, 135
And every hour with rude and bitter taunts
Abuse King Richard and his harmless friends.
We had a father that once call'd ye brother,
A grandsire too that titled you his son,
But could they see how you have wrong'd King 140
Richard,
Their ghosts would haunt ye, and in dead of night
Fright all your quiet sleeps with horrid fears.
I pray, stand up, we honor reverend years
In meaner subjects. Good uncle, rise, and tell us 145
What further mischiefs are there now devis'd
To torture and afflict your sovereign with.

YORK
[*Rises*] My royal lord, even by my birth, I swear,
My father's tomb, and faith to heaven I owe,
Your uncles' thoughts are all most honorable; 150
And to that end, the good Protector sends me
To certify your sacred Majesty

RICHARD II, PART ONE, II.I

The peers of England now are all assembled
To hold a parliament at Westminster,
And humbly crave your Highness would be there   155
To sit in Council, touching such affairs
As shall concern your country's government.

KING
Have they so soon procur'd a parliament?
Without our knowledge, too? 'Tis somewhat strange!
Yet say, good uncle, we will meet them straight.   160

YORK
The news to all will be most wish'd and welcome.
I take my leave, and to your Grace I swear
As I am subject loyal, just and true,
We'll nothing do to hurt the realm nor you.

KING
We shall believe you, uncle. [*To Bagot*] Go, attend   165
him.

Exit York attended by Bagot

Yes, we will meet them, but with such intent
As shall dismiss their sudden parliament
Till we be pleas'd to summon and direct it.
Come, sirs, to Westminster, attend our state,   170
This day shall make you ever fortunate.
The third of April! Bushy, note the time:
Our age accomplish'd, crown and kingdom's mine!

Exeunt

Act II Scene II

[Westminster]

Flourish of trumpets. Enter Queen Anne, attended by the Duchesses of Gloucester and Ireland, Woodstock with petitions and the Mace, Lancaster, Arundel Surrey and Sir Thomas Cheney. The Duke of York meets them in haste.

WOODSTOCK
Now, brother York, what says King Richard, ha?   1

YORK
His Highness will be here immediately.

WOODSTOCK
Go, cousin Surrey, greet the parliament,
Tell them the King is coming. Give these petitions
To th' knights and burgesses o' the lower house,   5
Sent from each several shire of all the kingdom.
These copies I will keep and show his Highness.
Pray make haste.

SURREY
I will, my lord.

Exit Surrey

QUEEN
Pity King Richard's youth, most reverend uncles,   10
And in your high proceedings gently use him.
Think of his tender years; what's now amiss
His riper judgment shall make good and perfect
To you and to the kingdom's benefit.

RICHARD II, PART ONE, II.II

YORK
Alack, sweet Queen, you and our lord the King   15
Have little cause to fear our just proceedings.
We'll fall beneath his feet and bend our knees,
So he cast off those hateful flatterers
That daily ruinate his state and kingdom.

WOODSTOCK
Go in, sweet ladies, comfort one another.   20
This happy parliament shall make all even,
And plant sure peace betwixt the King and realm.

QUEEN
May heaven direct your wisdoms to provide
For England's honor and King Richard's good!

YORK
Believe no less, sweet queen. Attend her Highness.   25

*Exeunt Queen Anne and the Duchesses of Gloucester
and Ireland, attended*

ARUNDEL
The King is come, my lords.

WOODSTOCK
Stand from the door, then. Make way, Cheney.

*Sound a flourish. Enter King Richard with Bushy
bearing books and papers, Bagot, Green, Scroop
and others*

GREEN
Yonder's your uncles, my lord.

KING
Ay, with our plain Protector,

RICHARD II, PART ONE, II.II

Full of complaints, sweet Green, I'll wage my crown! 30

BAGOT
Give them fair words and smooth awhile:
The toils are pitch'd, and you may catch them quickly.

KING
Why, how now, uncle! What, disrob'd again
Of all your golden, rich habiliments?

WOODSTOCK
Ay, ay, good coz, I'm now in my t'other hose. 35
I'm now myself, Plain Thomas, and by th' rood
In these plain hose I'll do the realm more good
Than these that pill the poor to jet in gold.

KING
Nay, be not angry, uncle.

WOODSTOCK
Be you then pleas'd, good coz, to hear me speak, 40
And view thy subjects' sad petitions.
See here, King Richard, whilst thou livest at ease,
Lulling thyself in nice security,
Thy wronged kingdom's in a mutiny!
From every province are the people come 45
With open mouths, exclaiming on the wrongs
Thou and these upstarts have impos'd on them!
Shame is decipher'd on thy palace gates,
Confusion hangeth o'er thy wretched head,
Mischief is coming and in storms must fall, 50
Th' oppression of the poor to heaven doth call!

KING
Well, well, good uncle, these your bitter taunts
Against my friends and me will one day cease.
But what's the reason you have sent for us?

RICHARD II, PART ONE, II.II

LANCASTER
To have your Grace confirm this parliament   55
And set your hand to certain articles
Most needful for your state and kingdom's quiet.

KING
Where are those articles?

ARUNDEL
The states and burgesses o' th' parliament
Attend with duty to deliver them.   60

YORK
Please you ascend your throne, we'll call them in.

KING
We'll ask a question first, and then we'll see them,
For trust me, reverend uncles, we have sworn
We will not sit upon our royal throne
Until this question be resolv'd at full.   65
Reach me that paper, Bushy. Hear me, princes:

Bushy hands him a paper

We had a strange petition here deliver'd us.
A poor man's son, his father being deceas'd,
Gave him in charge unto a rich man's hands
To keep him and the little land he had   70
Till he attain'd to one-and-twenty years.
The poor revenue amounts but to three crowns,
And yet th' insatiate churl denies his right
And bars him of his fair inheritance.
Tell me, I pray: will not our English laws   75
Enforce this rich man to resign his due?

WOODSTOCK
There is no let to bar it, gracious sovereign.

RICHARD II, PART ONE, II.II

Afore my God, sweet prince, it joys my soul
To see your Grace in person thus to judge his cause.

YORK
Such deeds as this will make King Richard shine   80
Above his famous predecessor kings
If thus he labor to establish right.

KING
The poor man then had wrong, you all confess?

WOODSTOCK
And shall have right, my liege, to quit his wrong.

KING
Then, Woodstock, give us right, for we are wrong'd!   85
Thou art the rich, and we the poor man's son.
The realms of England, France, and Ireland
Are those three crowns thou yearly keep'st from us.
Is't not a wrong when every mean man's son
May take his birthright at the time expir'd,   90
And we, the principal, being now attain'd
Almost to two-and-twenty years of age,
Cannot be suffer'd to enjoy our own,
Nor peaceably possess our father's right?

WOODSTOCK
Was this the trick, sweet prince? Alack the day,   95
You need not thus have doubled with your friends.
The right I hold, even with my heart I render,
And wish your Grace had claim'd it long ago—
Thoud'st rid mine age of mickle care and woe.
And yet I think I have not wrong'd your birthright,   100
For if the times were search'd I guess your Grace
Is not so full of years till April next.
But be it as it will. Lo, here, King Richard,
I thus yield up my sad Protectorship.

RICHARD II, PART ONE, II.II

Gives up the Mace

A heavy burden hast thou ta'en from me. 105
Long may'st thou live in peace and keep thine own,
That truth and justice may attend thy throne.

KING
Then in the name of heaven we thus ascend it,
And here we claim our fair inheritance
Of fruitful England, France, and Ireland, 110
Superior Lord of Scotland, and the rights
Belonging to our great dominions!
Here, uncles, take the crown from Richard's hand
And once more place it on our kingly head:
This day we will be new enthronised. 115

WOODSTOCK
With all our hearts, my lord. Trumpets, be ready!

Flourish of trumpets. Woodstock crowns Richard

ALL
Long live King Richard, of that name the second,
The sovereign lord of England's ancient rights!

KING
We thank ye all. [*Sits*] So, now we feel ourself! 120
Our body could not fill this chair till now,
'Twas scanted to us by Protectorship.
But now we let ye know King Richard rules
And will elect and choose, place and displace,
Such officers as we ourself shall like of. 125
And first, my lords, because your age is such
As pity 'twere ye should be further press'd
With weighty business of the common weal,
We here dismiss ye from the Council table
And will that you remain not in our court. 130

RICHARD II, PART ONE, II.II

Deliver up your staves; and hear ye, Arundel,
We do discharge ye of the Admiralty.
Scroop, take his office and his place in Council.

SCROOP
I thank your Highness.

YORK
Here, take my staff, good cousin.   135
York thus leaves thee.
Thou lean'st on staves that will at length deceive thee.

LANCASTER
There lie the burden of old Lancaster,
And may he perish that succeeds my place!

KING
So, sir, we will observe your humor.   140
Sir Henry Green, succeed our uncle York,
And Bushy, take the staff of Lancaster.

BUSHY
I thank your Grace. His curses frights not me,
I'll keep it to defend your Majesty.

WOODSTOCK
What transformation do mine eyes behold,   145
As if the world were topsy-turvy turn'd!
Hear me, King Richard!

KING
Plain Thomas, I'll not hear ye.

GREEN
Ye do not well to move his Majesty.

RICHARD II, PART ONE, II.II

WOODSTOCK
Hence, flatterer, or by my soul I'll kill thee! 150
Shall England, that so long was governed
By grave experience of white-headed age,
Be subject now to rash, unskillful boys?
Then force the sun run backward to the east,
Lay Atlas' burden on a pigmy's back, 155
Appoint the sea his times to ebb and flow—
And that as easily may be done as this!

KING
Give up your Council staff, we'll hear no more.

WOODSTOCK
My staff, King Richard? See, coz, here it is.
Full ten years' space within a prince's hand, 160
A soldier and a faithful Councilor,
This staff hath always been discreetly kept;
Nor shall the world report an upstart groom
Did glory in the honors Woodstock lost.
And therefore, Richard, thus I sever it! 165
There, let him take it, shiver'd, crack'd and broke,
As will the state of England be ere long
By thus rejecting true nobility!
Farewell, King Richard. I'll to Plashy, brothers,
If ye ride through Essex, call and see me. 170
If once the pillars and supporters quail,
How can the strongest castle choose but fail?

LORDS
And so will he ere long. Come, come, let's leave
them.

BUSHY
Ay, ay, your places are supplied sufficiently! 175

Exeunt the Lords

RICHARD II, PART ONE, II.II

SCROOP
Old doting graybeards! 'Fore God, my lord, had they
not been your uncles, I'd broke my Council staff
about their heads.

GREEN
We'll have an Act for this. It shall be henceforth
counted high treason for any fellow with a gray beard   180
to come within forty foot of the court gates!

BAGOT
Ay, or a great-bellied doublet! We'll alter the
kingdom presently.

GREEN
Pox on't, we'll not have a beard amongst us! We'll
shave the country and the city too, shall we not,   185
Richard?

KING
Do what ye will, we'll shield and buckler ye!
We'll have a guard of archers to attend us,
And they shall daily wait on us and you.
Send proclamations straight in Richard's name   190
T'abridge the laws our late Protector made.
Let some be sent to seek Tresilian forth.

BAGOT
Seek him? Hang him! He lurks not far off, I warrant.
And this news come abroad once, ye shall have him
here presently.   195

KING
Would he were come! His counsel would direct you
well.

RICHARD II, PART ONE, II.II

GREEN
Troth, I think I shall trouble myself but with a few
counselors. What cheer shall we have to dinner,
King Richard?   200

KING
No matter what today, we'll mend it shortly.
The hall at Westminster shall be enlarg'd,
And only serve us for a dining room
Wherein I'll daily feast ten thousand men.

GREEN
An excellent device! The commons has murmur'd   205
against us a great while, and there's no such means
as meat to stop their mouths.

SCROOP
'Sfoot, make their gate wider! Let's first filch their
money and bid them to dinner afterwards!

GREEN
'Sblood, and I were not a Councilor, I could find in   210
my heart to dine at a tavern today. Sweet king, shall's
be merry?

SCROOP
We must have money to buy new suits, my lord. The
fashions that we wear are gross and stale. We'll go sit
in Council to devise some new.   215

ALL
A special purpose to be thought upon! It shall be the
first thing we'll do!

KING
Come, wantons, come. If Gloucester hear of this,
He'll say our Council guides us much amiss.

Dismiss the parliament our uncles call'd,   220
And tell the peers it is our present pleasure
That each man parts unto his several home.
When we are pleas'd, they shall have summons sent
And with King Richard hold a parliament.
Set forward.   225

GREEN
You of the Council, march before the King;
I will support his arm.

KING
Gramercy, Green.

Flourish. Exeunt omnes.

Act II Scene III

[The Queen's apartment, Westminster]

*Enter Queen Anne, the Duchess of Gloucester, the
Duchess of Ireland, and maids with shirts and bands
and other linen*

QUEEN
Tell me, dear aunt, has Richard so forgot   1
The types of honor and nobility
So to disgrace his good and virtuous uncles?

DUCHESS OF GLOUCESTER
Madam, 'tis true. No sooner had he claim'd
The full possession of his government,   5
But my dear husband and his noble brethren
Were all dismissed from the Council table,
Banish'd the court, and even before their faces
Their offices bestow'd on several grooms.

The Tragedy of King Richard II, Part One

RICHARD II, PART ONE, II.III

DUCHESS OF IRELAND
My husband, Ireland, that unloving lord,   10
God pardon his amiss, he now is dead.
King Richard was the cause he left my bed.

QUEEN
No more, good cousin. Could I work the means,
He should not so disgrace his dearest friends.
Alack the day! Though I am England's Queen,   15
I meet sad hours and wake when others sleep.
He meets content, but care with me must keep.
Distressed poverty o'erspreads the kingdom:
In Essex, Surrey, Kent and Middlesex
Are seventeen thousand poor and indigent   20
Which I have number'd; and, to help their wants,
My jewels and my plate are turn'd to coin
And shar'd amongst them. Oh, riotous Richard,
A heavy blame is thine for this distress,
That dost allow thy polling flatterers   25
To gild themselves with others' miseries!

DUCHESS OF GLOUCESTER
Wrong not yourself with sorrow, gentle Queen,
Unless that sorrow were a helping means
To cure the malady you sorrow for.

QUEEN
The sighs I vent are not mine own, dear aunt.   30
I do not sorrow in mine own behalf,
Nor now repent with peevish frowardness
And wish I ne'er had seen this English shore,
But think me happy in King Richard's love.
No, no, good aunt, this troubles not my soul: 35
'Tis England's subjects' sorrow I sustain.
I fear they grudge against their sovereign.

DUCHESS OF GLOUCESTER
Fear not that, madam, England's not mutinous;

RICHARD II, PART ONE, II.III

'Tis peopled all with subjects, not with outlaws.
Though Richard, much misled by flatterers, 40
Neglects and throws his scepter carelessly,
Yet none dares rob him of his kingly rule.

DUCHESS OF IRELAND
Besides, your virtuous charity, fair Queen,
So graciously hath won the commons' love,
As only you have power to stay their rigor. 45

QUEEN
The wealth I have shall be the poor's revenue
As sure as 'twere confirm'd by parliament.
This mine own industry, and sixty more
I daily keep at work, is all their own.
The coin I have, I send them. Would 'twere more! 50
To satisfy my fears, or pay those sums
My wanton lord hath forc'd from needy subjects,
I'd want myself. Go, let those trunks be fill'd
With those our labors to relieve the poor.
Let them be carefully distributed. 55
For those that now shall want, we'll work again,
And tell them ere two days they shall be furnish'd.

Enter Cheney

CHENEY
What, is the court removing? Whither goes that trunk?

MAID
'Tis the queen's charity, sir, of needful clothing
To be distributed amongst the poor. 60

CHENEY
[*Aside*] Why, there's one blessing yet, that England hath
A virtuous queen, although a wanton king.

RICHARD II, PART ONE, II.III

Good health, sweet princess! Believe me, madam,
You have quick utterance for your huswifery, 65
Your Grace affords good pennyworths, sure, ye sell
so fast!
Pray heaven your gettings quit your swift return.

QUEEN
Amen, for 'tis from heaven I look for recompense.

CHENEY
No doubt, fair Queen, the righteous powers will quit 70
you
For these religious deeds of charity.
But to my message: [*To Duchess of Gloucester*]
Madam, my lord the Duke
Entreats your Grace prepare with him to horse. 75
He will this night ride home to Plashy House.

DUCHESS OF GLOUCESTER
Madam, ye hear I'm sent for.

QUEEN
                Then begone:
Leave me alone in desolation.

DUCHESS OF IRELAND
[*To Duchess of Gloucester*] Adieu, good aunt, I'll 80
see ye shortly there:
King Richard's kindred are not welcome here.

QUEEN
Will ye all leave me, then? Oh, woe is me,
I now am crown'd a queen of misery.

DUCHESS OF GLOUCESTER
Where did'st thou leave my husband, Cheney? Speak. 85

RICHARD II, PART ONE, II.III

CHENEY
Accompanied with the Dukes of York and Lancaster
Who, as I guess, intends to ride with him,
For which he wish'd me haste your Grace's presence.

DUCHESS OF GLOUCESTER
Thou see'st the passions of the Queen are such
I may not too abruptly leave her Highness; 90
But tell my lord I'll see him presently.

QUEEN
Saw'st thou King Richard, Cheney? Prithee, tell me,
What revels keeps his flattering minions?

CHENEY
They sit in Council to devise strange fashions,
And suit themselves in wild and antic habits 95
Such as this kingdom never yet beheld:
French hose, Italian cloaks, and Spanish hats,
Polonian shoes with peaks a handful long,
Tied to their knees with chains of pearl and gold.
Their plumed tops fly waving in the air 100
A cubit high above their wanton heads.
Tresilian with King Richard likewise sits
Devising taxes and strange shifts for money
To build again the hall at Westminster
To feast and revel in; and when abroad they come, 105
Four hundred archers in a guard attends them.

QUEEN
Oh, certain ruin of this famous kingdom!
Fond Richard, thou build'st a hall to feast in
And starvest thy wretched subjects to erect it!
Woe to those men that thus incline thy soul 110
To these remorseless acts and deeds so foul!

A flourish within

RICHARD II, PART ONE, III.I

DUCHESS OF GLOUCESTER
The trumpets tell us that King Richard's coming.
I'll take my leave, fair Queen, but credit me,
Ere many days again I'll visit ye.

DUCHESS OF IRELAND
I'll home to Langley with my uncle York, 115
And there lament alone my wretched state.

Exeunt Duchesses

QUEEN
Bless'd heaven conduct ye both. Queen Anne alone
For Richard's follies still must sigh and groan.

Exit Queen attended

Act III Scene I

[London: The Court]

Sound a sennet. Enter King Richard, Bagot, Bushy, Green, Scroop, very richly attired in new fashions, a guard of archers after them; and Tresilian with Blank Charters whispering with the King.

KING
Come, my Tresilian. 1
Thus like an emperor shall King Richard reign,
And you so many kings attendant on him.
Our guard of archers, keep the doors, I charge ye,
Let no man enter to disturb our pleasures! 5
Thou told'st me, kind Tresilian, th'ad'st devis'd
Blank Charters to fill up our treasury,
Opening the chests of hoarding cormorants
That laugh to see their kingly sovereign lack.

RICHARD II, PART ONE, III.i

Let's know the means we may applaud thy wit. 10

TRESILIAN
[*Shows Blank Charters*] See here, my lord: only with
parchment, innocent sheepskins. Ye see here's no
fraud, no clause, no deceit in the writing.

ALL
Why, there's nothing writ!

TRESILIAN
There's the trick on't! 15
These Blank Charters shall be forthwith sent
To every shrieve through all the shires of England,
With charge to call before them presently
All landed men, freeholders, farmers, graziers,
Or any else that have ability. 20
Then in your Highness' name they shall be charg'd
To set their names and forthwith seal these Blanks.
That done, these shall return to court again,
But cartloads of money soon shall follow them.

SCROOP
Excellent, Tresilian! 25

BUSHY
Noble Lord Chief Justice!

BAGOT
Where should his Grace get such a Councilor!

GREEN
Not if his beard were off! Prithee, Tresilian, off with
it! 'Sfoot, thou see'st we have not a beard amongst us!
Thou send'st out barbers there to poll the whole 30
country; 'sfoot, let some shave thee!

The Tragedy of King Richard II, Part One

RICHARD II, PART ONE, III.i

BUSHY
'Twould become thee better, i'faith, and make thee
look more grim when thou sit'st in judgment.

TRESILIAN
I tell ye, gallants, I will not lose a hair for my
lordships' and King Richard's favor, nor for the   35
Pope's revenues!

A GUARD
By your leave there, give way to the Queen!

Enter the Queen

KING
Now, Anne a' Beame, how cheers my dearest Queen?
Is't holiday, my love? Believe me, lords,
'Tis strange to take her from her sempst'ry,   40
She and her maids are all for housewif'ry.
Shalt work no more, sweet Nan, now Richard's King,
And peer and people all shall stoop to him.
We'll have no more protecting uncles, trust me!
Prithee, look smooth and bid these nobles welcome.   45

QUEEN
Whom my lord favors must to me be welcome.

KING
These are our Councilors, I tell ye, lady,
And these shall better grace King Richard's court
Than all the doting heads that late controll'd us.
Thou see'st already we begin to alter   50
The vulgar fashions of our homespun kingdom.
I tell thee, Nan, the states of Christendom
Shall wonder at our English royalty!
We held a Council to devise these suits:
Sir Henry Green devis'd this fashion shoe,   55

The Tragedy of King Richard II, Part One

RICHARD II, PART ONE, III.I

Bushy this peak, Bagot and Scroop set forth
This kind coherence 'twixt the toe and knee
To have them chain'd together lovingly,
And we, as sovereign, did confirm them all.
Suit they not quaintly, Nan? Sweet queen, resolve me.   60

QUEEN
I see no fault that I dare call a fault.
But would your Grace consider with advice
What you have done unto your reverend uncles?
My fears provoke me to be bold, my lord:
They are your noble kinsmen, to revoke   65
Their sentence were—

KING
                  An act of folly, Nan!
Kings' words are laws: if we infringe our word,
We break our law. No more of them, sweet queen.

TRESILIAN
Madam, what's done was with advice enough.   70
The King is now at years, and hath shook off
The servile yoke of mean Protectorship.

BUSHY
His Highness can direct himself sufficient.
Why should his pleasures then be curb'd by any,
As if he did not understand his state?   75

KING
They tell thee true, sweet love. Come, ride with me
And see today my hall at Westminster,
Which we have builded now to feast our friends.

GREEN
Do, do, good madam. Prithee, sweet king, let's ride
somewhither and it be but to show ourselves. 'Sfoot,   80

RICHARD II, PART ONE, III.I

our devices here are like jewels kept in caskets, or
good faces in masks that grace not the owners because
they're obscur'd. If our fashions be not publish'd,
what glory's in the wearing?

KING
We'll ride through London only to be gaz'd at.   85
Fair Anne a' Beame, you shall along with us;
At Westminster shalt see my sumptuous hall,
My royal tables richly furnished,
Where every day I feast ten thousand men!
To furnish out which feast I daily spend   90
Thirty fat oxen and three hundred sheep,
With fish and fowl in numbers numberless.
Not all our chronicles shall point a king
To match our bounty, state, and royalty;
Or let all our successors yet to come   95
Strive to exceed me, and if they forbid it,
Let records say, only King Richard did it!

QUEEN
Oh, but my lord, 'twill tire your revenues
To keep this festival a year together!

KING
As many days as I write 'England's King,'   100
We will maintain that bounteous festival.
[*To Tresilian*] Send them abroad with trusty officers,
And Bagot, see a messenger be sent
To call our uncle Woodstock home to th' court.
Not that we love his meddling company,   105
But that the ragged commons loves his plainness,
And should grow mutinous about these Blanks,
We'll have him near us. Within his arrow's length
We stand secure: we can restrain his strength.
See it be done. Come, Anne, to our great hall,   110
Where Richard keeps his gorgeous festival.

RICHARD II, PART ONE, III.I

Trumpets sound. Exeunt. Manet Tresilian

TRESILIAN
Within there, ho!

Enter Crosby and Fleming

CROSBY
Your lordship's pleasure?

TRESILIAN
What, are those Blanks dispatch'd?

FLEMING
They're all truss'd up, my lord, in several packets. 115

TRESILIAN
Where's Nimble? Where's that varlet?

Enter Nimble in peaked shoes with knee-chains

NIMBLE
As nimble as a morris-dancer, now my bells are on!
How do ye like the rattling of my chains, my lord?

TRESILIAN
Oh, villain, thou wilt hang in chains for this!
Art thou crept into the court fashion, knave? 120

NIMBLE
Alas, my lord, ye know I have follow'd your lordship
without e'er a rag since ye ran away from the court
once; and I pray, let me follow the fashion a little, to
show myself a courtier.

TRESILIAN
Go, spread those several Blanks throughout the 125
kingdom,

RICHARD II, PART ONE, III.I

And here's commission with the Council's hands
With charge to every shrieve and officer
T'assist and aid you. And when they're seal'd and
  sign'd, 130
See ye note well such men's ability
As set their hands to them. Inquire what rents,
What lands, or what revenues they spend by th' year,
And let me straight receive intelligence.
Besides, I'd have you use yourselves so cunningly 135
To mark who grudges or but speaks amiss
Of good King Richard, myself, or any of his new
  Councilors.
Attach them all for privy whisperers
And send them up. I have a trick in law 140
Shall make King Richard seize into his hands
The forfeiture of all their goods and lands.
Nimble, take thou these Blanks, and see
You take especial note of them.

NIMBLE
I'll take the ditty, sir, but you shall set a note to't, 145
for if any man shall speak but an ill word of anything
that's written here—

TRESILIAN
Why, ass, there's nothing.

NIMBLE
And would ye have them speak ill of nothing? That's
strange! But I mean, my lord, if they should but give 150
this paper an ill word, as to say, 'I will tear this
paper,' or worse, 'I will rend this paper,' or fouler
words than that, as to say, 'I will bumfiddle your
paper!' If there be any such, I have a black book for
them, my lord, I warrant ye. 155

RICHARD II, PART ONE, III.i

TRESILIAN
Be it your greatest care to be severe.
Crosby and Fleming, pray be diligent.

CROSBY
We shall, my lord.

NIMBLE
But how if we meet with some ignoramus fellows,
my lord, that cannot write their minds? What shall   160
they do?

TRESILIAN
If they but set to their marks, 'tis good.

NIMBLE
We shall meddle with no women in the Blanks,
shall we?

TRESILIAN
Rich widows, none else; for a widow is as much as   165
man and wife.

NIMBLE
Then a widow's a hermaphrodite, both cut and
long-tail! And if she cannot write, she shall set her
mark to it.

TRESILIAN
What else, sir?   170

NIMBLE
But if she have a daughter, she shall set her mother's
mark to't?

TRESILIAN
Meddle with none but men and widows, sir, I charge

ye.

NIMBLE
Well, sir, I shall see a widow's mark, then. I ne'er saw   175
none yet!

TRESILIAN
You have your lessons perfect, now begone:
Be bold and swift in execution.

NIMBLE
Goodbye, my lord. We will domineer over the vulgar
like so many Saint Georges over the poor dragons.   180

Exit Tresilian

Come, sirs, we are like to have a flourishing
commonwealth, i' faith!

Exeunt

Act III Scene II

[Plashy House, Essex]

Enter Woodstock, Lancaster and York

WOODSTOCK
Come, my good brothers, here at Plashy House   1
I'll bid you welcome with as true a heart
As Richard with a false and mind corrupt
Disgrac'd our names and thrust us from his court.

LANCASTER
Beshrew him that repines, my lord, for me,   5
I liv'd with care at court, I now am free.

The Tragedy of King Richard II, Part One

RICHARD II, PART ONE, III.II

YORK
Come, come, let's find some other talk, I think not on't.
I ne'er slept soundly when I was amongst them,
So let them go. This house of Plashy, brother,   10
Stands in a sweet and pleasant air, i' faith.
'Tis near the Thames and circled round with trees
That in the summer serve for pleasant fans
To cool ye, and in winter strongly break
The stormy winds that else would nip ye too.   15

WOODSTOCK
And in faith, old York,
We have all need of some kind wintering:
We are beset, heaven shield, with many storms.
And yet these trees at length will prove to be
Like Richard and his riotous minions,   20
Their wanton heads so oft play with the winds
Throwing their leaves so prodigally down,
They'll leave me cold at last. And so will they
Make England wretched and, i'th'end, themselves.

LANCASTER
If Westminster Hall devour as it has begun,   25
'Twere better it were ruin'd lime and stone.

WOODSTOCK
Afore my God, I late was certified
That at one feast was serv'd ten thousand dishes!

YORK
He daily feasts, they say, ten thousand men,
And every man must have his dish at least.   30

WOODSTOCK
Thirty fat oxen and three hundred sheep
Serve but one day's expenses!

The Tragedy of King Richard II, Part One

RICHARD II, PART ONE, III.II

LANCASTER
A hundred scarcely can suffice his guard,
A camp of soldiers feeds not like those bowmen!

WOODSTOCK
But how will these expenses be maintain'd? 35

YORK
Oh, they say there are strange tricks come forth
To fetch in money. What they are, I know not.

WOODSTOCK
You've heard of the fantastic suits they wear?
Never was English king so habited.

LANCASTER
We could allow his clothing, brother Woodstock, 40
But we have four kings more are equal'd with him.
There's Bagot, Bushy, wanton Green, and Scroop,
In state and fashion without difference.

YORK
Indeed, they're more than kings, for they rule him.

WOODSTOCK
Come, come, our breaths reverberate the wind. 45
We talk like good divines, but cannot cure
The grossness of the sin. Or shall we speak
Like all-commanding, wise astronomers,
And flatly say, such a day shall be fair,
And yet it rains, whether he will or no? 50
So may we talk, but thus will Richard do.

Enter Cheney with Blank Charters

LANCASTER
How now, Cheney, what drives thee on so fast?

RICHARD II, PART ONE, III.II

CHENEY
If I durst, I would say, my lord,
Tresilian drives me on haste so ill!
I'm still the pursuivant of unhappy news: 55
Here's Blank Charters, my lord, I pray behold them,
Sent from King Richard and his Councilors.

WOODSTOCK
Thou mak'st me blank at very sight of them!
What are these?

LANCASTER
They appear in shape of obligations. 60

CHENEY
They are no less. The country's full of them.
Commissions are come down to every Shrieve
To force the richest subjects of the land
To set their hands and forthwith seal these Blanks
That shall confirm a due debt to the King, 65
And then the bond must afterwards be paid
As much or little as they please to 'point it.

LANCASTER
Oh, strange, unheard-of, vile taxation!

WOODSTOCK
Who is't can help my memory a little?
Has not this e'er been held a principle, 70
'There's nothing spoke or done that has not been' ?

YORK
It was a maxim ere I had a beard.

WOODSTOCK
'Tis now found false, an open heresy.
This is a thing was never spoke nor done!

RICHARD II, PART ONE, III.II

Blank Charters call ye them? If any age 75
Keep but a record of this policy—
I phrase it too, too well, flat villainy—
Let me be chronicl'd Apostata,
Rebellious to my God and country both!

LANCASTER
How do the people entertain these Blanks? 80

CHENEY
With much dislike, yet some for fear have sign'd
them. Others there be refuse and murmur strangely.

WOODSTOCK
Afore my God, I cannot blame them for it:
He might as well have sent defiance to them.
Oh, vulture England, wilt thou eat thine own? 85
Can they be rebels call'd, that now turn head?
I speak but what I fear, not what I wish!
This foul oppression will withdraw all duty,
And in the commons' hearts hot rancors breed
To make our country's bosom shortly bleed. 90

LANCASTER
What shall we do to seek for remedy?

YORK
Let each man hie him to his several home
Before the people rise in mutiny,
And in the mildest part of lenity
Seek to restrain them from rebellion— 95
For what can else be look'd for? Promise redress;
That eloquence is best in this distress.

LANCASTER
York counsels well. Let's haste away,
The time is sick, we must not use delay.

RICHARD II, PART ONE, III.II

YORK
Let's still confer by letters.   100

WOODSTOCK
Content, content,
So friends may parley even in banishment.
Farewell, good brothers! Cheney, conduct them forth.

Exeunt all but Woodstock

Adieu, good York and Gaunt, farewell forever!
I have a sad presage comes suddenly   105
That I shall never see these brothers more.
On earth, I fear, we never more shall meet.
Of Edward the Third's seven sons we three are left
To see our father's kingdom ruinate.
I would my death might end the misery   110
My fear presageth to my wretched country.
The commons will rebel, without all question,
And, 'fore my God, I have no eloquence
To stay this uproar. I must tell them plain,
We all are struck but must not strike again.   115

Enter a Servant

How now? What news?

SERVANT
There's a horseman at the gate, my lord. He comes
from the King, he says, to see your Grace.

WOODSTOCK
To see me, say'st thou? A' God's name, let him come,
so he brings no Blank Charters with him! Prithee, bid   120
him 'light and enter.

RICHARD II, PART ONE, III.II

SERVANT
I think he dares not for fouling on his feet, my lord.
I would have had him 'light, but he swears as he's a
courtier he will not off on's horse' back till the inner
gate be open.   125

WOODSTOCK
Passion of me, that's strange! I prithee, give him
satisfaction, open the inner gate. What might this
fellow be?

SERVANT
Some fine fool. He's attir'd very fantastically, and
talks as foolishly.   130

WOODSTOCK
Go, let him in, and when you have done, bid Cheney
come and speak with me.

SERVANT
I will, my lord. Come on, sir, ye may ride into my
lord's cellar now, and ye will, sir.

Enter a Spruce Courtier on horseback

COURTIER
Prithee, fellow, stay and take my horse!   135

SERVANT
I have business for my lord, sir, I cannot.

Exit Servant

COURTIER
A rude swain, by heaven! But stay, here walks
another. Hear'st-ta thou, fellow, is this Plashy House?

RICHARD II, PART ONE, III.II

WOODSTOCK
Ye should have ask'd that question before ye came in,
sir. But this is it. 140

COURTIER
The hinds are all most rude and gross! I prithee, walk
my horse.

WOODSTOCK
I have a little business, sir.

COURTIER
Thou shalt not lose by't. I'll give thee a tester for thy
pains. 145

WOODSTOCK
I shall be glad to earn money, sir.

COURTIER
Prithee, do, and know thy duty. Thy head's too saucy.

WOODSTOCK
Cry ye mercy, I did not understand your worship's
calling!

COURTIER
The Duke of Gloucester lies here, does he not? 150

WOODSTOCK
Marry, does he, sir.

COURTIER
Is he within?

WOODSTOCK
He's not far off, sir, he was here even now.

RICHARD II, PART ONE, III.II

COURTIER
Ah, very good. Walk my horse well, I prithee, h'as
travel'd hard and he's hot, i' faith. I'll in and speak   155
with the Duke, and pay thee presently.

WOODSTOCK
I make no doubt, sir. [*Exit Courtier*] Oh, strange
metamorphosis! Is't possible that this fellow, that's
all made of fashions, should be an Englishman? No
marvel if he know not me, being so brave, and I so   160
beggarly! Well, I shall earn money to enrich me now,
and 'tis the first I earn'd, by the rood, this forty year.

Walks the horse

Come on, sir, you have sweat hard about this haste,
yet I think you know little of the business! Why so I
say? You're a very indifferent beast; you'll follow any   165
man that will lead you. Now truly, sir, you look but
e'en leanly on it. You feed not in Westminster Hall
'a-days, where so many sheep and oxen are devour'd.
I'm afraid they'll eat you shortly, if you tarry amongst
them! You're prick'd more with the spur than the   170
provender, I see that. I think your dwelling be at
Hackney when you are at home, is't not? You know
not the Duke neither, no more than your master, and
yet I think you have as much wit as he, i' faith! Say a
man should steal ye and feed ye fatter, could ye run   175
away with him lustily? Ah, your silence argues a
consent, I see! By the Mass, here comes company.
We had been both taken if we had, I see.

Re-enter Cheney, Courtier and Servant

CHENEY
Saw ye not my lord at the gate, say ye? Why, I left
him there but now.   180

RICHARD II, PART ONE, III.II

COURTIER
In sooth, I saw no creature, sir, only an old groom
I got to walk my horse.

CHENEY
A groom, say ye? 'Sfoot, 'tis my lord, the Duke! What
have ye done? [*To Woodstock*] This is somewhat too
coarse, your Grace should be an ostler to this fellow!   185

COURTIER
I do beseech your Grace's pardon. The error was in
the mistake that your plainness did deceive me.
Please it your Grace to redeliver.

WOODSTOCK
No, by my faith, I'll have my money first. A promise
is a debt.   190

COURTIER
I know your Grace's goodness will refuse it.

WOODSTOCK
Think not so nicely of me. Indeed, I will not!

COURTIER
If so you please, there is your tester.

WOODSTOCK
If so you please, there is your horse, sir. Now pray
you tell me, is your haste to me?   195

COURTIER
Most swift and serious from his Majesty.

WOODSTOCK
What, from King Richard, my dear lord and kinsman?
[*To Servant*] Go, sirrah, take you his horse, lead him

RICHARD II, PART ONE, III.II

to the stable, meat him well. I'll double his reward,
there's twelve pence for ye. 200

SERVANT
I thank your Grace.

Exit Servant with the horse

WOODSTOCK
Now, sir, your business.

COURTIER
His Majesty commends him to your Grace. [*Bows and
flourishes his hat*]

WOODSTOCK
This same's a rare fashion you have got at court! Of
whose devising was't, I pray? 205

COURTIER
I assure your Grace, King Richard's Council sat three
days about it!

WOODSTOCK
By my faith, their Wisdoms took great pains, I assure
ye! The state was well employ'd the whiles, by th'
rood. Then this at court is all the fashion now? 210

COURTIER
The King himself doth wear it, whose most gracious
Majesty sent me in haste.

WOODSTOCK
[*Indicating Courtier's shoe*] This peak doth strangely
well become the foot.

COURTIER
This peak the King doth likewise wear, being a 215

RICHARD II, PART ONE, III.II

Polonian peak; and me did his Highness pick from
forth the rest.

WOODSTOCK
He could not have pick'd out such another, I assure
ye.

COURTIER
I thank your Grace that picks me out so well!   220
But, as I said, his Highness would request—

WOODSTOCK
But this most fashionable chain, that links as it were
the toe and knee together?

COURTIER
In a most kind coherence, so it like your Grace, for
these two parts, being in operation and quality   225
different, as, for example, the toe a disdainer or
spurner, the k-nee a dutiful and most humble orator,
this chain doth, as it were, so toeify the k-nee, and so
k-neeify the toe, that between both it makes a most
methodical coherence or coherent method.   230

WOODSTOCK
'Tis most excellent, sir, and full of art. Please ye, walk
in.

COURTIER
My message tender'd, I will tend your Grace.

WOODSTOCK
Cry ye mercy, have you a message to me?

COURTIER
His Majesty, most affectionately, and like a royal   235
kinsman, entreats your Grace's presence at the court.

RICHARD II, PART ONE, III.III

WOODSTOCK
Is that your message, sir? I must refuse it, then.
My English plainness will not suit that place,
The court's too fine for me. My service here
Will stand in better stead, to quench the fire   240
Those Blanks have made. I would they were all burnt,
Or he were hang'd that first devis'd them, sir,
They stir the country so! I dare not come,
And so excuse me, sir. If the King think it ill,
He thinks amiss; I am Plain Thomas still.   245
The rest I'll tell ye as ye sit at meat.
Furnish a table, Cheney, call for wine.
Come, sir, ye shall commend me to the King.
Tell him I'll keep these parts in peace to him.

Exeunt omnes

Act III Scene III

[The market square, Dunstable]

*Enter Master Simon Ignorance, the Bailey of
Dunstable, Crosby, Fleming, and Nimble, with
Blanks. Officers with bills in attendance*

CROSBY
Despatch, good Master Bailey, the market's almost   1
done, you see. 'Tis rumor'd that the Blanks are come
and the rich chuffs begin to flock out o' the town
already. You have seen the High Shrieve's warrant
and the Council's commission, and therefore I charge   5
ye in the king's name, be ready to assist us.

IGNORANCE
Nay, look ye, sir, be not too pestiferous, I beseech ye!
I have begun myself and seal'd one of your Blanks.
I know my place and calling, my name is Ignorance

and I am Bailey of Dunstable. I cannot write nor read, 10
I confess it, no more could my father, nor his father,
nor none of the Ignorance this hundred year, I assure
ye.

NIMBLE
Your name proclaims no less, sir, and it has been a
most learned generation. 15

IGNORANCE
Though I cannot write, I have set my mark. *Ecce
signum*! Read it, I beseech ye.

NIMBLE
The mark of Simon Ignorance, the Bailey of
Dunstable, being a sheep-hook with a tarbox at end
on't. 20

IGNORANCE
Very right. It was my mark ever since I was an
innocent and therefore, as I say, I have begun, and
will assist ye, for here be rich whoresons i' the town,
I can tell ye, that will give ye the slip and ye look not
to it. 25

FLEMING
We therefore presently will divide ourselves. You two
shall stay here whilst we, Master Ignorance, with
some of your brethren, the men of Dunstable, walk
through the town noting the carriage of the people.
They say there are strange songs and libels cast about 30
the market place against my lord Tresilian and the rest
of the King's young Councilors. If such there be,
we'll have some aid and attach them speedily.

IGNORANCE
Ye shall do well, sir, and for your better aiding, if you

can but find out my brother, Master Ignoramus, he   35
will be most pestiferous unto ye, I assure ye.

CROSBY
I'm afraid he will not be found, sir, but we'll inquire.
Come, fellow Fleming. And Nimble, look to the
whisperers, I charge ye!

NIMBLE
I warrant ye. [*Exeunt Crosby and Fleming*] Come,   40
Master Bailey, let your billmen retire till we call them,
and you and I will here shadow ourselves and write
down their speeches. [*Officers hide themselves*]

IGNORANCE
Nay, you shall write and I will mark, sir.

*Enter a farmer, a butcher and Cowtail, a rich grazier,
very hastily*

And see, see, here comes some already, all rich   45
chubbs, by the Mass. I know them all, sir.

FARMER
Tarry, tarry, good neighbors, take a knave with ye!
What a murrain! Is there a bear broke loose i' the
town, that ye make such haste from the market?

COWTAIL
A bear? No, nor a lion baited neither. I tell ye,   50
neighbor, I am more afraid of the bee than the bear.
There's wax to be us'd today, and I have no seal about
me. I may tell you in secret, here's a dangerous world
towards. Neighbor, you're a farmer, and I hope here is
none but God and good company. We live in such a   55
state, I am e'en almost weary of all, I assure ye.
Here's my other neighbor, the butcher, that dwells at

RICHARD II, PART ONE, III.III

Hockley, has heard his landlord tell strange tidings.
We shall be all hoisted and we tarry here, I can tell ye!

NIMBLE
They begin to murmur. I'll put them down all for   60
whisperers. Master Bailey, what's he that talks so?

IGNORANCE
His name is Cowtail, a rich grazier, and dwells here
hard by at Leighton Buzzard.

NIMBLE
Cowtail, a grazier, dwelling at Leighton Buzzard,
Master Bailey?   65

IGNORANCE
Right, sir. Listen again, sir.

FARMER
Ah, sirrah? And what said the good knight, your
landlord, neighbor?

BUTCHER
Marry, he said—but I'll not stand to anything, I tell
ye that aforehand. He said that King Richard's new   70
Councilors, God amend them, had crept into honester
men's places than themselves were, and that the
King's uncles and the old lords were all banish'd the
court. And he said flatly we should never have a
merry world as long as it was so.   75

NIMBLE
[*Aside*] Butcher, you and your landlord will be both
hang'd for it!

BUTCHER
And then he said that there's one Tresilian, a lawyer,

that has crept in amongst them and is now a lord,
forsooth, and he has sent down into every county 80
of England a sort of black chapters!

FARMER
Black chapters? A' God's name, neighbor, out of
what black book were they taken?

COWTAIL
Come, come, they are Blank Charters, neighbors. I
heard of them afore, and therefore I made such haste 85
away. They're sent down to the High Shrieve, with
special charge that every man that is of any credit
or worship in the county must set their hands and
seal to them, for what intent I know not. I say no
more. I smell something. 90

FARMER
Well, well, my masters, let's be wise: we are not all
one man's sons. They say there are whispering
knaves abroad. Let's hie us home, for I assure ye,
'twas told me where I broke my fast this afternoon
that there were above three-score gentlemen in our 95
shire that had set their hands and seals to those Blank
Charters already.

COWTAIL
Now God amend them for it, they have given an ill
example we shall be forc'd to follow.

BUTCHER
I would my wife and children were at Jerusalem with 100
all the wealth! I'd make shift for one, I warrant them.
Come, neighbors, let's be gone.

NIMBLE
Step forward with your bills, Master Bailey! Not so

fast, sirs! I charge ye in the King's name to stand till
we have done with ye.   105

ALL
Saint Benedicite, what must we do now, trow?

IGNORANCE
Be not so pestiferous, my good friends and neighbors!
You are men of wealth and credit in the county, and
therefore, as I myself and others have begun, I charge
ye in his Highness' name presently to set your hands   110
and seals to these Blank Charters.

COWTAIL
Jesu, receive my soul, I'm departed!

FARMER
I'm e'en stroke to at heart too!

BUTCHER
Alas, sir, we are poor men, what should our hands do?

IGNORANCE
There is no harm, I warrant ye. What need you fear,   115
when ye see Bailey Ignorance has seal'd before ye?

COWTAIL
I pray ye, let us see them, sir.

NIMBLE
Here, ye bacon-fed pudding-eaters! Are ye afraid of a
sheepskin? [*Hands Blank to Cowtail*]

COWTAIL
Mass, 'tis somewhat darkly written.   120

FARMER
Ay, ay, 'twas done i'the night, sure.

RICHARD II, PART ONE, III.III

COWTAIL
Mass, neighbors, here's nothing that I see.

BUTCHER
And can it be any harm, think ye, to set our hands to
nothing? These Blank Charters are but little pieces of
parchment. Let's set our marks to them, and be rid of   125
a knave's company.

*Nimble offers ink, pen and sealing wax. Butcher signs,
then hands pen to Farmer*

FARMER
As good at first as last, we can be but undone. [*Signs*]

COWTAIL
Ay, and our own hands undoes us, that's the worst
on't. Lend's your pen, sir. [*Signs*]

BUTCHER
We must all venture, neighbors, there's no remedy.   130

NIMBLE
They grumble as they do it, I must put them down for
whisperers and grumblers. Come, have you done yet?

COWTAIL
Ay, sir. [*Aside*] Would you and they were sodden for
my swine!

NIMBLE
Here's wax, then. I'll seal them for ye, and you shall   135
severally take them off and then deliver them as your
deeds. [*Seals them*] Come, you boar's grease, take off
this seal here. So, this is your deed?

FARMER
Faith, sir, in some respect it is and it is not.

NIMBLE
And this is yours?

COWTAIL
Ay, sir, against my will, I swear.

NIMBLE
[*To Butcher*] Ox-jaw, take off this seal! You'll deliver your deed with a good conscience?

BUTCHER
There 'tis, sir, against my conscience, God's my witness! I hope ye have done with us now, sir.

NIMBLE
No, ye caterpillars, we have worse matters against ye yet! Sirrah, you know what your landlord told ye concerning my lord Tresilian and King Richard's new favorites; and, more than that, you know your own speeches. And therefore, Master Bailey, let some of your billmen away with them to the High Shrieve's, presently either to put in bail or be sent up to the court for privy whisperers.

IGNORANCE
Their offenses are most pestiferous. Away with them!

ALL
Now out, alas, we shall all to hanging, sure!

NIMBLE
Hanging? Nay, that's the least on't! Ye shall tell me that a twelve-month hence else!

Exeunt Officers with the three men

Stand close, Master Bailey, we shall catch more of

these traitors presently.

IGNORANCE
You shall find me most pestiferous to assist ye! And 160
so I pray ye, commend my service to your good lord
and master. Come, sir, stand close.

Enter a Schoolmaster and a Servingman

SERVINGMAN
Nay, sweet Master Schoolmaster, let's hear't again,
I beseech ye.

SCHOOLMASTER
Patientia, you're a servingman, I'm a scholar. I have 165
shown art and learning in these verses, I assure ye,
and yet if they were well search'd they're little better
than libels. But the carriage of a thing is all, sir: I have
cover'd them rarely.

SERVINGMAN
'Sfoot, the country's so full of intelligencers that two 170
men can scarce walk together but they're attach'd for
whisperers.

SCHOOLMASTER
This paper shall wipe their noses, and they shall not
say boo to a goose for't, for I'll have these verses
sung to their faces by one of my schoolboys, wherein 175
I'll tickle them all, i' faith. Shalt hear else, but first
let's look there be no pitchers with ears, nor needles
with eyes, about us.

SERVINGMAN
Come, come, all's safe, I warrant ye.

RICHARD II, PART ONE, III.III

SCHOOLMASTER
Mark, then. Here I come over them for their Blank   180
Charters, shalt hear else.

Will ye buy any parchment knives?
We sell for little gain:
Whoe'er are weary of their lives
They'll rid them of their pain.   185

Blank Charters they are call'd—
A vengeance on the villain!
I would he were both flay'd and bald:
God bless my lord Tresilian!

Is't not rare?   190

NIMBLE
Oh, rascals! They're damn'd three hundred fathom
deep already!

SCHOOLMASTER
Nay, look ye, sir, there can be no exceptions taken,
for this last line helps all, wherein with a kind of
equivocation I say, 'God bless my lord Tresilian!'   195
Do ye mark, sir? Now here, in the next verse, I run
o'er all these flatterers i' the court by name. Ye shall
see else:

A poison may be Green,
But Bushy can be no maggot: 200
God mend the King and bless the Queen
And 'tis no matter for Bagot.

For Scroop, he does no good;
But if you'll know the villain,
His name is now to be understood: 205
God bless my lord Tresilian!

How like ye this, sir?

SERVINGMAN
Most excellent, i'faith, sir.

NIMBLE
Oh, traitors! Master Bailey, do your authority!

IGNORANCE
Two most pestiferous traitors! Lay hold of them,   210
I charge ye!

Officers arrest them

SERVINGMAN
What mean ye, sir?

NIMBLE
Nay, talk not, for if ye had a hundred lives they were
all hang'd! Ye have spoke treason in the ninth degree.

SCHOOLMASTER
Treason? *Patientia*, good sir, we spoke not a word!   215

IGNORANCE
Be not so pestiferous, mine ears have heard your
examinations, wherein you utter'd most shameful
treason, for ye said, 'God bless my lord Tresilian!'

SCHOOLMASTER
I hope there's no treason in that, sir.

NIMBLE
That shall be tried! Come, Master Bailey, their hands   220
shall be bound under a horse's belly and sent up to
him presently. They'll both be hang'd, I warrant them.

RICHARD II, PART ONE, III.III

SERVINGMAN
Well, sir, if we be, we'll speak more ere we be
hang'd, in spite of ye.

NIMBLE
Ay, ay, when you're hang'd speak what you will, we   225
care not. Away with them!

Exeunt Schoolmaster and Servingman with Officers

Ye see, Master Bailey, what knaves are abroad now
you are here! 'Tis time to look about, ye see.

IGNORANCE
I see there are knaves abroad indeed, sir. I speak for
mine own part, I will do my best to reform the   230
pestiferousness of the times. And as for example I
have set my mark to the Charters, so will I set mine
eyes to observe these dangerous cases.

Enter one a-whistling

NIMBLE
Close again, Master Bailey, here comes another
whisperer, I see. Oh, villain, he whistles treason!   235
I'll lay hold of him myself!

Seizes whistler

WHISTLER
Out, alas! What do ye mean, sir?

NIMBLE
A rank traitor, Master Bailey! Lay hold on him, for
he has most erroneously and rebelliously whistled
treason!   240

RICHARD II, PART ONE, III.III

WHISTLER
Whistl'd treason? Alas, sir, how can that be?

IGNORANCE
Very easily, sir! There's a piece of treason that flies up and down the county in the likeness of a ballad, and this being the very tune of it, thou hast whistl'd treason. 245

WHISTLER
Alas, sir, ye know I spake not a word!

NIMBLE
That's all one. If any man whistles treason, 'tis as ill as speaking it. Mark me, Master Bailey: the bird whistles that cannot speak, and yet there be birds in a manner that can speak too. Your raven will call ye 250 black, your crow will call ye knave, Master Bailey, *ergo*, he that can whistle can speak, and therefore this fellow hath both spoke and whistl'd treason. How say you, Bailey Ignorance?

IGNORANCE
Ye have argued well, sir, but ye shall hear me sift him 255 nearer, for I do not think but there are greater heads in this matter. And therefore, my good fellow, be not pestiferous, but say and tell the truth, who did set you a-work? Or who was the cause of your whistling? Or did any man say to you, 'Go whistle'? 260

WHISTLER
Not any man, woman or child, truly, sir.

IGNORANCE
No? How durst you whistle, then? Or what cause had ye to do so?

RICHARD II, PART ONE, III.III

WHISTLER
The truth is, sir, I had lost two calves out of my
pasture, and being in search for them, from the top   265
of the hill I might spy you two i' the bottom here,
and took ye for my calves, sir; and that made me come
whistling down for joy, in hope I had found them.

NIMBLE
More treason yet, he take a courtier and a Bailey for
two calves! To Limbo with him, he shall be quarter'd   270
and then hang'd!

WHISTLER
Good Master Bailey, be pitiful!

IGNORANCE
Why, law ye, sir, he makes a pitiful fellow of a Bailey
too! Away with him! Yet stay awhile, here comes
your fellows, sir.   275

Enter Crosby and Fleming

CROSBY
Now, Master Bailey, are your Blanks sealed yet?

IGNORANCE
They are, sir. And we have done this day most strange
and pestiferous service, I assure ye, sir.

FLEMING
Your care shall be rewarded. Come, fellow Nimble,
we must to court about other employments. There are   280
already thirteen thousand Blanks signed and return'd
to the Shrieves, and seven hundred sent up to the court
for whisperers, out of all which my lord will fetch a
round sum, I doubt it not. Come, let's away.

RICHARD II, PART ONE, IV.I

NIMBLE
Ay, ay, we'll follow. Come, ye sheepbiter! Here's   285
a traitor of all traitors, that not only speaks but has
whistled treason! Come, come, sir, I'll spoil your
whistle, I warrant ye!

Exeunt omnes

Act IV Scene I

[London, the royal court]

*Enter Tresilian with writings, and a servant with
bags of money*

TRESILIAN
Sirrah, are the bags seal'd?   1

SERVANT
Yes, my lord.

TRESILIAN
Then take my keys and lock the money in my study
safe. Bar and make sure, I charge ye. So, begone.

SERVANT
I will, my lord.   5

TRESILIAN
So, seven thousand pounds
From Bedford, Buckingham and Oxford shires,
These Blanks already have return'd the King.
So then there's four for me and three for him—
Our pains in this must needs be satisfied!   10
Good husbands will make hay while the sun shines,
And so must we, for thus conclude these times:

RICHARD II, PART ONE, IV.I

So men be rich enough, they're good enough.
Let fools make conscience how they get their coin,
I'll please the King and keep me in his grace, 15
For princes' favors purchase land apace.
These Blanks that I have scatter'd in the realm
Shall double his revenues to the Crown.

Enter Bushy and Scroop, attended by archers

SCROOP
Now, Lord Tresilian, is this coin come yet?

BUSHY
King Richard wants money, you're too slack, 20
Tresilian.

TRESILIAN
Some shires have sent, and more, my lords, will
follow.
These sealed Blanks I now have turn'd to bonds,
And these shall down to Norfolk presently. 25
The chuffs with much ado have sign'd and seal'd,
And here's a secret note my men have sent
Of all their yearly 'states amounts unto,
And by this note I justly tax their bonds.
Here's a fat whoreson in his russet slops, 30
And yet may spend three hundred pounds by th' year,
The third of which the hogsface owes the King.
Here's his bond for't, with his hand and seal,
And so by this I'll sort each several sum,
The thirds of all shall to King Richard come. 35
How like you this, my lords?

SCROOP
Most rare, Tresilian! Hang 'em, codsheads. Shall they
spend money and King Richard lack it?

RICHARD II, PART ONE, IV.I

BUSHY
Are not their lives and lands and livings his? Then
rack them thoroughly! 40

TRESILIAN
Oh, my lords, I have set a trick afoot for ye. And ye
follow it hard and get the King to sign it, you'll be all
kings by it.

BUSHY
The farming out the kingdom? Tush, Tresilian, 'tis
half granted already, and had been fully concluded 45
had not the messenger returned so unluckily from the
Duke of Gloucester, which a little mov'd the King at
his uncle's stubbornness. But to make all whole, we
have left that smooth-fac'd, flattering Green to follow
him close, and he'll never leave till he has done it, 50
I warrant ye.

SCROOP
There's no question on't. King Richard will betake
himself to a yearly stipend, and we four by lease must
rent the kingdom!

BUSHY
Rent it, ay, and rack it too, ere we forfeit our leases, 55
and we had them once!

Enter Bagot

How now, Bagot, what news?

BAGOT
All rich and rare! The realm must be divided
presently, and we four must farm it. The leases are
a-making and for seven thousand pounds a month the 60
kingdom is our own, boys!

RICHARD II, PART ONE, IV.i

BUSHY
'Sfoot, let's differ for no price! And it were seventy
thousand pounds a month, we'll make somebody pay
for't!

SCROOP
Where is his Highness?   65

BAGOT
He will be here presently to seal the writings. He's
a little angry that the Duke comes not, but that will
vanish quickly. On with your soothest faces, ye
wenching rascals! Humor him finely, and you're all
made by it.   70

*Sound a flourish. Enter King Richard and Sir Henry
Green, attended by archers*

BUSHY
See, see, he comes, and that flattering hound Green
close at his elbow.

SCROOP
Come, come, we must all flatter if we mean to live by
it.

KING
Our uncle will not come, then?

GREEN
That was his answer, flat and resolute.   75

KING
Was ever subject so audacious?

BAGOT
And can your Grace, my lord, digest these wrongs?

RICHARD II, PART ONE, IV.i

KING
Yes—as a mother that beholds her child
Dismember'd by a bloody tyrant's sword!
I tell thee, Bagot, in my heart remains   80
Such deep impressions of his churlish taunts,
As nothing can remove the gall thereof
Till with his blood mine eyes be satisfied.

GREEN
'Sfoot, raise powers, my lord, and fetch him thence
perforce!   85

KING
I dare not, Green, for whilst he keeps i' the country
There is no meddling. He's so well belov'd
As all the realm will rise in arms with him.

TRESILIAN
'Sfoot, my lord, and you'd fain have him, I have a
trick shall fetch him from his house at Plashy, in spite   90
of all his favorites.

KING
Let's ha't, Tresilian, thy wit must help, or all's dash'd
else.

TRESILIAN
Then thus, my lord. Whilst the Duke securely revels i'
the country, we'll have some trusty friends disguise   95
themselves like masquers, and this night ride down to
Plashy and in the name of some near-adjoining
friends offer their sports to make him merry, which he
no doubt will thankfully accept. Then in the masque
we'll have it so devis'd, the dance being done and   100
the room voided, then upon some occasion single the
Duke alone, thrust him in a masquing suit, clap a
vizard on his face, and so convey him out o' the house
at pleasure!

RICHARD II, PART ONE, IV.I

SCROOP
How if he cry and call for help? 105

TRESILIAN
What serves your drums but to drown his cries? And
being in a masque, 'twill never be suspected.

GREEN
Good, i' faith! And to help it, my lord, Lapoole,
the Governor of Calais, is new ready to receive him.
Hurry him away to the Thames' side where a ship 110
shall be laid ready for his coming, so clap him under
hatches, hoist sails, and secretly convey him out o' the
realm to Calais! And so by this means ye shall prevent
all mischief, for neither of your uncles nor any of the
kingdom shall know what's become of him. 115

KING
I like it well, sweet Green, and by my crown
We'll be in the masque ourself, and so shall you!
Get horses ready, this night we'll ride to Plashy.
But see ye carry it close and secretly,
For whilst this plot's a-working for the Duke, 120
I'll set a trap for York and Lancaster.
Go, Tresilian, let proclamations straight be sent
Wherein thou shalt accuse the dukes of treason,
And then attach, condemn, and close imprison them.
Lest the commons should rebel against us, 125
We'll send unto the King of France for aid,
And in requital we'll surrender up
Our forts of Guisnes and Calais to the French.
Let crown and kingdom waste, yea life and all,
Before King Richard see his true friends fall! 130
Give order our disguises be made ready,
And let Lapoole provide the ship and soldiers.
We will not sleep, by heaven, till we have seiz'd him!

RICHARD II, PART ONE, IV.1

BUSHY
[*Aside to Green*] 'Sfoot, urge our suit again, he will
forget it else. 135

KING
These traitors once surpris'd, then all is sure:
Our kingdom quiet and your states secure.

GREEN
Most true, sweet King. And then your Grace, as you
promis'd, farming out the kingdom to us four, shall
not need to trouble yourself with any business. This 140
old turkey-cock, Tresilian, shall look to the law, and
we'll govern the land most rarely.

KING
So, sir:
The love of thee and these, my dearest Green,
Hath won King Richard to consent to that
For which all foreign kings will point at us, 145
And of the meanest subject of our land
We shall be censur'd strongly, when they tell
How our great father toil'd his royal person
Spending his blood to purchase towns in France,
And we, his son, to ease our wanton youth, 150
Become a landlord to this warlike realm,
Rent out our kingdom like a pelting farm,
That erst was held, as far as Babylon,
The maiden conqueress to all the world.

GREEN
'Sfoot, what need you care what the world talks? 155
You still retain the name of King, and if any disturb
ye, we four comes presently from the four parts of the
kingdom with four puissant armies to assist you.

RICHARD II, PART ONE, IV.I

KING
You four must be all then, for I think nobody else will
follow you, unless it be to hanging! 160

GREEN
Why, Richard, King Richard, will ye be as good as
your word, and seal the writings? 'Sfoot, an' thou
dost not, and I do not join with thine uncles and turn
traitor, would I might be turn'd to a toadstool!

KING
Very well, sir. They did well to choose you for their 165
orator, that has King Richard's love and heart in
keeping. Your suit is granted, sir. Let's see the
writings.

ALL
They're here, my lord!

KING
View them, Tresilian, then we'll sign and seal them. 170
Look to your bargain, Green, and be no loser, for if
ye forfeit or run behind-hand with me, I swear I'll
both imprison and punish ye soundly.

GREEN
Forfeit, sweet king? 'Sblood, I'll sell their houses ere
I'll forfeit my lease, I warrant thee! 175

KING
If they be stubborn, do, and spare not. Rack them
soundly and we'll maintain it. Remember ye not the
proviso enacted in our last parliament, that no statute,
were it ne'er so profitable for the commonwealth,
should stand in any force 'gainst our proceedings? 180

RICHARD II, PART ONE, IV.I

GREEN
'Tis true, my lord. Then what should hinder ye to accomplish anything that may best please your kingly spirit to determine?

KING
True, Green, and we will do it, in spite of them! Is't just, Tresilian? 185

TRESILIAN
Most just, my liege. These gentlemen here, Sir Henry Green, Sir Edward Bagot, Sir William Bushy, and Sir Thomas Scroop, all jointly here stand bound to pay your Majesty, or your deputy, wherever you remain, seven thousand pounds a month for this your 190 kingdom; for which your Grace, by these writings, surrenders to their hands all your crown lands, lordships, manors, rents, taxes, subsidies, fifteens, imposts, foreign customs, staples for wool, tin, lead, and cloth; all forfeitures of goods or lands confiscate; 195 and all other duties that is, shall, or may appertain to the king or crown's revenues; and for non-payment of the sum or sums aforesaid, your Majesty to seize the lands and goods of the said gentlemen above named, and their bodies to be imprisoned at your 200 Grace's pleasure.

KING
How like you that, Green? Believe me, if you fail, I'll not favor ye a day.

GREEN
I'll ask no favor at your hands, sir. Ye shall have your money at your day, and then do your worst, sir! 205

KING
'Tis very good. Set to your hands and seals. Tresilian,

we make you our deputy to receive this money. Look
strictly to them, I charge ye.

TRESILIAN
If the money come not to my hands at the time
appointed, I'll make them smoke for't. 210

GREEN
Ay, ay, you're an upright justice, sir, we fear ye not!
Here, my lord, they're ready, sign'd and seal'd.

TRESILIAN
Deliver them to his Majesty all together, as your
special deeds.

ALL
We do, with humble thanks unto his Majesty, that 215
makes us tenants to so rich a lordship!

KING
Keep them, Tresilian. Now will we sign and seal to
you. Never had English subjects such a landlord!

GREEN
Nor never had English king such subjects as we four,
that are able to farm a whole kingdom and pay him 220
rent for't!

KING
Look that ye do, we shall expect performance
speedily. [*Signs*] There's your indenture, sign'd and
seal'd, which as our kingly deed we here deliver.

GREEN
Thou never did'st a better deed in thy life, sweet 225
bully, thou may'st now live at ease! We'll toil for
thee and send thy money in tumbling.

RICHARD II, PART ONE, IV.I

KING
We shall see your care, sir. Reach me the map,
that we may allot their portions and part the realm
amongst them equally. You four shall here by us   230
divide yourselves into the nine-and-thirty shires and
counties of my kingdom, parted thus. Come stand by
me and mark those shires assign'd ye. Bagot, thy lot
betwixt the Thames and sea thus lies: Kent, Surrey,
Sussex, Hampshire, Berkshire, Wiltshire, Dorsetshire,   235
Somersetshire, Devonshire, Cornwall. Those parts are
thine as amply, Bagot, as the crown is mine.

BAGOT
All thanks, love, duty to my princely sovereign!

KING
[*To Bagot*] Bushy from thee shall stretch his
government over these lands that lie in Wales,   240
together with our counties of Gloucester, Worcester,
Hereford, Shropshire, Staffordshire and Cheshire.
[*To Bushy*] There's thy lot.

BUSHY
Thanks to my king that thus hath honor'd me!

KING
Sir Thomas Scroop, from Trent to Tweed thy lot is   245
parted thus: all Yorkshire, Derbyshire, Lancashire,
Cumberland, Westmoreland, and Northumberland.
Receive thy lot, thy state and government.

SCROOP
With faith and duty to your Highness' throne!

KING
Now, my Green, what have I left for thee?   250

The Tragedy of King Richard II, Part One

RICHARD II, PART ONE, IV.i

GREEN
'Sfoot, and you'll give me nothing, then good night,
landlord! Since ye have serv'd me last, and I be not
the last shall pay your rent, ne'er trust me!

KING
I kept thee last to make thy part the greatest. See here,
sweet Green, these shires are thine, even from the   255
Thames to Trent. Thou here shalt lie i' the middle of
my land.

GREEN
That's best i' the winter. Is there any pretty wenches
in my government?

KING
Guess that by this: thou hast London, Middlesex,   260
Essex, Suffolk, Norfolk, Cambridgeshire,
Hertfordshire, Bedfordshire, Buckinghamshire,
Oxfordshire, Northamptonshire, Rutlandshire,
Leicestershire, Warwickshire, Huntingdonshire, and
Lincolnshire. There's your portion, sir.   265

GREEN
'Slid, I will rule like a king amongst them,
And thou shalt reign like an emperor over us!

KING
Thus have I parted my whole realm amongst ye;
Be careful of your charge and government.
And now to attach our stubborn uncles!   270
Let warrants be sent down, Tresilian,
For Gaunt and York, Surrey and Arundel,
Whilst we this night at Plashy suddenly
Surprise plain Woodstock. Being parted thus,
We shall with greater ease arrest and take them.   275
Your places are not sure while they have breath,

Therefore pursue them hard. Those traitors gone,
The staves are broke the people lean upon,
And you may guide and rule them at your pleasures.
Away to Plashy, let our masque be ready! 280
Beware, Plain Thomas, for King Richard comes,
Resolv'd with blood to wash all former wrongs!

Flourish of trumpets. Exeunt omnes

Act IV Scene II

[Plashy House, Essex]

*Enter Woodstock and his Duchess with a Gentleman,
Cheney, and others prepared for a journey*

WOODSTOCK
The Queen so sick! Come, come, make haste good 1
wife,
Thou'lt be belated sure, 'tis night already!
On with thy cloak and mask! To horse, to horse!

DUCHESS OF GLOUCESTER
Good troth, my lord, I have no mind to ride. 5
I have been dull and heavy all this day,
My sleeps were troubled with sad dreams last night,
And I am full of fear and heaviness.
Pray, let me ride tomorrow.

WOODSTOCK
What, and the Queen so sick? Away, for shame! 10
Stay for a dream? Thou'st dreamt, I'm sure, ere this!

DUCHESS OF GLOUCESTER
Never so fearful were my dreams till now.
Had they concern'd myself, my fears were past,
But you were made the object of mine eye,

RICHARD II, PART ONE, IV.II

And I beheld you murder'd cruelly. 15

WOODSTOCK
Ha, murder'd?
Alack, good lady, did'st thou dream of me?
Take comfort, then, all dreams are contrary.

DUCHESS OF GLOUCESTER
Pray God it prove so, for my soul is fearful,
The vision did appear so lively to me. 20
Methought as you were ranging through the woods,
An angry lion with a herd of wolves
Had in an instant round encompass'd you
When, to your rescue, 'gainst the course of kind,
A flock of silly sheep made head 'gainst them, 25
Bleating for help, 'gainst whom the forest king
Rous'd up his strength, and slew both you and them.
This fear affrights me.

WOODSTOCK
Afore my God, thou'rt foolish. I'll tell thee all thy
dream. 30
Thou know'st last night we had some private talk
About the Blanks the country's tax'd withal,
Where I compar'd the state as now it stands,
Meaning King Richard and his harmful flatterers,
Unto a savage herd of ravening wolves, 35
The commons to a flock of silly sheep
Who, whilst their slothful shepherd careless stood,
Those forest thieves broke in and suck'd their blood.
And this thy apprehension took so deep,
The form was portray'd lively in thy sleep. 40
Come, come, 'tis nothing. What, are her horses ready?

CHENEY
They are, my lord.

RICHARD II, PART ONE, IV.II

WOODSTOCK
Where is the gentleman that brought this message?
Where lies the Queen, sir?

GENTLEMAN
At Sheen, my lord, most sick, and so much alter'd   45
As those about her fears her sudden death.

WOODSTOCK
Forfend it, heaven! Away, make haste, I charge ye.
[*To Duchess*] What, weeping now? Afore my God,
thou'rt fond! Come, come, I know thou art no augurer
of ill. Dry up thy tears. This kiss, and part. Farewell!   50

DUCHESS OF GLOUCESTER
That farewell from your lips to me sounds ill.
Where'er I go, my fears will follow still.

WOODSTOCK
See her to horseback, Cheney.

Exeunt Duchess and the rest. Manet Woodstock

'Fore my God, 'tis late,
And but th' important business craves such haste   55
She had not gone from Plashy House tonight.
But woe is me, the good Queen Anne is sick
And, by my soul, my heart is sad to hear it.
So good a lady, and so virtuous,
This realm for many ages could not boast of.   60
Her charity hath stay'd the commons' rage
That would ere this have shaken Richard's chair
Or set all England on a burning fire.
And 'fore my God I fear when she is gone
This woeful land will all to ruin run.   65

Re-enter Cheney

RICHARD II, PART ONE, IV.II

How now, Cheney, what, is thy lady gone yet?

CHENEY
She is, my lord, with much unwillingness,
And 'tis so dark I cannot blame her Grace.
The lights of heaven are shut in pitchy clouds
And flakes of fire run tilting through the sky   70
Like dim ostents to some great tragedy.

WOODSTOCK
God bless good Anne a' Beame! I fear her death
Will be the tragic scene the sky foreshows us.
When kingdoms change, the very heavens are
troubled.   75
Pray God King Richard's wild behavior
Force not the powers of heaven to frown upon us.
My prayers are still for him. What think'st thou,
Cheney?
May not Plain Thomas live a time to see   80
This state attain her former royalty?
'Fore God, I doubt it not! My heart is merry,
And I am suddenly inspir'd for mirth.
Ha, what sport shall we have tonight, Cheney?

CHENEY
I'm glad to see your Grace addicted so,   85
For I have news of sudden mirth to tell ye
Which, till I heard ye speak, I durst not utter.
We shall have a masque tonight, my lord.

WOODSTOCK
Ha, a masque say'st thou? What are they, Cheney?

CHENEY
It seems, my lord, some country gentlemen,   90
To show their dear affection to your Grace,
Proffer their sports this night to make you merry.

RICHARD II, PART ONE, IV.II

Their drums have call'd for entrance twice already.

WOODSTOCK
Are they so near? I prithee, let them enter.
Tell them we do embrace their loves most kindly. 95
Give order through the house that all observe them.

Exit Cheney

We must accept their loves, although the times
Are no way suited now for masques and revels.
What ho, within there!

Enter a Servant

SERVANT
My lord? 100

WOODSTOCK
Prepare a banquet. Call for lights and music.

Servant bows and exits

They come in love, and we'll accept it so.
Some sports does well, we're all too full of woe.

Re-enter Cheney and Servants with lights

CHENEY
They're come, my lord.

WOODSTOCK
They all are welcome, Cheney. Set me a chair, 105
We will behold their sports in spite of care.

*Cheney setst a chair, then exits. Flourish and winding
of horns, and a great shout. Enter Cynthia*

RICHARD II, PART ONE, IV.II

CYNTHIA
From the clear orb of our ethereal sphere
Bright Cynthia comes to hunt and revel here.
The groves of Calydon and Arden Woods
Of untam'd monsters, wild and savage herds, 110
We and our knights have freed, and hither come
To hunt these forests, where we hear there lies
A cruel tusked boar, whose terror flies
Through this large kingdom, and with fear and dread
Strikes her amazed greatness pale and dead. 115
And, having view'd from far these towers of stone,
We heard the people, midst their joy and moan,
Extol to heaven a faithful prince and peer
That keeps a court of love and pity here.
Reverend and mild his looks: if such there be, 120
This state directs, great prince, that you are he.
And ere our knights to this great hunting go,
Before your Grace they would some pastime show
In sprightly dancing. Thus they bade me say,
And wait an answer to return or stay. 125

WOODSTOCK
Nay, for heaven's pity, let them come, I prithee.
Pretty device, i'faith! Stand by, make room there!
Stir, stir, good fellows, each man to his task.

Exit Servants

We shall have a clear night, the moon directs the
masque. 130

*Music. Enter King Richard, Green, Bushy and Bagot,
like Diana's knights, led in by four other knights in
green, with horns about their necks and boar-spears
in their hands*

RICHARD II, PART ONE, IV.II

WOODSTOCK
Ha, country sports, say ye? 'Fore God, 'tis courtly.
A general welcome, courteous gentlemen,
And when I see your faces, I'll give each man more particular.
If your entertainment fail your merit, 135
I must ask pardon: my lady is from home
And most of my attendants waiting on her.
But we'll do what we can to bid you welcome.
Afore my God, it joys my heart to see
Amidst these days of woe and misery 140
Ye find a time for harmless mirth and sport.
But 'tis your loves, and we'll be thankful for't.
Ah, sirrah, ye come like knights to hunt the boar indeed,
And heaven, he knows, we had need of helping hands, 145
So many wild boars roots and spoils our lands,
That England almost is destroy'd by them.
I care not if King Richard hear me speak it:
I wish his Grace all good, high heaven can tell.
But there's a fault in some, alack the day, 150
His youth is led by flatterers much astray.
But he's our king and God's great deputy,
And if ye hunt to have me second ye
In any rash attempt against his state,
Afore my God, I'll ne'er consent unto it. 155
I ever yet was just and true to him,
And so will still remain. What's now amiss
Our sins have caus'd, and we must bide heaven's will.
I speak my heart: I am Plain Thomas still.
Come, come, a hall and music there! Your dance 160
being done,
A banquet stands prepar'd to bid you welcome.

Music. They dance. Re-enter Cheney in haste

RICHARD II, PART ONE, IV.II

WOODSTOCK
How now, Cheney, is this banquet ready?

CHENEY
There is no time, I fear, for banqueting, my lord!
I wish your Grace be provident, 165

A drum heard afar off

I fear your person is betray'd, my lord!
The house is round beset with armed soldiers!

WOODSTOCK
Ha, soldiers?
Afore my God, the commons all are up, then.
They will rebel against the King, I fear me, 170
And flock to me to back their bold attempts.
Go arm the household, Cheney!

Exit Cheney. The Players privately confer

Hear me, gentlemen!
'Fore God, I do not like this whispering!
If your intents be honest, show your faces. 175

KING
Guard fast the doors and seize him presently!
This is the cave that keeps the tusked boar
That roots up England's vineyards uncontroll'd.
Bagot, arrest him! If for help he cry,
Drown all his words with drums confusedly. 180

WOODSTOCK
Am I betray'd?

BAGOT
Ye cannot 'scape, my lord, the toils are pitch'd

And all your household fast in hold ere this.
Thomas of Woodstock, Duke of Gloucester,
Earl of Cambridge and of Buckingham, 185
I here arrest thee in King Richard's name
Of treason to the crown, his state and realm.

WOODSTOCK
I'll put in bail, and answer to the law.
Speak, is King Richard here?

ALL
No, no, my lord! Away with him! 190

WOODSTOCK
Villains, touch me not!
I am descended of the royal blood,
King Richard's uncle, his grandsire's son,
His princely father's brother!
Becomes it princes to be led like slaves? 195

KING
Put on a vizard! Stop his cries!

WOODSTOCK
Ha, who bids them so? I know that voice full well.
Afore my God, false men, King Richard's here!
Turn thee, thou headstrong youth, and speak again!
By thy dead father's soul, I charge thee, hear me, 200
So heaven may help me at my greatest need,
As I have wish'd thy good and England's safety.

BAGOT
You're still deceiv'd, my lord, the King's not here!

BUSHY
On with his masquing suit, and bear him hence!
We'll lead ye fairly to King Richard's presence. 205

RICHARD II, PART ONE, IV.III

WOODSTOCK
Nay, from his presence to my death you'll lead me!
And I am pleas'd I shall not live to see
My country's ruin and his misery.
Thou hear'st me well, proud King, and well may'st boast   210
That thou betray'd'st me here so suddenly,
For had I known thy secret treachery,
Nor thou, nor these thy flattering minions,
With all your strengths, had wrong'd plain Woodstock thus!   215
But use your wills. Your uncles, Gaunt and York,
Will give you thanks for this, and the poor commons,
When they shall hear of these your unjust proceedings.

KING
Stop's mouth, I say, we'll hear no more!   220

WOODSTOCK
Good heaven, forgive me, pray ye forbear awhile,
I'll speak but one word more, indeed I will!
Some man commend me to my virtuous wife,
Tell her her dreams have ta'en effect indeed:
By wolves and lions now must Woodstock bleed.   225

KING
Deliver him to Lapoole—the ship lies ready.
Convey him o'er to Calais speedily,
There use him as we gave directions.
Sound up your drums! Our hunting sports are done,
And when you're past the house, cast by your habits   230
And mount your horses with all swiftest haste.
The boar is taken, and our fears are past!

Drums. Exeunt omnes

Act IV Scene III

[Sheen Palace, Richmond]

Enter Crosby, Fleming and Nimble

CROSBY
Come, sirs, attend; my lord is coming forth. 1
The High Shrieves of Kent and Northumberland
With twenty gentlemen are all arrested
For privy whisperers against the state,
In which I know my lord will find some trick 5
To seize their goods, and then there's work for us.

NIMBLE
Nay, there will be work for the hangman first, then we
rifle their goods, and my lord seizes their lands! If
these seven hundred whisperers that are taken come
off lustily, he'll have the devil and all shortly! 10

Enter Tresilian with the Shrieves of Kent and Northumberland, guarded by Officers

FLEMING
See, see, they're coming.

TRESILIAN
Call for a marshal there! Commit the traitors!

SHRIEVE OF KENT
We do beseech your Honor, hear us speak.

TRESILIAN
Sir, we'll not hear ye, the proof's too plain against ye!
Becomes it you, sir, being Shrieve of Kent, 15
To stay the Blanks King Richard sent abroad,
Revile our messengers, refuse the Charters,

RICHARD II, PART ONE, IV.III

And spurn like traitors 'gainst the King's decrees?

SHRIEVE OF KENT
My lord, I plead our ancient liberties
Recorded and enroll'd in the king's Crown Office,   20
Wherein the men of Kent are clear discharg'd
Of fines, fifteens, or any other taxes,
Forever given them by the Conqueror.

TRESILIAN
You're still deceiv'd. Those Charters were not sent
To abrogate your ancient privilege,   25
But for his Highness' use they were devis'd
To gather and collect amongst his subjects
Such sums of money as they well might spare,
And he, in their defense, must hourly spend.
Is not the subjects' wealth at the King's will?   30
What, is he lord of lives and not of lands?
Is not his high displeasure present death?
And dare ye stir his indignation so?

SHRIEVE OF NORTHUMBERLAND
We are free-born, my lord, yet do confess
Our lives and goods are at the King's dispose,   35
But how, my lord, like to a gentle prince,
To take or borrow what we best may spare,
And not, like bond-slaves, force it from our hands.

TRESILIAN
Presumptuous traitors, that will we try on you!
Will you set limits to the King's high pleasure?   40
Away to prison! Seize their goods and lands!

SHRIEVE OF KENT
Much good may it do ye, my lord, the care is ta'en;
As good die there as here abroad be slain.

RICHARD II, PART ONE, IV.III

SHRIEVE OF NORTHUMBERLAND
Well, God forgive both you and us, my lord.
Your hard oppressions have undone the state   45
And made all England poor and desolate.

TRESILIAN
[*To Officers*] Why suffer ye their speech? To prison, hie!
There let them perish, rot, consume, and die!

Exeunt Officers with the Shrieves

Art thou there, Nimble?   50

NIMBLE
I am here, my lord, and since your lordship is now
employ'd to punish traitors, I am come to present
myself unto you.

TRESILIAN
What, for a traitor?

NIMBLE
No, my lord, but for a discoverer of the strangest   55
traitor that was ever heard of, for by the plain
arithmetic of my capacity, I have found out the very
words a traitor spoke that has whistl'd treason.

TRESILIAN
How is that, whistl'd treason?

NIMBLE
Most certain, my lord, I have a trick for't. If a carman   60
do but whistle, I'll find treason in it, I warrant ye.

TRESILIAN
Thou'rt a rare statesman, Nimble. Thou hast a

reaching head.

NIMBLE
I'll put treason into any man's head, my lord, let him
answer it as he can! And then, my lord, we have got 65
a schoolmaster that teaches all the country to sing
treason, and like a villain he says God bless your
lordship!

TRESILIAN
Thou'rt a most strange discoverer! Where are these
traitors? 70

NIMBLE
All in prison, my lord. Master Ignorance, the Bailey
of Dunstable, and I, have taken great pains about
them. Besides, here's a note of seven hundred
whisperers, most o' them sleepy knaves. We pull'd
them out of Bedfordshire. 75

TRESILIAN
Let's see the note. Seven hundred whispering traitors?
Monstrous villains! We must look to these.
Of all the sort, these are most dangerous
To stir rebellion 'gainst the King and us.
What are they, Crosby? Are the rebels wealthy? 80

CROSBY
Fat chuffs, my lord, all landed men, rich farmers,
graziers, and such fellows that, having been but a
little pinch'd with imprisonment, begin already to
offer their lands for liberty.

TRESILIAN
We'll not be nice to take their offers, Crosby, 85
Their lands are better than their lives to us,
And without lands they shall not ransom lives.

RICHARD II, PART ONE, IV.III

Go, sirs, to terrify the traitors more
Ye shall have warrants straight to hang them all;
Then, if they proffer lands and put in bail   90
To make a just surrender speedily,
Let them have lives, and after, liberty.
But those that have nor lands nor goods to pay,
Let them be whipp'd, then hang'd. Make haste, away.

NIMBLE
Well, then, I see my whistler must be whipp'd. He has   95
but two calves to live on, and has lost them too. As
for my schoolmaster, I'll have him march about the
market place with ten dozen of rods at his girdle the
very day he goes a-feasting, and every one of his
scholars shall have a jerk at him!   100

Enter Bagot

TRESILIAN
Away and leave us. Here comes Sir Edward Bagot.

NIMBLE
Come, sirs.

Exeunt Nimble, Crosby, and the others

BAGOT
Right happily met, my lord Tresilian.

TRESILIAN
You're well return'd to court, Sir Edward,
To this sad house of Sheen, made comfortless   105
By the sharp sickness of the good Queen Anne.

BAGOT
King Richard's come, and gone to visit her.
Sad for her weak estate, he sits and weeps.
Her speech is gone. Only at sight of him

RICHARD II, PART ONE, IV.III

She heav'd her hands and clos'd her eyes again, 110
And whether alive or dead is yet uncertain.

Enter Bushy

TRESILIAN
Here comes Sir William Bushy. What tidings, sir?

BUSHY
The King's a widower, sir. Fair Anne a' Beame
Hath breath'd her last farewell to all the realm.

TRESILIAN
Peace with her soul, she was a virtuous lady. 115
How takes King Richard this her sudden death?

BUSHY
Fares like a madman! Rends his princely hair,
Beats his sad breast, falls groveling on the earth
All careless of his state, wishing to die
And even in death to keep her company! 120
But that which makes his soul more desperate,
Amidst this heat of passion, weeping comes
His aunt, the Duchess, Woodstock's hapless wife,
With tender love and comfort,
At sight of whom his griefs again redoubled, 125
Calling to mind the lady's woeful state
As yet all ignorant of her own mishap.
He takes her in his arms, weeps on her breast,
And would have there reveal'd her husband's fall
Amidst his passions, had not Scroop and Green 130
By violence borne him to an inward room,
Where still he cries to get a messenger
To send to Calais to reprieve his uncle.

BAGOT
I do not like those passions.

The Tragedy of King Richard II, Part One

RICHARD II, PART ONE, IV.III

If he reveal the plot we all shall perish. Where is the   135
Duchess?

BUSHY
With much ado we got her leave the presence, with an
intent in haste to ride to Plashy.

TRESILIAN
She'll find sad comforts there. Would all were well!
A thousand dangers round enclose our state!   140

BAGOT
And we'll break through, my lord, in spite of fate.
Come, come, be merry, good Tresilian.

Enter King Richard, Green and Scroop, with archers

Here comes King Richard, all go comfort him.

SCROOP
My dearest lord, forsake these sad laments.
No sorrows can suffice to make her live.   145

KING
Then let sad sorrow kill King Richard too!
For all my earthly joys with her must die,
And I am kill'd with cares eternally,
For Anne a' Beame is dead, forever gone!
She was too virtuous to remain with me,   150
And heaven hath given her higher dignity.
Oh, God, I fear even here begins our woe:
Her death's but chorus to some tragic scene
That shortly will confound our state and realm.
Such sad events black mischiefs still attend,   155
And bloody acts, I fear, must crown the end.

BAGOT
Presage not so, sweet prince, your state is strong.

RICHARD II, PART ONE, IV.III

Your youthful hopes with expectation crown;
Let not one loss so many comforts drown.

KING
Despair and madness seize me! Oh, dear friends,   160
What loss can be compar'd to such a queen?
Go, ruin all! Down with this house of Sheen!
Pull down her buildings, let her turrets fall,
Forever lay it waste and desolate,
That English king may never here keep court,   165
But to all ages leave a sad report,
When men shall see these ruin'd walls of Sheen
And sighing, say, 'Here died King Richard's queen!'
For which we'll have it wasted lime and stone
To keep a monument of Richard's moan.   170
Oh, torturing grief!

BUSHY
Oh, dear my liege, all tears for her are vain oblations,
Her quiet soul rests in celestial peace.
With joy of that, let all your sorrows cease.

KING
Send post to Calais and bid Lapoole forbear   175
On pain of life to act our sad decree!
For heaven's love, go! Prevent the tragedy!
We have too much provok'd the powers divine,
And here repent thy wrongs, good uncle Woodstock,
The thought whereof confounds my memory!   180
If men might die when they would 'point the time,
The time is now King Richard would be gone,
For as a fearful thunderclap doth strike
The soundest body of the tallest oak,
Yet harmless leaves the outward bark untouch'd,   185
So is King Richard struck. Come, come, let's go.
My wounds are inward, inward burn my woe!

RICHARD II, PART ONE, V.I

Exeunt omnes

Act V Scene I

[The English fortress at Calais]

Enter Lapoole with a light, after him two Murderers

LAPOOLE
Come, sirs, be resolute. The time serves well   1
To act the business you have ta'en in hand.
The Duke is gone to rest, the room is voided,
No ear can hear his cries. Be fearless, bold,
And win King Richard's love with heaps of gold.   5
Are all your instruments for death made ready?

FIRST MURDERER
All fit to the purpose. See, my lord, here's first a towel
with which we do intend to strangle him; but if he
strive, and this should chance to fail, I'll mall his old
mazzard with this hammer, knock him down like an   10
ox, and after cut's throat. How like ye this?

LAPOOLE
No, wound him not,
It must be done so fair and cunningly
As if he died a common, natural death,
For so we must give out to all that ask.   15

SECOND MURDERER
There is no way then but to smother him.

LAPOOLE
I like that best. Yet one thing let me tell ye:
Think not your work contriv'd so easily
As if you were to match some common man.
Believe me, sirs, his countenance is such,   20

RICHARD II, PART ONE, V.I

So full of dread and lordly majesty,
Mix'd with such mild and gentle 'havior,
As will, except you be resolv'd at full,
Strike you with fear even with his princely looks.

FIRST MURDERER
Not an' he look'd as grim as Hercules,   25
As stern and terrible as the devil himself!

LAPOOLE
'Tis well resolv'd. Retire yourselves awhile,
Stay in the next withdrawing chamber there,
And when I spy the best advantage for ye, I'll call
ye forth.   30

SECOND MURDERER
Do but beckon with your finger, my lord, and like
vultures we come flying and seize him presently!

LAPOOLE
Do so.

Exeunt the Two Murderers

And yet, by all my fairest hopes, I swear
The boldness of these villains to this murder   35
Makes me abhor them and the deed forever!
Horror of conscience with the King's command
Fights a fell combat in my fearful breast.
The King commands his uncle here must die,
And my sad conscience bids the contrary,   40
And tells me that his innocent blood thus spilt
Heaven will revenge. Murder's a heinous guilt,
A seven-times crying sin. Accursed man!
The further that I wade in this foul act
My troubled senses are the more distract,   45
Confounded and tormented past my reason.

RICHARD II, PART ONE, V.I

But there's no lingering: either he must die
Or great King Richard vows my tragedy.
Then 'twixt two evils 'tis good to choose the least:
Let danger fright faint fools. I'll save mine own,   50
And let him fall to black destruction.

He draws the curtains

He sleeps upon his bed. The time serves fitly,
I'll call the murderers in. Sound music there,
To rock his senses in eternal slumbers.

Music within

Sleep, Woodstock, sleep. Thou never more shalt   55
wake.
This town of Calais shall forever tell,
Within her castle walls Plain Thomas fell.

Exit Lapoole. Thunder and lightning. Enter the Ghost of the Black Prince

GHOST OF THE BLACK PRINCE
Night, horror, and th'eternal shrieks of death
Intended to be done this dismal night,   60
Hath shook fair England's great cathedral,
And from my tomb elate at Canterbury
The ghost of Edward the Black Prince is come
To stay King Richard's rage, my wanton son.
Thomas of Woodstock, wake! Thy brother calls thee!   65
Thou royal issue of King Edward's loins,
Thou art beset with murder! Rise and fly!
If here thou stay, death comes and thou must die.
Still dost thou sleep? Oh, I am naught but air!
Had I the vigor of my former strength,   70
When thou beheld'st me fight at Crécy Field,
Where, hand-to-hand, I took King John of France

The Tragedy of King Richard II, Part One

RICHARD II, PART ONE, V.I

And his bold sons my captive prisoners,
I'd shake these stiff supporters of thy bed
And drag thee from this dull security! 75
Oh, yet for pity, wake! Prevent thy doom!
Thy blood upon my son will surely come,
For which, dear brother Woodstock, haste and fly,
Prevent his ruin and thy tragedy!

Thunder. Exit Ghost of the Black Prince. Enter the Ghost of Edward the Third

GHOST OF EDWARD THE THIRD
Oh, sleep'st thou so soundly and pale death so nigh? 80
Thomas of Woodstock, wake, my son, and fly!
Thy wrongs have rous'd thy royal father's ghost
And from his quiet grave King Edward's come
To guard thy innocent life, my princely son.
Behold me here: sometime fair England's lord. 85
Seven warlike sons I left; yet, being gone,
Not one succeeded in my kingly throne.
Richard of Bordeaux, my accursed grandchild,
Cut off your titles to the kingly state
And now your lives and all would ruinate. 90
Murders his grandsire's sons—his father's brothers!—
Becomes a landlord to my kingly titles,
Rents out my crown's revenues, racks my subjects
That spent their bloods with me in conquering France,
Beheld me ride in state through London streets, 95
And at my stirrup lowly footing by
Four captive kings to grace my victory.
Yet that nor this his riotous youth can stay,
Till death hath ta'en his uncles all away.
Thou fifth of Edward's sons, get up and fly! 100
Haste thee to England, close and speedily!
Thy brothers, York and Gaunt, are up in arms,
Go join with them, prevent thy further harms.
The murderers are at hand—awake, my son!

This hour foretells thy sad destruction. 105

Exit Ghost of Edward the Third

WOODSTOCK
Oh, good angels, guide me! Stay, thou blessed spirit,
Thou royal shadow of my kingly father!
Return again, I know thy reverend looks,
With thy dear sight once more recomfort me,
Put by the fears my trembling heart foretells, 110
And here is made apparent to my sight
By dreams and visions of this dreadful night.
Upon my knees I beg it. Ha, protect me, heaven!
The doors are all made fast: 'twas but my fancy.
All's whist and still, and nothing here appears 115
But the vast circuit of this empty room.
Thou blessed hand of mercy, guide my senses!
Afore my God, methought as here I slept,
I did behold in lively form and substance
My father Edward and my warlike brother, 120
Both gliding by my bed, and cried to me
To leave this place, to save my life and fly.
Lighten my fears, dear Lord! I here remain
A poor old man, thrust from my native country,
Kept and imprison'd in a foreign kingdom. 125
If I must die, bear record, righteous heaven,
How I have nightly wak'd for England's good,
And yet to right her wrongs would spend my blood.
Send thy sad doom, King Richard, take my life,
I wish my death might ease my country's grief. 130

Enter Lapoole and the Murderers

LAPOOLE
We are prevented. Back, retire again,
He's risen from his bed. What fate preserves him?
[*To Woodstock*] My lord, how fare you?

RICHARD II, PART ONE, V.I

WOODSTOCK
Thou can'st not kill me, villain! 135
God's holy angel guards a just man's life
And with his radiant beams as bright as fire
Will guard and keep his righteous innocence.
I am a prince, thou dar'st not murder me!

LAPOOLE
Your Grace mistakes, my lord. 140

WOODSTOCK
What art thou? Speak!

LAPOOLE
Lapoole, my lord, this city's governor.

WOODSTOCK
Lapoole, thou art King Richard's flatterer.
Oh, you just gods, record their treachery,
Judge their foul wrongs that under show of friendship 145
Betray'd my simple, kind intendiments!
My heart misgave it was no time for revels
When you like masquers came disguis'd to Plashy,
Join'd with that wanton king to trap my life—
For that I know's the end his malice aims at! 150
This castle, and my secret sending hither,
Imports no less. Therefore, I charge ye, tell me
Even by the virtue of nobility,
And partly, too, on that allegiance
Thou ow'st the offspring of King Edward's house, 155
If aught thou know'st to prejudice my life,
Thou presently reveal, and make it known.

LAPOOLE
Nay, good my lord, forbear that fond suspicion!

RICHARD II, PART ONE, V.1

WOODSTOCK
I tell thee, Poole, there is no less intended.
Why am I sent thus from my native country, 160
But here at Calais to be murdered?
And that, Lapoole, confounds my patience.
This town of Calais, where I spent my blood
To make it captive to the English king,
Before whose walls great Edward lay encamp'd 165
With his seven sons, almost for fourteen months;
Where the Black Prince, my brother, and myself,
The peers of England, and our royal father,
Fearless of wounds, ne'er left till it was won—
And was't to make a prison for his son? 170
Oh, righteous heavens, why do you suffer it?

LAPOOLE
Disquiet not your thoughts, my gracious lord.
There is no hurt intended, credit me,
Although a while your freedom be abridg'd.
I know the King: if you would but submit 175
And write your letters to his Majesty,
Your reconcilement might be easily wrought.

WOODSTOCK
For what should I submit or ask his mercy?
Had I offended, with all low submission
I'd lay my neck under the blade before him 180
And willingly endure the stroke of death.
But if not so, why should my fond entreaties
Make my true loyalty appear like treason?
No, no, Lapoole, let guilty men beg pardons;
My mind is clear. And I must tell ye, sir, 185
Princes have hearts like pointed diamonds
That will in sunder burst afore they bend,
And such lives here, though death King Richard
  send!
Yet fetch me pen and ink, I'll write to him, 190

Not to entreat, but to admonish him,
That he forsake his foolish ways in time,
And learn to govern like a virtuous prince,
Call home his wise and reverend Councilors,
Thrust from his court those cursed flatterers   195
That hourly works the realm's confusion.
This counsel if he follow may in time
Pull down those mischiefs that so fast do climb.

LAPOOLE
Here's pen and paper, my lord, will't please ye write?

WOODSTOCK
Anon I will. Shut to the doors and leave me.   200
Goodnight, Lapoole, and pardon me, I prithee,
That my sad fear made question of thy faith.
My state is fearful, and my mind was troubled,
Even at thy entrance, with most fearful visions,
Which made my passions more extreme and hasty.   205
Out of my better judgment I repent it,
And will reward thy love. Once more, good night.

LAPOOLE
Good rest unto your Grace. [*Aside*] I mean in death.
This dismal night thou breath'st thy latest breath.
He sits to write. I'll call the murderers in,   210
To steal behind and closely strangle him.

Exit Lapoole

WOODSTOCK
So help me, heaven, I know not what to write,
What style to use, nor how I should begin.
My method is too plain to greet a king.
I'll nothing say to excuse or clear myself,   215
For I have nothing done that needs excuse,
But tell him plain, though here I spend my blood,

RICHARD II, PART ONE, V.I

I wish his safety and all England's good.

Enter both the Murderers

FIRST MURDERER
Creep close to his back, ye rogue, be ready with the
towel, when I have knock'd him down, to strangle   220
him.

SECOND MURDERER
Do it quickly whilst his back is towards ye, ye damn'd
villain! If thou let'st him speak but a word we shall
not kill him.

FIRST MURDERER
I'll watch him for that. Down on your knees and   225
creep, ye rascal.

WOODSTOCK
Have mercy, God! My sight o' the sudden fails me.
I cannot see my paper,
My trembling fingers will not hold my pen.
A thick congealed mist o'erspreads the chamber: 230
I'll rise and view the room.

SECOND MURDERER
Not too fast for falling! [*Strikes him*]

WOODSTOCK
What villain hand hath done a deed so bad,
To drench his black soul in a prince's blood?

FIRST MURDERER
Do ye prate, sir? Take that and that! Zounds, put the   235
towel about's throat and strangle him quickly, ye
slave, or by the heart of hell, I'll fell thee too!

RICHARD II, PART ONE, V.I

SECOND MURDERER
'Tis done, ye damn'd slave! Pull, ye dog, and pull thy
soul to hell in doing it, for thou hast kill'd the truest
subject that ever breath'd in England! 240

FIRST MURDERER
Pull, rogue, pull! Think of the gold we shall have for
doing it, and then let him and thee go to the devil
together! Bring in the featherbed and roll him up in
that till he be smother'd and stifled and life and soul
press'd out together! Quickly, ye hellhound! 245

SECOND MURDERER
[*Brings featherbed*] Here, here, ye cannibal! Zounds,
he kicks and sprawls! Lie on's breast, ye villain!

FIRST MURDERER
Let him sprawl and hang! He's sure enough for
speaking. Pull off the bed now, smooth down his hair
and beard. Close his eyes and set his neck right. Why, 250
so, all fine and cleanly. Who can say that this man
was murder'd now?

Enter Lapoole

LAPOOLE
What, is he dead?

SECOND MURDERER
As a door-nail, my lord. What will ye do with his
body? 255

LAPOOLE
Take it up gently, lay him in his bed;
Then shut the door as if he there had died.

RICHARD II, PART ONE, V.I

FIRST MURDERER
It cannot be perceived otherwise, my lord. Never was
murder done with such rare skill. At our return, we
shall expect reward, my lord.   260

LAPOOLE
'Tis ready told. Bear in the body, then return and take
it.

Exeunt Murderers with the body and featherbed

Within there, ho!

Enter Soldiers

SOLDIERS
My lord?

LAPOOLE
Draw all your weapons, soldiers, guard the room!   265
There's two false traitors enter'd the Duke's chamber,
Plotting to bear him thence, betray the castle,
Deliver up the town and all our lives
To the French forces that are hard at hand
To second their attempts. Therefore, stand close,   270
And as they enter, seize them presently.
Our will's your warrant: use no further words,
But hew them straight in pieces with your swords!

SOLDIER
I warrant ye, my lord, and their skins were scal'd with
brass we have swords will pierce them. Come, sirs, be   275
ready.

Re-enter the Two Murderers

FIRST MURDERER
Come, ye miching rascal, the deed's done and all

things perform'd rarely. We'll take our reward, steal
close out o' the town, buy us fresh geldings, then
spur, cut and ride till we are past all danger, I warrant   280
thee.

LAPOOLE
Give their reward there! Quick, I say!

SOLDIER
Down with the traitors! Kill the villains!

FIRST AND SECOND MURDERERS
Hell and the devil! Zounds! Hold, ye rascals!

Soldiers kill the Murderers

LAPOOLE
Drag hence their bodies, hurl them in the sea!   285
The black reward of death's a traitor's pay!

Exeunt Soldiers with their bodies

So, this was well perform'd! Now who but we
Can make report of Woodstock's tragedy?
Only he died a natural death at Calais—
So must we give it out, or else King Richard   290
Through Europe's kingdoms will be hardly censur'd.
His headstrong uncles, York and Lancaster,
Are up, we hear, in open arms against him;
The gentlemen and commons of the realm,
Missing the good old Duke, their plain Protector,   295
Break their allegiance to their sovereign lord
And all revolt upon the barons' sides.
To help which harm, I'll o'er to England straight,
And with th' old troops of soldiers ta'en from Calais,
I'll back King Richard's power, for should he fail,   300
And his great uncles get the victory,

His friends are sure to die. But if he win,
They fall and we shall rise, whilst Richard's king!

Exit

Act V Scene II

[Near King Richard's camp]

Drums. March within. Enter Tresilian and Nimble with armor

TRESILIAN
These proclamations we have sent abroad, 1
Wherein we have accus'd the Dukes of treason,
Will daunt their pride and make the people leave them.
I hope no less, at least. Where art thou, Nimble? 5

NIMBLE
So loaden with armor I cannot stir, my lord!

TRESILIAN
Whose drums were those that beat even now?

NIMBLE
King Richard's drums, my lord. The young lords are pressing soldiers.

TRESILIAN
Oh, and do they take their press with willingness? 10

NIMBLE
As willing as a punk that's press'd on a feather-bed, they take their pressing apiece with great patience. Marry, the lords no sooner turn their backs but they run away like sheep, sir,

RICHARD II, PART ONE, V.II

TRESILIAN
They shall be hang'd like dogs for't! 15
What, dares the slaves refuse their sovereign?

NIMBLE
They say the proclamation's false, my lord,
And they'll not fight against the King's friends.

TRESILIAN
So, I fear'd as much. And since 'tis come to this,
I must provide betime and seek for safety, 20
For now the King and our audacious peers
Are grown to such a height of burning rage
As nothing now can quench their kindled ire
But open trial by the sword and lance,
And then, I fear, King Richard's part will fail. 25
Nimble, our soldiers run, thou sayest?

NIMBLE
Ay, by my troth, my lord, and I think 'tis our best
course to run after them, for if they run now, what
will they do when the battle begins? If we tarry here
and the King's uncles catch us, we are sure to be 30
hang'd. My lord, have ye no trick of law to defend us?
No demur, or writ of error, to remove us?

TRESILIAN
Nimble, we must be wise.

NIMBLE
Then let's not stay to have more wit beaten into our
heads. I like not that, my lord! 35

TRESILIAN
I am a man for peace, and not for war.

NIMBLE
And yet they say you have made more wrangling i'
the land than all the wars has done these seven years!

TRESILIAN
This battle will revenge their base exclaims.
But hear'st thou, Nimble, I'll not be there today.   40
One man amongst so many is no maim,
Therefore I'll keep aloof till all be done.
If good, I stay; if bad, I run away.
Nimble, it shall be so. I'll neither fight nor die,
But thus resolv'd, disguise myself and fly.   45

NIMBLE
'Tis the wisest course, my lord, and I'll go put off
mine armor that I may run lustily too.

Exeunt

Act V Scene III

[Radcot Bridge]

*Enter with drum and colors Lancaster, York, Arundel
Surrey, Cheney and Soldiers, with the Duchess of
Gloucester weeping*

LANCASTER
Go to our tents, dear sister, cease your sorrows.   1
We will revenge our noble brother's wrongs,
And force that wanton tyrant to reveal
The death of his dear uncle, harmless Woodstock,
So traitorously betray'd.   5

YORK
It was an easy task to work on him,
His plainness was too open to their view.

RICHARD II, PART ONE, V.III

He fear'd no wrong because his heart was true.
Good sister, cease your weeping, there's none here
But are as full of woe and touch'd as near. 10
Conduct and guard her, Cheney, to the tent.
[*To Duchess*] Expect to hear severest punishment
On all their heads that have procur'd his harms,
Struck from the terror of our threatening arms.

DUCHESS OF GLOUCESTER
May all the powers of heaven assist your hands, 15
And may their sins sit heavy on their souls,
That they in death this day may perish all
That traitorously conspir'd good Woodstock's fall!

LANCASTER
If he be dead, by good King Edward's soul,
We'll call King Richard to a strict account 20
For that, and for his realm's misgovernment!

Exit the Duchess of Gloucester escorted by Cheney

You peers of England, rais'd in righteous arms,
Here to re-edify our country's ruin,
Join all your hearts and hands, never to cease
Till with our swords we work fair England's peace! 25

ARUNDEL
Most princely Lancaster, our lands and lives
Are to these just proceedings ever vow'd!

SURREY
Those flattering minions that o'erturns the state
This day in death shall meet their endless fate!

YORK
Never such vipers were endur'd so long 30
To grip and eat the hearts of all the kingdom!

RICHARD II, PART ONE, V.III

LANCASTER
This day shall here determinate all wrongs!
The meanest man tax'd by their foul oppressions
Shall be permitted freely to accuse,
And right they shall have to regain their own, 35
Or all shall sink to dark confusion!

Drums sound within

ARUNDEL
How now, what drums are these?

Enter Cheney

CHENEY
To arms, my lords! The minions of the King
Are swiftly marching on to give ye battle!

LANCASTER
They march to death then, Cheney. Dare the traitors 40
Presume to brave the field with English princes?

YORK
Where is King Richard? He was resolv'd but lately
To take some hold of strength and so secure him.

CHENEY
Knowing their states were all so desperate,
It seems they have persuaded otherwise, 45
For now he comes with full resolve to fight.
Lapoole this morning is arriv'd at court
With the Calais soldiers and some French supplies
To back this now-intended enterprise.

LANCASTER
Those new supplies have spurr'd their forward hopes 50
And thrust their resolutions boldly on

The Tragedy of King Richard II, Part One

RICHARD II, PART ONE, V.III

To meet with death and sad destruction.

Drums sound

YORK
Their drums are near. Just heaven, direct this deed,
And as our cause deserv's, our fortunes speed!

*They march about. Then enter with drums and colors
King Richard, Bagot, Bushy, Green, Scroop, Lapoole,
and Soldiers. They march about also*

KING
Although we could have easily surpris'd, 55
Dispers'd and overthrown your rebel troops
That draw your swords against our sacred person,
The highest God's anointed deputy,
Breaking your holy oaths to heaven and us,
Yet of our mild and princely clemency 60
We have forborne, that by this parliament
We might be made partaker of the cause
That mov'd ye rise in this rebellious sort.

LANCASTER
Hast thou, King Richard, made us infamous
By proclamations false and impudent? 65
Hast thou condemn'd us in our absence too
As most notorious traitors to the crown?
Betray'd our brother Woodstock's harmless life,
And sought base means to put us all to death?
And dost thou now plead doltish ignorance 70
Why we are banded thus in our defense?

GREEN
Methinks your treasons to his Majesty,
Raising his subjects 'gainst his royal life,
Should make ye beg for mercy at his feet!

RICHARD II, PART ONE, V.III

KING
You have forgotten, uncle Lancaster, 75
How you in prison murdered cruelly
A friar Carmelite because he was
To bring in evidence against your Grace
Of most ungracious deeds and practices?

LANCASTER
And you, my lord, remember not so well 80
That by that Carmelite at London once,
When at a supper, you'd have poison'd us.

YORK
For shame, King Richard, leave this company
That like dark clouds obscure the sparkling stars
Of thy great birth and true nobility! 85

ARUNDEL
Yield to your uncles! Who but they should have
The guidance of your sacred state and Council?

BAGOT
Yield first your heads, and so he shall be sure
To keep his person and his state secure!

KING
And, by my crown, if still you thus persist, 90
Your heads and hearts ere long shall answer it!

ARUNDEL
Not till ye send for more supplies from France,
For England will not yield ye strength to do it!

YORK
Thou well may'st doubt their loves, that lost their
hearts! 95
Ungracious prince, cannot thy native country
Find men to back this desperate enterprise?

RICHARD II, PART ONE, V.III

LANCASTER
His native country? Why, that is France, my lords!
At Bordeaux was he born, which place allures
And ties his deep affections still to France. 100
Richard is English blood, not English born!
Thy mother travail'd in unhappy hours
When she at Bordeaux left her heavy load.
The soil is fit for wines, not fit for men,
And England now laments that heavy time. 105
Her royalties are lost, her state made base,
And thou no king but landlord now become
To this great state that terror'd Christendom.

KING
I cannot brook these braves! Let drums sound death,
And strike at once to stop this traitor's breath! 110

BAGOT
Stay, my dear lord! And once more hear me, princes.
The King was minded, ere this brawl began,
To come to terms of composition.

LANCASTER
Let him revoke the proclamations,
Clear us of all supposed crimes of treason, 115
Reveal where our good brother Gloucester keeps,
And grant that these pernicious flatterers
May by the law be tried, to quit themselves
Of all such heinous crimes alleg'd against them,
And we'll lay down our weapons at thy feet. 120

KING
Presumptuous traitors!

ALL
Traitors!

RICHARD II, PART ONE, V.IV

KING
Again we double it: rebellious traitors!
Traitors to heaven and us! Draw all your swords
And fling defiance to those traitorous lords! 125

KING'S MEN
Let our drums thunder and begin the fight!

LORDS' MEN
Just heaven protect us and defend the right!

Exeunt omnes

Act V Scene IV

[The battlefield]

Alarum. Enter Green and Cheney, armed

CHENEY
Stand, traitor! For thou can'st not 'scape my sword! 1

GREEN
What villain fronts me with the name of traitor?
Was't thou, false Cheney? Now, by King Richard's love,
I'll tilt thy soul out for that base reproach! 5
I would thy master and the late Protector,
With both his treacherous brothers, Gaunt and York,
Were all oppos'd with thee to try these arms!
I'd seal't on all your hearts!

CHENEY
This shall suffice to free the kingdom from thy 10
villainies!

They fight. Enter Arundel

The Tragedy of King Richard II, Part One

RICHARD II, PART ONE, V.IV

ARUNDEL
Thou hunt'st a noble game, right warlike Cheney!
Cut but this ulcer off, thou heal'st the kingdom.
Yield thee, false traitor, most detested man,
That settest King Richard 'gainst his reverend uncles   15
To shed the royal bloods and make the realm
Weep for their timeless desolation!
Cast down thy weapons, for by this my sword,
We'll bear thee from this place, alive or dead!

GREEN
Come both, then! I'll stand firm and dare your worst!   20
He that flies from it, be his soul accurs'd!

They fight and Green is slain

ARUNDEL
So may the foes of England fall in blood!
Most dissolute traitor! Up with his body, Cheney,
And hale it to the tent of Lancaster.

Enter King Richard, Bagot, Bushy, Scroop and Soldiers

CHENEY
Stand firm, my lord, here's rescue!   25

ARUNDEL
We'll bear his body hence, in spite of them!

They fight. To them enter Lancaster, York and Surrey, and beats the King's men all away. Manet Richard with Green's corpse

KING
Oh, princely youth, King Richard's dearest friend!
What heavy star this day had dominance

To cut off all thy flow'ring youthful hopes!
Prosper, proud rebels, as you dealt by him! 30
Hard-hearted uncles, unrelenting churls,
That here have murder'd all my earthly joys!
Oh, my dear Green, wert thou alive to see
How I'll revenge thy timeless tragedy
On all their heads that did but lift a hand 35
To hurt this body that I held so dear!
Even by this kiss and by my crown, I swear!

Alarum within. Re-enter Bagot, Bushy and Scroop to the King

BAGOT
Away, my lord, stand not to wail his death!
The field is lost! Our soldiers shrink and fly,
Lapoole is taken prisoner by the lords. 40
Hie to the Tower! There is no help in swords!

SCROOP
Still to continue war were childishness.
Their odds a mountain, ours a molehill is.

BUSHY
Let's fly to London and make strong the Tower!
Loud proclamations post throughout the camp 45
With promise of reward to all that take us.
Get safety for our lives, my princely lord,
If here we stay, we shall be all betray'd!

KING
Oh, my dear friends, the fearful wrath of heaven
Sits heavy on our heads for Woodstock's death. 50
Blood cries for blood; and that almighty hand
Permits not murder unreveng'd to stand.
Come, come, we yet may hide ourselves from worldly strength,

But heaven will find us out, and strike at length. 55
Each lend a hand to bear this load of woe
That erst King Richard lov'd and tender'd so.

Exeunt bearing the body of Green

Act V Scene V

[A field near the Lords' camp]

Enter Tresilian and Nimble, disguised

TRESILIAN
Where art thou, Nimble? 1

NIMBLE
As light as a feather, my lord! I have put off my
shoes, that I might run lustily. The battle's lost and
the young lords prisoners. What shall we do, my
lord? Yonder's a stream. We may run along that and 5
ne'er be seen, I warrant.

TRESILIAN
I did suspect no less, and so 'tis fall'n.
The day is lost and dash'd are all our hopes.
King Richard's taken prisoner by the peers.
Oh, that I were upon some steepy rock 10
Where I might tumble headlong to the sea
Before those cruel lords do seize on me!

NIMBLE
Oh, that I were transform'd into a mouse that I might
creep into any hole i' the house and I car'd not!

TRESILIAN
Come, Nimble, 'tis no time to use delay. 15

RICHARD II, PART ONE, V.V

I'll keep me in this poor disguise awhile
And so, unknown, prolong my weary life
In hope King Richard shall conclude my peace.

Trumpets within

Hark, hark, the trumpets call the soldiers back:
Retreat is sounded! Now the time serves fit   20
And we may steal from hence. Away, good Nimble!

NIMBLE
Nay, stay my lord! 'Slid, and ye go that way,
farewell; but an' you'll be rul'd by me, I have
thought of a trick that ye shall 'scape them all
most bravely.   25

TRESILIAN
Bethink thyself, good Nimble. Quickly, man!

NIMBLE
I'll meditate, my lord, and then I'm for ye.
[*Aside*] Now, Nimble, show thyself a man of valor!
Think of thy fortunes: 'tis a hanging matter if thou
conceal him. Besides, there's a thousand marks for   30
him that takes him, with the dukes' favors and free
pardon. Besides, he's but a coward, he would ne'er
have run from the battle else. Saint Tantony, assist
me! I'll set upon him presently. [*To Tresilian*] My
lord, I have thought upon this trick: I must take ye   35
prisoner.

TRESILIAN
How, prisoner?

NIMBLE
There's no way to 'scape else. Then must I carry ye to
the King's uncles, who presently condemns ye for a

traitor, sends ye away to hanging, and then 'God bless   40
my lord Tresilian!'

TRESILIAN
Wilt thou betray thy master, villain?

NIMBLE
Ay, if my master be a villain! You think 'tis nothing
for a man to be hang'd for his master? You heard not
the proclamation?   45

TRESILIAN
What proclamation?

NIMBLE
Oh, sir, all the country's full of them—that whosoever
sees you and does not presently take ye and bring ye
to the Lords shall be hang'd for his labor. Therefore,
no more words, lest I raise the whole camp upon ye!   50
Ye see one of your own swords of justice drawn over
ye, therefore go quietly lest I cut your head off and
save the hangman a labor.

TRESILIAN
Oh, villain!

NIMBLE
No more words. Away, sir!   55

Exeunt

Act V Scene VI

[The Lords' camp]

*Sound a retreat, then a flourish. Enter victoriously
with drums and colors Lancaster, Arundel, Surrey,*

The Tragedy of King Richard II, Part One

RICHARD II, PART ONE, V.VI

Cheney and Soldiers, with Lapoole, Bushy and Scroop as prisoners

LANCASTER
Thus princely Edward's sons, in tender care 1
Of wanton Richard and their father's realm,
Have toil'd to purge fair England's pleasant field
Of all those rancorous weeds that chok'd the grounds
And left her pleasant meads like barren hills. 5
Who is't can tell us which way Bagot fled?

ARUNDEL
Some say to Bristowe, to make strong the castle.

LANCASTER
See that the port's belay'd. He'll fly the land,
For England hath no hold can keep him from us.
Had we Tresilian hang'd, then all were sure! 10
Where slept our scouts, that he escap'd the field?

CHENEY
He fled, they say, before the fight began.

LANCASTER
Our proclamations soon shall find him forth,
The root and ground of all these vile abuses.

Enter Nimble with Tresilian bound and guarded

LANCASTER
How now, what guard is that? What traitor's there? 15

NIMBLE
The traitor now is ta'en.
I here present the villain,
And if ye needs will know his name,
God bless my lord Tresilian!

CHENEY
Tresilian, my lord, attach'd and apprehended by his   20
man!

NIMBLE
Yes, and it please ye, my lord, 'twas I that took him.
I was once a trampler in the law after him, and I thank
him he taught me this trick, to save myself from
hanging.   25

LANCASTER
Thou'rt a good lawyer, and hast remov'd the cause
from thyself fairly.

NIMBLE
I have remov'd it with a *Habeas Corpus*, and then I
took him with a *Surssararis* and bound him in this
bond to answer it. Nay, I have studied for my   30
learning, I can tell ye, my lord. There was not a stone
between Westminster Hall and Temple Bar but I have
told them every morning.

ARUNDEL
What moved thee, being his man, to apprehend him?

NIMBLE
Partly for these causes: first, the fear of the   35
proclamation, for I have plodded in Plowden and
can find no law that doth protect this traitor from your
Graces' justice. And second, for the money promis'd,
and third, because he did most treacherously
command the murder of the Duke of Gloucester,   40
Thomas of Woodstock.

Hands a parchment to Lancaster

RICHARD II, PART ONE, V.VI

LANCASTER
Oh, 'tis a warrant for my brother's death!

NIMBLE
Aye, writ of my Lord Chief Injustice here.

LANCASTER
[*Reading*] 'See thou no marks nor violence show
upon him, that we may say he naturally died.' 45
[*To Tresilian*] Oh, scoundrel, for this shalt thou most
violent and unnaturally die!

Shows parchment to Surrey and Arundel

SURREY
Oh, monstrous!

ARUNDEL
Thou false traitor and injurious villain,
To hell's eternal torments art thou damn'd! 50

TRESILIAN
Great lords, I plead the ancient privilege of law
To put in bail and appeal the charge.

LANCASTER
By Heav'n, we'll hear no more, the proof's too plain.
Away with him to Radcot Castle and death's pain!

TRESILIAN
Mercy, great Lancaster! Oh, help me, Nimble! 55

NIMBLE
God bless my lord Tresilian.

Exit Tresilian with Soldiers

RICHARD II, PART ONE, V.VI

LANCASTER
Now, Bushy, freely speak thy mind.
What dost thou know of noble Gloucester's death?

BUSHY
I ever honor'd and rever'd the worthy Duke.
'Twas Bagot, Scroop, Tresilian and the rest   60
Contriv'd against my Lord Protector's life.

SCROOP
Nay, by Lapoole was he most cruelly kill'd.

LAPOOLE
Not so, my lords, at Callice was our watch
Deceiv'd by murd'rers that his Majesty did send,
Who chok'd the goodly kind old man. Yet still   65
I do repent that in my rage I slew
The villains both and cast their bloody limbs
From off the battlements into the sea.

ARUNDEL
So art thou doubly damn'd, Lapoole,
For Woodstock's bloody death and theirs.   70

LAPOOLE
But yet have mercy lords, it was the King
Commanded us. It is the King who is to blame!

LANCASTER
King Richard did decree it, sayest thou? We'll fetch
him in.

CHENEY
The Duke of York attends him. I'll be their conduct.   75

Exit Cheney

RICHARD II, PART ONE, V.VI

LAPOOLE
His Majesty did order Woodstock's death.

BUSHY
Aye, 'twas the King. 'Beware, Plain Thomas,'
Thus said he, 'for Richard comes
To wash away with blood all former wrongs!'
'Tis true, my lords, King Richard did require it. 80

*Re-enter Cheney with King Richard chained, York
bearing his crown and scepter, and Soldiers. Scroop
and Bushy kneel*

KING
I pray you, mock me not. You see I am a king in
chains.

They rise

YORK
King Richard, though our prisoner, art thou still
The first of princely Edward's royal blood,
And we your faithful subjects, staunch and true. 85
Nay, coz, turn not thy kingly face away,
We yet do bear the sad and heavy death
Of Thomas Woodstock, thy kind uncle and our kin.

KING
I am so weary, sirs [*He sits*] I mourn him also, uncle.
God rest good Gloucester's soul. 90

LANCASTER
Stand up, Richard. These traitors here maintain
That you decreed thy father's brother's death.
Here is thy warrant with Tresilian's seal.

KING
Why then they lie, 'twas done without my wish,

RICHARD II, PART ONE, V.VI

For Gloucester's grievous death I urg'd it not. 95
Bushy, thou know'st I did command no gall
To our belov'd Protector should befall.

BUSHY
He did, my lords, and we endeavor'd so.

LANCASTER
Yet is he dead.

KING
Good uncles, I acknowledge my disgrace, 100
I did neglect my duty in that case.

YORK
Your duty, nephew? Aye, and what of ours,
Whose honor and allegiance thus are torn
Betwixt our murder'd kinsman and our king?

KING
I am thy kinsman, uncle, and your king, 105
And with thee grieve most sore for Woodstock's
death.
But, uncle York, and you most noble peers,
Anointed am I still with holy oil,
Thy coronation oaths, my crown, and scepter royal. 110
Nor tears, nor blood nor waters in the sea
Can off my kingly brow take them from me.

ARUNDEL
He is our king, whom we may not depose,
Lest harshly plucking we destroy fair England's rose.

YORK
What says our brother Lancaster? 115

LANCASTER
Edmund, I do believe he wish'd no harm,

RICHARD II, PART ONE, V.VI

We'll pardon him as God shall pardon us
That righteously have sought to cleanse this land.
Besides, Tresilian and Lapoole hath both confess'd;
To end the matter here methinks 'tis best. 120
[*To Soldiers*] See execution's done, take him away.
The sable night of death shall close his day.

Lapoole is taken away

Although of Woodstock's murder you're acquit,
Thy kingdom, Richard, must be set aright,
For all the Commons and assembl'd peers 125
In univocal clamor do require it. Take off his chains.

KING
[*To Soldier*] Thank you, sir. What must I do, my lords?

ARUNDEL
Dismiss these baneful flatterers your court,
Cancel the proclamations of our treachery, 130
Receive us back into your Council's heart.
Then all shall be as it first was before,
And thy bright crown and kingdom we'll restore.

KING
Hear all, we do revoke our royal word,
Vacate the proclamations and abjure the charge, 135
Recall our uncles Lancaster and York,
And to our Council re-admit these earls.
[*To Bushy and Scroop*] With Bagot art thou now dismiss'd the court,
Remov'd from office and thy powers revok'd. 140
Come not again near to us by ten mile.

SURREY
The Commons beg revocation of the Charters, sir.

RICHARD II, PART ONE, V.VI

KING
We do repent us now of those Blank Charters,
Repeal the law, and further here proclaim
We grieve most sore the death of our Protector, 145
Good, plain and loving Thomas, villainously slain.

York hands him the crown. Richard sets it on his head

Redeem'd, restored and renew'd, we vow
In fresh humility our realm to crown
With justice, truth and amity of God.
No more a pelting farm, yet once again 150
An England that's a royal seat of kings.
God save the soul of Thomas Woodstock!

ALL
God save the soul of Thomas Woodstock!

KING
And now, my lords, to Windsor, if you will,
For there awaits, we hear, the Commons and the peers 155
With whom we would be sweetly reconcil'd,
That peace may claim new fruits and harvests mild.
Away! Let neither king nor kingdom rest
Until, like Woodstock, we be plainer dressed.

Exeunt omnes

The Tragedy of King Richard II, Part One

Text Notes

Act I Scene I

s.d. *Several*: Includes the sense of 'in the dark,' supported by the call for lights. Cf. *King John*, V.vi.0.s.d. 'Enter Bastard and Hubert, severally [as in the dark]' L.A. Beaurline (ed.): *King John* (C.U.P., 1990), p. 163.
19 *Carous'd*: Toast his health.
40 *Diadem*: Crown. The Black Prince died in 1376 before he could succeed his father, Edward III. His son Richard was appointed king by a special act of parliament, over John of Gaunt, Duke of Lancaster, technically the next in line. The seeds of the Wars of the Roses may be found here.
46 *Strings*: Sinews.
47 *Livelihood*: Manly vigor.
48 *Wanton*: Childishly cruel, irresponsible. Note how the word acquires additional shades of meaning as the story evolves.
51 *Minions*: Favorites.
55 *King and Sovereign*: In 1371 or 1372 John of Gaunt married Constance, eldest daughter of Peter the Cruel of Castile, gaining a claim to the Castilian throne and thereafter styling himself King of Castile.
56 *Vile*: Lowly.
58 *Invoke*: Prayer.
67 *Elects*: Chooses.
69 *Confound*: Defeat, overthrow.
71 *My royal father*: Edward III.
74 *Prevent*: Anticipate; forestall; stop (all 16th-Century meanings, OED).
85 *Prize*: A captured enemy ship.
87 *You all can tell!* The fleet action referred to is probably the Battle of Cadzand, 17 March 1387.
87 *Tell*: Count, report.
89 *Carracks*: Galleons, armed naval transports.
93 *Mark*: A form of currency worth 13 shillings and four pence, or two-thirds of one Pound.
104 *Jet*: Strut, swagger.
105 *Frieze*: Coarse woolen cloth.
118 *Prosecute*: Put into effect.
126 *Our Lady*: The Virgin Mary.
129 *Front*: Confront, especially in defiance.
153 *Wanton humor*: Disturbed psychological condition.

154	*Cur'd*: Cured.
155	*Let blood*: Letting blood or controlled bleeding was considered a cure.
159	*Spill*: Kill.
160	*Nonage*: Under-age, not yet adult or 21 years old.
167	*Dissolute*: Negligent; also sexually self-indulgent.
172	*Should beautify*: That beautifies.
173	*Conceit*: Understand.
181	*Countenance*: Favor.
186	*Conceit*: Understand.
188	*Anne a' Beame*: Anne of Bohemia, daughter of the Holy Roman Emperor, Charles IV (1347-78). Her marriage to Richard and early death has become the stuff of romantic historical fiction.
193	*Discountenance*: Spoil by showing disapproval (with a play on countenance/frown, l.181).
193	*Ignorant*: Ignore, pretend unawareness.
206	*Smooth*: Pleasant.
212	*Bravery*: Fine clothes.
220	*Brave*: Finely dressed, with an ironic pun on courage. Gloucester himself elaborates the pun in l. 228 and again at I.iii.69
223	*Sumpter*: Wear on one's back, together with an oblique reference to Elizabethan sumptuary laws.
223	*Gaudy*: Luxurious.
226	*Habit*: Attire.

Act I Scene II

4	*Mad*: Irritate, bother.
8	*Carmelite*: In 1384, a Carmelite friar named John Latimer accused John of Gaunt of plotting Richard II's assassination. May McKissack notes that the incident was the start of the 'Woodstock affair,' and 'the first recorded breach between Richard and his uncle Thomas of Woodstock, who is said to have broken into the royal chamber in a rage and sworn that he would kill anybody, the king not excepted, who tried to impute treason to his brother of Lancaster.' (May McKissack: *The Fourteenth Century 1307-1399* (1959) p. 434; Nigel Saul: *Richard II* (1997) pp. 131-2. Latimer was eventually taken into custody by Gaunt and horribly tortured to death. See also V.iii.77.
9	*Limbo Patrum*: 'The Limbo of Fathers.' In Catholic theol-

ogy, a region bordering Hell for the adult unbaptized (cf. *Limbo Infantum*, The Limbo of Infants).
21 *Brook*: Put up with.
25 *Footcloth*: A brightly decorated saddle cloth laid over the back of horses ridden by dignitaries. It hung down to the ground on either side.
30 *Legit* or *non legit*? Not 'legitimate or not legitimate?' but with a hard *g*, meaning 'Can he read or not?' This refers to the so-called 'neck verse' literacy test granting defendants who could read the Bible the right to be tried in an ecclesiastical court rather than face the harsher lay courts Tresilian so horrifically describes.
35 *Rhadamanth*: In Greek mythology, one of the judges in the lower world, hence a severe magistrate.
42 *Wanton*: Frivolous, pleasure-loving.
43 *Beadles*: Minor justice officers; stupidly officious.
61 *Delicate*: Delicacy.
65 *Put on*: Confirmed.
67 *Janus-like*: Two-faced like the Roman god of doorways, who looked simultaneously in opposite directions.
69 *Leaves*: Pages, but also with the 16th-Century sense of having two leaves like a door. Cf. Janus-like, l. 67.
77 *Buckram*: A complex pun, since the word meant variously coarse cloth, a false appearance of strength, and a lawyer's bag.
77 *Scribe*: Penman or copyist.
79 *Monsieur*: Perhaps ironically pronounced 'Mon-*Sir*'.
87 *Uncaput*: No-head, dolt. An apparent neologism. Cf. German *dummkopf*.
92 *I ... Honor:* Foreshadowing Nimble's betrayal in Act V.
105 *Arrant*: A complex pun. *Arrant* derives from *errant*, i.e., wandering, so an *arrant thief* originally meant an outlaw roving the countryside, a highwayman. The word also carried the sense of *thorough, genuine*.
107 *Highway lawyer*: A qualified lawyer, with an oblique reference to *arrant*, l. 105. A popular saying was: 'From Westminster Hall to the Temple each day/the River of Thames was made a Highway.' In V.vi.30-3 Nimble remarks of his legal training: 'Nay, I have studied for my learning, I can tell ye, my lord, there was not a stone between Westminster and Temple Bar but I have told them every morning.'
118 *Buckram*: See l. 77.

The Tragedy of King Richard II, Part One

119	*Pleading lawyer*: A working attorney.
125	*Remove her*: Help her move house.
129	*Habeas Corpus, Surssararys*: Legal terms without semantic relevance. See V.vi.29.
137	*Fig*: Fig of Spain, a contemptuous gesture in which the thumb is thrust between the first two fingers of the same hand.

Act I Scene III

s.d.	*Very Brave*: See I.i.220.
22	*Misconstrued*: MS 'misconstred,' an archaic spelling of interest to scholars but confusing to a modern audience.
22 s.d	*King moves to silence Woodstock*. A major theme in the play.
24	*Wanton*: Wild, unsettled.
30	*Wag*: A mischievous boy, often used as a term of endearment.
33	*True English-bred...kind*. See 'Hidden Iambics,' *A Short History of the Text*.
34	*Double*: Ambivalent.
35	*By the rood*: By Christ's cross.
52	*Gramercy*: Great thanks.
63	*Sit aside*: The practice of women riding side-saddle was brought to England by Anne of Bohemia.
69	*So Brave*: Bold (but with a pun on Woodstock's new clothes).
81	*Hatch'd*: Fabric decorated with gold or silver bands.
95	*Mount and curvet*: Rise and leap.
95	*Bucephalus*: Alexander the Great's charger.
100	*These*: i.e., his own.
101	*Brave*: Look good.
105	*T'other hose*: The other, or second of two sets of leggings, probably farm or work pants (Jamieson, *Etymological Dictionary of the Scottish Language*).
106	*Frieze*: See I.i.105.
114	*Jet...Pride*: Swagger in ostentatious display.
117	*Pill*: Rob, impoverish (Cf. pillage).
118	commons: The common people, vs. the Commons, the Lower House of Parliament.
129	*These*: i.e., Green and Bagot.
133	*London...sacked by them*: The Peasants' Revolt, 1381, led by Wat Tyler and John Ball. The young Richard II played a

The Tragedy of King Richard II, Part One

        historic role defusing the rebellion.
140   *Brave*: See I.i.220.
142   *Tickle*: Chastise, taunt.
143   *Dote*: Speak or think foolishly as an old man.
148   *Outrageous*: Angry, outraged.
149   *Outrage*: Ill-treated beyond reasonable bounds (with an ironic pun, of course, on l. 148).
153-61 *Here's Arundel...* Refers to the naval battle of Cadzand, 17 March 1387.
158   *Pride*: Arrogance, power.
170   *Cankers*: Inner rottenness, gangrene.
175   *Encounter*: Challenge.
190   *The English Cross*: The cross of St George.
194   *Kites*: A bird that preys upon others; also a vague term of detestation.
195   *Fraught*: Freight.
204   *Deject*: Lower, demean.
213   *Beshrew*: Curse or blame greatly.
213   *Churls*: Unmannerly people.
224   *Brook these braves*: Endure these insults.
227   *Outbraved*: Outfaced
249   *Essex*: The site of Plashy House, Woodstock's family seat. This partly explains his readiness in Act IV to assume that the maskers may be rebels against the king come to elicit his support.
251   *Shrieves*: County sheriffs, responsible for law and order.
252   *Commons:* Lower House of Parliament
260   *commons*: The people.
264   *Wanton*: Irresponsible.
275   *Deeds*: Requests.

Act II Scene I
2   *Pride*: Strength
3   *Edward*: MS gives Thomas.
6,10 *Proudest*: Mightiest.
7   *Buckler*: Protect (Cf. *Buckler*, a small, round shield).
11   *Seeks*: As MS, an example of the Elizabethan 'plural verb,' agreeing in number with 'uncles.'
15   *Dated*: Appointed.
23   *Stay*: Support
25   *Confound*: Defeat, overthrow.
27   *Brave*: Challenge, defy

30	*Resolve us*: Explain to us.
40	*Hale*: Haul, drag.
53 s.d	*Bushy... book*: Some editors place this s.d after l. 38. See *Text and Variorum Notes* (2006).
55	*The Moniment of English Chronicles*. Some eds. give *Monument*. Bushy's anonymous text appears to be fictitious—a scheme on the part of the minions to manipulate Richard into prematurely claiming his throne. Almost all its details are either incredible or inaccurate, including the year of Richard II's birth—a crux in the plot—and a wildly improbable version of Poitiers. See 75-83.
63	*Mortimer ... treachery*: Also historically untrue. A.P. Rossiter plausibly suggests the story derives from Holinshed's account of the execution of Hugh Spencer.
72	*Doubtful fear*: Uncertain outcome.
75-83	*Then ... my Lord*: The factual and arithmetical errors in this breathless account seem to be deliberate. They include a wrong date for Poitiers (1356), exaggerated claims of victory over a French army of 68,000 by 7,750 Englishmen, who within an hour killed 6,000 and took 11,700 prisoners, including 1,700 nobles. The dramatic point seems to be Richard's naive acceptance of the same fictitious chronicle's incorrect record of his birthday.
90	*Hap*: Chance, especially good luck.
107	*1365*: Also incorrect, and perhaps the point of all these errors. Richard II was actually born 6 January 1367 at the abbey of St Andrew, Bordeaux. He is thus only 20 years old, as Woodstock reminds him in II.ii.100-2. Cf. also 'nonage King,' I.i.156. Interestingly enough, Henry Bullingbrook's birthday was 3 April, 1366.
116	*Two-and-twenty*: The MS gives *(22)*. The form used here completes the line as an iambic pentameter.
135	*Malign*: Plot, conspire.
141-5	*York kneels...Rises*: Not in MS, but Richard twice urges York to rise.

Act II Scene II

30	*Wage*: wager.
32	*The toils are pitched*: A complex pun. *Toils* means *nets* (i.e., a trap) which are therefore pitched (or thrown). But it can also mean to *argue*, *struggle* or *battle*, with *pitch* carry-

The Tragedy of King Richard II, Part One

	ing the additional sense of set, as in *pitched battle*.
38	*Pill*: Rob (v), *pillage* being the spoils.
41	*Sad*: Grievous.
43	*Lulling*: Deluding.
49	*Confusion*: Civil discord.
59	*States and burgesses*: Peers and knights.
73	*Insatiate churl*: Greedy miser.
76	*Resign his due*: Pay what is owed the young man.
77	*Let*: Hindrance.
94	*Our father's right*: Unconsciously ironic, since Edward the Black Prince died before becoming king. A special act of parliament in 1376 designated Richard his grandfather's successor, thus excluding John of Gaunt who, by primogeniture, was next in line.
96	*Doubled*: Dealt evasively.
99	*Mickle*: Much.
102	*Is not so full of years*: Not of legal age, i.e., twenty-one. Note that Woodstock is in fact correct.
104	*Sad*: Heavy, burdensome.
115	*Enthronished*: Set upon the throne. The word appears to be a neologism developed for the sake of rhyme and meter.
131	*Staves*: Lengths of decorated wood symbolizing government office.
137	*Deceive*: Ensnare, but also mislead and defraud.
140	*Humor*: Sentiment, attitude.
149	*Move*: Provoke.
153	*Boys*: Knaves, varlets (contemptuous).
160	*Prince's hand*: I.e., his own.
163	*Groom*: Immature male (contemptuous).
169	*Plashy*: Plashy House, Woodstock's country residence in Essex.
171	*Quail*: Break down, collapse.
179	*An Act*: A law.
184	*Pox*: Syphilis, i.e., a curse.
187	*Buckler*: Protect.
188	*Guard of archers*: A praetorian guard of 400 Cheshire archers attended Richard after 1397. Some called him 'Dickun,' perhaps too intimately. This may be reflected when Green, his favorite favorite, is allowed to familiarly call him 'Richard' (IV.i.161).
194	*And ... once*: As soon as this news is out.
199	*Cheer*: Food.

212 *Merry*: In a happy mood, but also with the sense of flirtatious: cf. *The Merry Wives of Windsor.*
218 *Wantons*: Ironic, but tinged now with the word's sensual connotations, reinforced by 'merry' in l. 212.
222 *Parts*: Departs.

Act II Scene III
2 *Types*: Emblems of rank.
9 *Grooms*: Immature young men (contemptuous).
10 *My husband, Ireland*: Robert de Vere, Duke of Ireland, Marquess of Dublin, 9th Earl of Oxford (1362-92], Richard II's homosexual lover. He divorced his wife in 1387, the year of the play. Historically, he approximates the role assigned to Green in this drama. See also my *Text and Variorum Notes* (2006).
16 *Meet*: Keep.
17 *Meets*: Experiences (v), with a play on 'meet,' l. 16.
25 *Polling*: Taxing, thieving.
27 *Duchess of Gloucester*: In the MS ll. 27-69 are cut and there is no indication of who speaks which lines, though the context makes it clear. For discussion, see *Text and Variorum Notes* (2006),
32 *Frowardness*: Refractory, perverse.
45 *Stay their rigor*: Check their anger (also violence, severity).
48 *This ... industry*: 'My personal diligence,' but, as the parenthetical phrase suggests, including 'these workers of mine,' the maids.
49 *Their own*: i.e, the poor's.
52 *Wanton*: Fiscally wasteful, but with a pun on 'wanting,' i.e., both needful and lacking in good qualities, retroactively elaborated by 'want myself,' (l. 53) and 'those that now shall want' (l. 56).
58 *Removing*: Taking up another residence.
65 *Utterance*: Disposal of goods.
65 *Husewifery*: Articles of household use (but also domestic economy).
66 *Pennyworths*: Money's worth.
67 *Fast*: Firmly, rapidly, determinedly.
68 *Pray heaven your gettings quit your swift return.* 'May your earnings bring a quick reward.' Note that *swift* puns on *fast,* and *quit* (financial remittance) puns on *earn-*

The Tragedy of King Richard II, Part One

ings.
72   Square bracket indicates the end of the cut beginning at l. 27. See *A Short History of the Text.*
75   *Prepare*: Make ready for a journey (*OED*, 1).
95   *Antic habits*: Bizarre clothes.
98   *Polonian shoes with peaks*: In the fashionable Polish style, with extended toes. See also *Text and Variorum Notes* (2006).
101 *Wanton*: Absurd, ridiculous. Note how this word's meanings are gradually expanded.
111 *Remorseless*: Cruel, unfeeling.
113 *Credit me*: Believe me.
114 *Ere many days again I'll visit ye*: Heavy with unconscious irony, since the next time the Duchess visits the Queen it is to attend her fatal illness.
115 *Langley*: King's Langley, the Duke of York's country estate in Hertfordshire.

Act III Scene I
s.d.   *A guard of archers*. See II.ii.188.
7   *Blank Charters*: The most notorious tax innovation of Richard II's reign, in effect blank checks whose amounts were later inserted by the Crown and then forcibly collected as a legal and often ruinous debt.
8   *Cormorants*: Insatiably greedy subjects.
10   *Means*: Reasons.
13 s.d. *All*: As MS. However, this and similar group declarations are not meant to be chanted in unison; rather they're a generalized set of similar remarks. Nothing is lost (and much may be gained) if a director allows his actors to *ad lib* a little, e.g., 'Forsooth, Tresilian!' 'They're all blank!' etc.
17   *Shrieve*: Sheriff or local authority.
20   *Else*: Others.
20   *Ability*: The ability to pay, i.e., wealthy.
41   *Housewif'ry*: Domestic work.
45   *Look smooth*: Be nice.
56   *Peak*: Long, pointed extensions to the toe of a shoe. Cf. II.iii.93-94.
57   *Kind coherence*: Naturally united, as in kinship.
60   *Quaintly*: Ingeniously.
60   *Resolve*: Answer.

The Tragedy of King Richard II, Part One

71   *At years*: An adult.
83   *Published*: Shown openly.
91-2 *Thirty ... numberless*. Richard's followers, at a time of widespread famine, were said to number over 10,000, fed daily by 300 Westminster cooks. One feast in September, 1387, the year of the play, included '14 oxen lying in salte, 2 oxen ffreyssh, 120 carcas of shepe fressh, 12 bores, 14 calvys, 140 pigges, 3 ton of salt veneson, 50 swannes, 210 gees, 60 dozen hennes, 400 conygges (large rabbits) 100 dozen peions (pigeons) and 11 thousand egges.' (Lorna Sass: *To the King's Taste. Richard II's Book of Feasts and Recipes. Adapted for Modern Cooking* (London: J. Murray, 1976), pp. 19-20.)
96   *Forbid*: Challenge or prohibit.
98   *Tire*: Exhaust.
100 *As ... King*: "As long as I'm King of England," with the unintended irony of his imminent deposition.
107 *Should*: In case they may.
108 *Arrow's length*. In addition to a bow-drawn missile, an arrow was the leading shoot of a plant or tree. Richard means to keep an eye on Gloucester by having him near.
115 *Truss'd up*: Tied with cord.
117 *Morris-dancer*: English folk dancer.
127 *Commission*: Legal warrant.
127 *Hands*: Signatures.
131 *Ability*: See l. 20.
134 *Intelligence*: Information.
135 *Cunningly*: Skillfully.
139 *Attach*: Arrest.
139 *Privy*: Secret.
140 *Send them up*: Convey them to court for trial. Cf. III.iii.106.
145 *Ditty*: Writing, with a possible pun on 'ditty,' a song, playing off the word 'note.' This creates an interesting doubling with the Schoolmaster's song, consistent with all the other doublings in the play. Cf. also *dittay,* in Scottish law the grounds for an indictment.
154 *Bumfiddle*: Use it to clean up after a bowel movement.
155 *Black book*: Book of laws, such as the *Black Book of the Admiralty*, compiled by Edward III; also ironically a list of rogues and villains. Cf. Webster, *The White Devil*, III.ii.31-8.
162 *Marks*: Ideographic signatures, e.g., a 'sheephook with a

The Tragedy of King Richard II, Part One

tarbox at end on't,' III.iii.17.

163 *Meddle ... widows*. Possibly referring to the habit of some tax collectors who, on the pretext of assessing a young woman's age (and hence liability for tax), reached under their clothes to check for pubic hair. In *Jacke Straw* (1594) the practice becomes a major cause of the revolt.

167 *Cut and long-tail*: Humorous vulgarities for female and male.

175 *Mark*: Target, with a prurient meaning playing on l. 171

Act III Scene II

Loc. *Plashy*: The only scene location noted in the MS, which also has no act or scene divisions. Plashy, now Pleshey, is a village seven miles N.E. of Chelmsford, and in fact nowhere near the Thames (see l. 11).

17 *Wintering*: Protection from the cold.
21 *Wanton*: Irresponsible to the point of treachery.
22 *Prodigally*: Wastefully.
27 *Late was certified*: Reliably informed.
38 *Fantastic*: Extravagantly devised.
39 *Habited*: Clothed.
42 *Wanton*: Homosexually lascivious.
45 *Reverberate*: Re-echo the wind, i.e., are empty of sound.
46 *Divines*: Soothsayers giving advice.
47 *Grossness*: Monstrousness.
48 *Astronomers*: Astrologers, i.e., those who predict the future.
54 *On haste*: MS gives *one halfe*, but I think Rossiter is correct and that *one halfe* is a scribal error for *on haste*. Lancaster has just asked Cheney what it is that drives him on so fast. Rossiter nevertheless emends to *on behalf*, because Shakespeare writes 'in an unjust behalf' in *1 Henry IV*, I.iii. 173.
54 *So ill*: Unhappily.
55 *Pursuivant*: Herald or messenger.
58 *Blank*: To pale, be disconcerted.
59 *What [are] these...?* The phrase is difficult to make out in MS. Frijlinck, Rossiter, and Corbin and Sedge give 'what must these', but Halliwell and Keller earlier saw 'what myscheefes?' and 'what myscheef?'. I try to keep as much as possible of what is still legible (not much), while making sense of the line. Lancaster's 'They appear in shape of obligations,' also works better as a response to 'What [are]

The Tragedy of King Richard II, Part One

60 *Obligations*: Legal contracts for the payment of money.
62 *Commissions*: Warrants.
67 *'Point*: Appoint, nominate. See also *A Short History of the Text* about the editorial redrafting of these lines.
78 *Let ... Apostata*: Let me go down in history as a renegade. This key declaration deliberately calls into question Woodstock's chronicled reputation as a troublemaker and rebel. The revision is supported by John Gower's *Cronica Tripertita*. See discussion in *A Short History of the Text*.
80 *Entertain*: Receive, i.e., react to.
82 *Strangely*: Hostile or unfriendly.
84 *Defiance*: Declaration of aversion or contempt.
86 *Turn head*: Confront their pursuers; defy and resist.
89 *Rancors*: Hatreds.
105 *Presage, Presageth*: Presentiment.
109 *Ruinate*: Ruined.
115 *Strike again*: Strike back in reply.
121 *'Light: Alight*, dismount.
122 *On, on's*: Of, of his.
126 *Passion of me*: My suffering like Christ's upon the cross, i.e., an exclamation.
134 *Cellar*: A storage area, either above or below ground.
134 s.d. *Spruce*: One who affects the manners of the royal court, an upstart. The character clearly resembles Osric. See *A Short History of the Text*.
137 *Rude swain*: Inexperienced or untrained servingman.
138 *Hear'st-ta thou*: 'Do you hear?' The final *-ta*: in *hear's-ta* indicates a *T* pronounced with exaggerated clarity.
144 *Tester*: A coin worth sixpence.
147 *Saucy*: Impertinent.
149 *Calling*: Vocation and/or social standing.
160 *Brave*: Smartly dressed (ironic).
165 *Indifferent*: Impartial.
166 *Now... it*: You seem rather thin.
168 *'A-days*: Now-a-days.
171 *I ... not?:* i.e., merely a hired horse.
176 *Lustily*: With energetic pleasure, though at IV.iii.7-10 Carpenter glosses the word as 'easily,' a sense that also works here.
178 *We ... see:* We would both have been caught.
184 *Coarse*: Inappropriate.

The Tragedy of King Richard II, Part One

185 *Ostler*: Servant who tends horses.
188 *Redeliver*: i.e., return my horse to me.
189 *A promise ... debt*: A familiar saying of the time.
192 *Nicely*: Foolishly.
199 *Meat*: Feed.
204 *This same's*: The Courtier's hat.
214 *Peak*: In MS the word is spelled *picke*, as is the word 'pick,' to choose, allowing for a series of witty puns on *peak/pick*.
217 *Polonian*: In the Polish style.
224 *Kind coherence*: See III.i.56.
227 *K-nee*. On the analogy of *hears-ta*, l.138, Rossiter suggests 'k-nee' and 'k-neeify.'
238 *Suit*: A pun on clothing/appropriateness.

Act III Scene III

s.d. *Bailey*: Bailiff, town official similar to mayor.
      Bills: Pikes.
3   *Chuffs*: Rustics, boors; any person disliked; a miser; a contemptuous reference to wealthy rural people. The word is related to *chough*, a bird of the crow family, often applied to any small, chattering species.
7   *Pestiferous*: Pestilential, i.e., plague-bearing. Bailey Ignorance throws the word around throughout this scene as a generalized term, used more for its 'big-word' sound than any sense. Cf. Dogberry.
16-   *Ecce signum!*: Behold the sign! (With an ironic Biblical
17   echo, *ecce homo*?)
30   *Strange*: Hostile, unfriendly.
46   *Chubbs*: Fools.
48   *Murrain*: Turmoil, fuss (lit. pestilence, disease, esp. bovine).
56   *State*: An unconsciously ironic pun by Cowtail on 'condition' and 'political entity.'
59   *Hoisted*: OED gives a variety of contemporary meanings, including *strung up on a rope*; *destroyed by one's own means* ('hoist with his own petard,' *Hamlet*, III.iv.207); and *forcibly removed* ('We'll quickly hoise Duke Humphrey from his seat,' *2 Henry VI*, I.i.169). Corbin and Sedge note Middleton (1607), 'overtaxed, surcharged.' Given the probable composition date of *1 Richard II*, 1592-3, the connection with *2 Henry VI* is perhaps especially significant.
69   *I'll not ... anything*: I will not swear to its accuracy.

The Tragedy of King Richard II, Part One

71 *Amend*: A malapropism for 'Amen,' perhaps also a subtle political pun by the playwright.
75 *Merry*: Pleasant, agreeable.
80 *County*: MS gives *country*.
101 *I'd make shift for one*: I'd be all right on my own.
127 *As good at first as last*: First or last, what's the difference? Cf. the proverb, 'As good do it at first as last.'
133 *Sodden*: Boiled or stewed. See *Text and Variorum Notes* (2006) for variations.
136 *Deliver*: Complete. Cf. Richard's, 'our kingly deed we here deliver,' (IV.i.192).
162 *Come, sir, stand close*. In MS, this is followed by an illegible fragment beginning with 'I see…' Nothing more can be made out. I opt to delete rather than conjecture.
167 *Well search'd*: Examined closely.
168 *Carriage*: Performance or tenor.
168 *Cover'd them rarely*: Concealed the libels skillfully.
173 *Their*: i.e., the authorities.
176 *Tickle*: Tease, equivocate
176 *Shalt hear else*: You'll really hear something, especially its underlying meaning.
182 *Will ye buy any parchment knives?* An original tune for this song may be found in an Appendix to *1 Richard II* (2006).
188 *Bald*: There is some debate about this word, apparently used as a verb and thus a semi-neologism. Paired with 'flay'd,' it seems to mean 'have his hair torn out.' For discussion, see *Text and Variorum Notes* (2006).
190 *Rare*: Excellent.
193 *Exceptions*: Objections. Cf. *Henry V*, IV.ii.25: "'Tis positive against all exceptions…'
195 *Equivocation*: Saying one thing while giving the impression of saying another.
200 *Maggot*: In MS, 'faggot,' which these days unfortunately gets a laugh for the wrong reasons. My suggestion avoids a gratuitous distraction, even though a minor pun (*Bushy / faggot*) gets lost.
214 *The ninth degree*: Ultimate level of seriousness, but perhaps another bit of legal mumbo-jumbo by Nimble—cf. I.ii.128 and V.vi.26.
217 *Examinations*: A Dogberry-like malapropism for 'explanations,' overheard by Nimble and Ignorance, but also

	perhaps a subtle political pun.
222	*Him*: Tresilian.
230	*Mine own [part]:* The damaged MS shows *I peake for myne owne p*. Halliwell gives *I speake for myne own part*, which I follow, encouraged by the fact that Dogberry uses the same phrase: '... but truly, for mine own part, if I were as tedious as a king, I could find in my heart to bestow it all of your worship.' (III.v.19-22.)
239	*Whistled*: Perhaps spoken without an emphasis on the final *-ed*. MS gives *whistled* and *whisselld* in adjacent lines.
255	*Sift*: Question closely.
256	*Greater heads*: Supplied by earlier editors, since the original is obscured.
269	*Take*: MS *sic*. Elizabethan noun-verb discord.
270	*Limbo*: Prison (*OED*, 2). In Newgate there was a cell called Limbo, 'a dark Opace [opaque?] wild room' lit by a single candle on a large black rock known as the Black Dog of Newgate.
273	*Be pitiful*: 'Take pity,' but also ambiguous. The Bailiff is merciless yet deserves contemptuous pity.
274	*Law ye, sir*: An exclamation, with a legal pun. Some editors emend to 'Why, look ye sir!' but this is unnecessary, since *law* or *la* was a common exclamation of surprise. Cf. *Love's Labor's Lost*, V.ii.414: '...so God help me, law!'
285	*Sheepbiter*: Shifty, thievish fellow. But see my *Text and Variorum Notes* (2006) for additional possible meanings.
288	*Whistle*: A grim pun, since 'whistle' was also a jocular word for the mouth or throat. Cf. To wet one's whistle.

Act IV Scene I

20	*Slack*: Slow, remiss.
26	*Chuffs*: See III.iii.3.
28	*'States*: Estates, i.e., property, wealth.
30	*Russet slops*: Coarse peasant garments, especially coats and pants.
34	*Sort ... sum*: Figure out what each one owes
40	*Rack*: Charge extortionate rent.
44	*Farming*: A familiar legal practice among the nobility, in which a peer in need of immediate cash sold the lease of a relatively minor piece of property, usually to a wealthy commoner. The new owner recouped and often exceeded his investment by rent-racking the existing tenants.

The Tragedy of King Richard II, Part One

53   *Stipend*: Fixed payment.
54-5 *Ere ... once*: Once we've got them.
58   *Rich and rare*: i.e., excellent news.
59   *A-making*: Are being drawn up.
62   *'Sfoot! ... price!:* 'Christ's foot! Let's not argue over the cost!'
68   *Soothest*: Most flattering, pleasant.
85   *Perforce*: Forcibly.
92   *Let's ... else*: Some editions give this speech to Green. See *Text and Variorum Notes* (2006).
96   *Masquers*: Masked entertainers and revelers.
101   *Single*: Isolate, a hunting term consistent with the imagery used during the masque itself, IV.ii.103 ff.
103   *Vizard*: Mask.
142   *Rarely*: Excellently (but with an ironic authorial pun on *unusually*).
150   *Wanton*: Fiscally irresponsible.
158   *Puissant*: Powerful.
162   *'Sfoot ... toadstool*: Refuse, and I'll become a traitor and make common cause with your uncles.
189   *Remain*: Dwell; located physically.
193   *Subsidies*: Financial grants by Parliament to the monarch.
193   *Fifteens*: A tax of one-fifteenth imposed on personal property.
193   *Imposts*: Taxes levied on merchandise.
193   *Foreign customs*: Import taxes.
194   *Staples*: Chief articles of consumption; warehouses storing exportable goods; commercial centers. (All given by OED.)
195   *Forfeitures*: Penalties or fines.
237   *Those ... mine*: MS sets as a couplet, emphasizing the unconsciously ironic sense.
251-3 *Since...me.* Since you've served me last I'll pay you last, believe me!
271   *Attach*: Arrest.

Act IV Scene II
4   *Mask*: Head cover.
6, 8 *Heavy, heaviness*: Sad, depressed.
18   *Contrary*: Express the opposite of their apparent meaning.
45   *Sheen*: A palace in Richmond, Surrey.
49   *Augurer*: One able to predict the future.

The Tragedy of King Richard II, Part One

55	*Craves*: Demands.
80	*Live a time*: Live long enough.
85	*Addicted*: Given up so (to mirth).
96	*Observe them*: Take care of them properly.
103	*Sports:* Entertainment.
107	*Clear orb ... sphere*: The moon.
119	*Pity*: Compassion.
121	*This state directs*: Woodstock viewing the masque, his 'chair of state' showing that he is the local lord.
129	*The moon directs*: The moon gives its light and so obliquely does Queen Elizabeth I, since she was conventionally identified with the moon.
133-4	*And ... more particular*: When you unmask at the end I'll acknowledge each of you personally.
135	*If...merit*: If my hospitality is less than you deserve.
165	*Provident*: A neat pun: frugal and foresighted (OED 1,
166	*Betray'd*: Surrounded by enemies.
182	*Toils are pitched*: The trap is sprung.
185	*Earl of Cambridge*: Incorrect. Woodstock's brother Edmund was created Earl of Cambridge on 13 November 1362.
196	*Vizard*: Mask, gag.
230	*Habits*: Disguises used during the masque.

Act IV Scene III

9-11	*If... shortly*: If these 700 prisoners are successfully robbed, Tresilian will soon have it all.
16	*Stay*: Resist, refuse.
22	*Fifteens*: See IV.i.193.
24	*The Conqueror*: William the Conqueror (1027?-87), whose Norman armies occupied England in 1066.
33	*Indignation*: Anger.
39	*That ... you*: We'll put you on trial for that.
42	*The ... ta'en*: We have already accepted (and grieved over) that.
49	*Consume*: Decompose, waste away.
60	*Carman*: Carters or carriers, famous for whistling as they worked.
62	*Reaching head*: Having great mental reach, esp. of plans (OED, 2).
74	*Sleepy knaves*: Dull or stupid people of low social standing.

	The phrase triggers a series of puns.
74	*Out of Bedfordshire*: A pun: sleepy knaves, pulled out of bed; also perhaps a variation on the humorous saying, 'To go to Bedfordshire,' i.e., to be off to bed.
81	*Chuffs*: See III.iii.3.
85	*Nice*: Finicky (especially about money).
98	*Rods...girdle*: Beaten on the rump and back by 120 sticks, probably a melodramatic exaggeration.
99	*The ... a-feasting*: The day he is hanged (?).
100	*Have a jerk at him*: Have a chance to beat him.
108	*Estate*: Condition of health.
140	*A thousand ... state*: A deliberately ambiguous line. Tresilian means the situation of the favorites is threatened, but also unwittingly evokes the dangers posed to England.
162-170	*Go, ruin all!* Holinshed, *Chronicles* III, p. 481, writes: 'This year [1394 – the play moves the date back to 1387] on Whit-sundaie being the seaventh of June, queene Anne departed this life, to the great greefe of her husband king Richard, who loved her intirelie. She deceased at Sheen, and was buried at Westminster, upon the south side of saint Edwards shrine. The king took such a conceit with the house of Shene, where she departed this life, that he caused the buildings to be throwne down and defaced, whereas the former kings of this land, being wearie of the citie, used customablie thither to resort, as to a place of pleasure, and serving highlie to their recreation.'
172	*Oblations*: Offerings, prayers.
176	*Sad*: Established or settled; also mournful, grave.
179	*Thy wrongs*: i.e., the injustices done to you.
180	*Confounds*: Upsets, disturbs.
181	*'point*: Appoint.

Act V Scene I

3	*Voided*: Empty (except for Woodstock).
9	*Strive*: Struggle, resist.
9	*Mall*: Hit, as with a mallet, so perhaps rhymes with *pal*.
10	*Mazzard*: Head (jocular).
13	*Fair*: Showing no marks.
13	*Cunningly*: Skillfully.
18	*Contrived*: Accomplished.
19	*As if ... man*: As though you were dealing with an ordinary

The Tragedy of King Richard II, Part One

22   *'Havior*: Behavior.
50   *Mine own*: My own life.
63   *Elate*: Raised.
64   *Wanton*: Out of control, evil.
74   *Stiff ... bed*: i.e., bed posts.
80   *Oh!*: The MS does not clearly assign a speaker. The groan could thus emanate from Woodstock or either of the departing or arriving spirits. I give it to Edward III, allowing the Black Prince to exit with a strong concluding couplet.
92   *Racks*: Extorts.
95-7 *Beheld me ride in state*: In 1356, after the Battle of Poitiers, Edward III led his captives in triumph through the streets of London.
100 *Fifth of Edward's sons*: Woodstock was actually the seventh son, but for the sake of rhythm I leave the MS unchanged. It is also true that two of Edward III's sons died young, so Woodstock was the fifth to survive into adulthood.
105 *Sad*: Inevitable, but also tragic, burdensome, etc.
115 *Whist and still*: Quiet and peaceful.
146 *Intendiments*: Attentive consideration.
147 *Misgave*: Suspected.
149 *Wanton*: Raging murderously.
153 *Virtue of nobility*: As a man of rank and honor, one noble to another.
158 *Fond*: Foolish, simple.
162 *Confounds*: Exhausts.
173 *Credit me*: Believe me.
179 *Under the blade*: For discussion, see *A Short History of the Text*.
202 *Sad*: Weary.
202 *Faith*: Honesty, good will.
213 *Style*: Manner of greeting.
235 *Prate*: Chatter, speak to little purpose.
236 *About's*: As MS, though I feel strongly that an actor should give the *S* its fullest weight and say *about his*.
248 *He's ... speaking*: It's safe to say he's dead.
253 *Dead as a door-nail*: Cf. '*Falstaff*: What, is the old king dead? / *Pistol*: As nail in door.' (*2 Henry IV*, V.iii.120-1).
261 *Told*: Counted up, with perhaps a pun on 'predicted.'

265	*Draw ... soldiers*: *Draw all* means not *all your weapons* but *all of you*.
274	*Scal'd*: Plated.
277	*Miching*: Skulking.
290	*Hardly*: Severely.

Act V Scene II

3	*Daunt their pride*: Weaken their strength and confidence.
9	*Pressing soldiers*: Forcibly conscripting men.
11	*Punk*: Prostitute.
21	*Audacious*: Wicked, defiant.
32	*Demur*: A legal plea admitting the facts but avoiding the consequence.
32	*Writ of Error*: Legal document, usually from the monarch.
33	*Remove*: Relieve, excuse.
39	*Base exclaims*: Worthless charges.
41	*Maim*: Loss, disability.
43	*If bad, I run away*: MS gives 'away I run,' probably a transposition error by the copyist.
47	*Lustily*: Energetic enthusiasm.

Act V Scene III

3	*Wanton*: Uncontrolled.
23	*Re-edify*: Rebuild.
29	*Endless fate*: Eternal death.
31	*Grip*: Bite.
32	*Determinate*: Clearly define, put an end to.
33	*Tax'd...oppressions*: A neatly ambiguous phrase embracing both the Blank Charters and the general strain of living under Richard's rule.
43	*Hold of strength*: Strong hold.
52	*Sad*: Inevitable.
s.d.	*They march about also*: MS gives 'They march about (all'.
64	*Infamous*: Deprived of civil rights following a criminal conviction.
65	*Impudent*: Shameless.
79	*Ungracious*: Irreligious, disgraceful.
102	*Travail'd*: Labor giving birth. MS gives 'trauelld,' which could be 'travelled,' though this makes less sense in context. Dover Wilson notes that Elizabethan *travel / travail* do not differ in form (*King Richard II*, Notes, p. 146).

106 *Royalties*: Monarchical rule.
109 *Brook these braves*: Endure these bullies, assassins (OED, 5.1b).
114 *Terms of Composition*: Settlement, peace agreement.

Act V Scene IV
2 *Fronts*: Confronts.
5 *Tilt*: Thrust.
9 *Seal't*: Seal it, i.e., drop hot wax and then brand the word traitor on all your hearts.
14 *Timeless desolation*: Eternal loss.
20 *Dissolute*: Overindulgent in sensual pleasures (OED), referring to Green's homosexual liaison with the king.
21 *Hale*: Haul.
22 *Rescue*: i.e., an attempt to recover Green's body.
25 *Heavy*: Tragic, full of grief.
28 *Churls*: Brutal people.
41 *The Tower*: The Tower of London, in those days a royal fortress.
43 *Take us*: Conduct or follow us, i.e., support, help.
47 *Heavy*: Grievously.
48 *Almighty hand*: i.e., of heaven.

Act V Scene V
2-6 The MS's right margin and several words are damaged, requiring considerable editorial reconstruction. Drawing chiefly on Everitt, I supply *the young lords* and *stream*. See *Text and Variorum Notes* (2006) for discussion.
3 *Lustily*: With energetic enthusiasm.
17 *Unknown*: Unrecognized.
25 *Bravely*: Splendidly, but with an ironic pun.
28 *Valor*: Social importance.
33 *Saint Tantony*: Saint Antony, often spelled *Saint Tantony*, was traditionally followed everywhere by his pig, hence the proverb, 'To follow like Saint Antony's pig.'

Act V Scene VI
2 *Wanton*: Careless, irresponsible.
7 *Bristowe*: Bristol.
8 *Belay'd*: Surrounded.
29 *Surssararis*: According to the OED, *surserara* is an 'obs. corruption of *Certiorari*,' a writ from a superior to an

inferior court. OED refers the reader to *siserary* which, in addition to its legal meaning, includes the senses of suddenly, promptly, vengeance, a severe rebuke or scolding, a sharp blow, and a torrent of language. All or any of these could be appropriate in this context. Note also the trope on 'bond' and 'bound' and how the whole phrase looks back to I.ii.129.

35 *Causes*: Reasons.
36 *Plowden*: Edmund Plowden (1518-85), authoritative Elizabethan jurist known for the phrase, 'the case is altered.' Note *3 Henry VI*, IV.iii.31, 'Ay, but the case is alter'd.' and the Plowden reference in *Hamlet*, V.i.15-22.
37-159 A conjectural emendation concluding the play. Its elements are discussed in *A Short History of the Text*.

The Tragedy of King Richard II, Part One

A Short History of the Text

The most fertile ground is the flexible *via media* between line-to-line fidelity and idiosyncratic appropriation.
—George Steiner

*T*he Tragedy of King Richard the Second, Part One, as we have noted, is an anonymous, untitled and incomplete history play, fols. 161-185 in a 349-page, leather-bound volume owned by the British Library, London, catalogued as Egerton 1994.

The anthology is a treasure trove of fifteen anonymous early-English plays and a masque. In addition to *1 Richard II*, Eg.1994 includes *Edmund Ironside*, edited and ascribed to Shakespeare by Eric Sams.[1]

The B.L. purchased the volume from the estate of Lord Charlemont in 1865. Following Chambers, most scholars believe that after the closing of the theaters in 1642, Egerton 1994 belonged to William Cartwright the younger, an actor and book seller who bequeathed it to Dulwich College. Later it passed into the possession of Lord Charlemont, who may have stolen it.

Persuasive inferences about the play's origins and early history can and have been drawn from clues found in the heavily edited MS, which evidently passed through the hands of stage managers, actors, prompters and government censors. Their notes, cuts and insertions, and the reasonable inferences we may draw from them about the MS's history, including its author, are all exciting dramas in themselves. Their hidden protagonist of course is William Shakespeare.

Wolfgang Keller, the manuscript's second editor (1899),

---

[1] Eric Sams (ed.): *Shakespeare's Lost Play Edmund Ironside* (1985). See also Chambers, *William Shakespeare 1*, p. 92, and F.S. Boas, *Shakespeare & the Universities* (1923) pp. 97-8.

suggested that *1 Richard II* might be of an earlier vintage than the other plays in Egerton 1994, since its leaves are independently numbered, trimmed and mounted two to a page to fit the folio format. He added, however, that 'The only certain thing we can say of the original...is that it must have existed long before Eg. 1994.' [2]

This remains the commonsensus, as does Ribner's judgment that the MS continues to be 'one of the most important original documents we possess for the study of the Elizabethan theatre.' [3]

In the 1920's, Sir E.K. Chambers followed Keller and his predecessor Halliwell in calling the play *1 Richard II*, hinting at Shakespeare's hand. But F.S. Boas hotly contested this in *Shakespeare & the Universities* (1923), insisting that the drama be retitled *Woodstock* precisely to discourage the notion that the author of *Lear* and *Hamlet* could ever write such mediocre stuff.

The Malone Society's editor, W.P. Frijlinck, who considered Shakespeare the likely author, thus tactfully called her 1929 transcription both *1 Richard II* and *Woodstock*. In 1946 however A.P. Rossiter firmly supported Boas's title and ascription to 'ANON,' as he emphatically expressed it, settling the debate for a generation.

Shakespeare's possible role in the play was not considered again until Everitt's error-filled edition in 1965, also the last time anyone attempted a transcript directly from the deteriorating manuscript itself.

List of Editions and Codes
The following editions and reference codes are used throughout this book. '*1 Richard II*' refers to the untitled

---

[2] Keller, Introduction, p. 4. An English translation appears in my *1 Richard II*, Vol. III (2006).
[3] Irving Ribner: *The English History Play in the Age of Shakespeare* (1964), p. 134.

MS, and '*2 Richard II*' to Shakespeare's canonical drama. Unless otherwise indicated, all references are to the text in this volume or *The Riverside Shakespeare* (1997).

APR   A.P. Rossiter (ed.): *Woodstock, a Moral History* (London: Chatto & Windus, 1946).

ARM   William A. Armstrong (ed.): *Woodstock (Anonymous)*, in *Elizabethan History Plays* (London, New York and Toronto: Oxford University Press, 1965).

BLN   A.H. Bullen (ed.): *A Collection of Old English Plays in Four Volumes*, Vol. I (London: Wyman & Sons, 1882-5), Appendix 1, pp. 427-8.

BUL   Geoffrey Bullough (ed.): 'from *Thomas of Woodstock*,' in *Narrative and Dramatic Sources of Shakespeare,* Vol. III (London and New York: Routledge & Kegan Paul and Columbia University Press, 1960), pp. 460-91.

CAR   Frederick Ives Carpenter: 'Notes on the Anonymous *Richard II*,' *The Journal of Germanic Philology*, Vol. III, No. 2 (Bloomington: Journal Publishing Co., 1900) pp. 138-42.

COR   Peter Corbin and Douglas Sedge (eds.): *Thomas of Woodstock or Richard the Second, Part One* (Manchester and New York: Manchester University Press, 2002).

EBE   E.B. Everitt (ed.): *Thomas of Woodstock or 1 Richard II*, in *Six Early Plays Related to the Shakespeare Canon* (Copenhagen: *Anglistica*, Vol. XIV, Rosenkilde and Bagger, 1965).

HAL   [J.O. Halliwell, ed.]: *A Tragedy of King Richard the Second, Concluding with the Murder of the Duke of Gloucester at Calais. A Composition Anterior to Shakespeare's Tragedy on the Same Reign, Now First*

Printed from a Contemporary Manuscript. (London: Printed by T. Richards, Great Queen Street. 1870).

KEL Wolfgang Keller (ed.): *Richard II. Erster Teil. Ein Drama aus Shakespeares Zeit* (*Jahrbuch der Deutschen Shakespeare-Geselschaft* XXXV, ed. Alois Brandl und Wolfgang Keller, Berlin 1899).

MEE Michael Egan (ed.): *The Tragedy of Richard II, Part One* (New York: Edwin Mellen Press, 4 vols., 2006).

NOT George Parfitt and Simon Shepherd (eds.): *Thomas of Woodstock* (Nottingham Drama Texts, Nottingham University Press, 1977) *Thomas of Woodstock: An English History Play of Shakespeare's Time Otherwise Known As A Tragedy of King Richard the Second, The First Part of the Reign of King Richard the Second, Woodstock: A Moral History* and *Woodstock.* (Doncaster: The Brynmill Press, 1988).

OXF *Thomas of Woodstock*, compiled by Louis Ule, reviewed by M.W.A. Smith (ca. 1998-2001).

WPF Wilhelmina P. Frijlinck (ed.): *The First Part of the Reign of King Richard the Second or Thomas of Woodstock* (London: Printed for the Malone Society by J. Johnson at the Oxford University Press, 1929).

Condition of the MS

The MS has deteriorated and is deteriorating. More than a century ago, Wolfgang Keller, the German scholar who prepared the work's second edition (1899), sometimes disagreed with his predecessor J.O. Halliwell, noting that, for example,

Die Stelle ist ganz verwischt, und es wärenicht unmöglich, daß H. der ein Vierteljahrhundert vor mir arbeitete, sie

besser gelesen hätte.[4]

And also later:

So liest H. Heute ist am Rande nichts mehr zu erkennen. Vielleicht stand Yorke *da.*[5]

A sense of the continuing rate of loss may be gathered from the fact that in 2002 editors Peter Corbin and Douglas Sedge found the word *fellow* (III.ii.185) to be completely 'obliterated,'[6] which I can confirm, whereas in 1929 Frijlinck saw *f*, in 1899 Keller could make out *fel*, and in 1870 Halliwell confidently transcribed *fellow*.

Keller's difficulties make Frijlinck's Malone Society recreation of the text 30 years later, using fonts to represent the script, an even more remarkable achievement, despite her access to primitive photographic technology.[7]

A.P. Rossiter (1946) also worked from the original, introducing several fundamental changes to the text and its organization. E.B. Everitt published an uneven and inaccurate transcription in 1965.

---

[4] 'This part [of the MS page] is completely obliterated, and it's not impossible that H[alliwell], who worked a quarter-century before me, read it more clearly.' (All translations by Michael Egan.)

[5] 'Thus reads H[alliwell]. Today nothing more can be seen in the margin. Perhaps *Yorke* stood there.'

[6] Corbin and Sedge, p. 116n.

[7] Frijlinck used 'rotographs...[which] as a rule appeared to be clearer than the original and have enabled several words to be deciphered which it would have been difficult to make out in the manuscript itself. On the other hand it was found that the apparent legibility of the rotographs was at times speciously misleading, since they failed of course to reproduce the colour of the original, and in several cases what had been assumed to be traces of letters proved on further examination to be dirt.' (Frijlinck, p. xxxiii.)

My four-volume *The Tragedy of Richard II, Part One,*
(2006), winner of the Adele Mellen Award for Distinguished
Scholarship, was the first close look at the manuscript itself
in over half a century. It remains, together with the revised
and updated version in this volume, the only rendering based
on a digital analysis of the original. The British Library generously provided both access to the fragile manuscript and
full-size photoscans capable of conversion into a variety of
digital formats.

The Art of Transcription
The MS's condition is so poor, and its handwriting often
so ambiguous and enigmatic, that even simple transcription
becomes quite difficult. The copyist's scrawl barely distinguishes between certain letters or even combinations of letters, resulting in errors like the *blocke/blade*, *hears/heaps*
and other confusions discussed below.

The looped diphthong *oo*, for instance, tends to resemble
the letter *a*, 'a peculiarity that has led to some misreadings
by former editors,' as Frijlinck drily remarks.[8] Later at MS
IV.i.10 she admits her own inability to distinguish between
the copyist's *e* and 'a very small *d*.'[9]

Rossiter echoes, lamenting 'the manuscript's *e/d* confusions.'[10] Commenting on I.ii.124, where the word *Roope*
(rope) is misread as *raixe* and *raxe* by Halliwell, Keller and
Carpenter, he notes that 'even an expert can take *-oo-* for *-ai-*
in English hand.'[11]

These and related difficulties have led to widely divergent
and even contradictory texts.

Consider, for example, the five contrasting versions of
Nimble's speech at I.ii.79-86, set out for comparison below.

[8] Frijlinck, p. vii.
[9] Frijlinck, p. 61 n.
[10] Rossiter, p. 182.
[11] Rossiter, p. 185.

The Tragedy of King Richard II, Part One

An early iteration perhaps of Falstaff's Nym, as indeed Tresilian may be of the fat knight, Nimble is responding to his master's teasing hint that he has been spectacularly promoted to the land's top legal office, Lord Chief Justice.

An inexpert reader might reasonably assume the accuracy of any of the following, starting with Frijlinck's literal recreation of the original. But in fact there are substantial differences between them all, in punctuation, emphasis, vocabulary, spelling, implicit characterization and thus overall semantics. Not one editor, however, provides any descriptive or explanatory notes.

W.P. Frijlinck (1929)
Neither S^r: nor mounsier: nor Signior: what should I call him, tro, hees monsterously translated sodaynly: at first when we were schoolefellows, then I calld hime sirra, but sence he became my m^r. I payrd away the .a. and serud him wth the Sur: what title he has gott now, I knowe not, but Ile try ffurther. has yor worshipp any Imployment for me.

J.O. Halliwell (1870)
Neither Sir, nor mounsier, nor signior, what should I call him, tro, hees monstrously translated sodaynly: at first when we were schoole fellows, then I calld hime Sirra, but sence he became my master, I payrd away the a. and serud him with the Sur. what title he has gott now, I knowe not, but Ile try ffurther Has your worshipp any Imployment for me

Wolfgang Keller (1899)
Neither S*ir*, nor Mounsier, nor Signior; what should I call him, tro? Hee's monstrously translated sodaynly. At first, when we were schoole-fellows, then I calld hime sirra; but sence he became my m*aste*r, I payrd away the a and serud him with the Sur: what title he has gott now, I knowe not, but I'le try further. Has *your* worshipp any imployment for me?

A.P. Rossiter (1946)
Neither Sir: nor Monsieur: nor Signior. What should I call him? Troth, he's monstrously translated suddenly! At first, when we were schoolfellows then I called him Sirrah, but since he became

186

my master I pared away the Ah and served him with the Sir. What title he has got now, I know not, but I'll try further...Has your worship any employment for me?

E.B. Everitt (1965)
Neither sir nor monsieur, nor signior? What should I call him, trow? He's monsterously translated suddenly. At first when we were schoolfellows then I called him sirrah, but since he became my master, I pared away the *ah* and served him with the 'sir.' What title he has got now, I know not, but I'll try further. Has your worship any employment for me?

In light of these differences, I acknowledge doubt in its place but make what I like to think are reasoned choices. Editorial decisions are after all only judgments, albeit informed, and good alternatives may always suggest themselves.

Here's how I render Nimble's speech, beginning with a new stage direction and ending in another:

[*Aside*] Neither Sir, nor Monsieur, nor Signior! What should I call him? Trow, he's monstrously translated suddenly! At first, when we were schoolfellows, then I call'd him Sirrah, but since he became my master I par'd away the Ah and serv'd him with the Sir. What title he has got now, I know not, but I'll try further. [*To Tresilian*] Has your Worship any employment for me?
—*1 Richard II*, I.ii.75-80

Words and Meanings
Transcription difficulties also affect individual words and sentences, transforming the meaning of entire passages and hence the play.

At I.iii.230, for example, Woodstock refers to 'The inly passions boiling in my breast,' a key statement contributing to the Forsterian 'roundness' of his character. But Halliwell transcribes the second word as *Julye* and Keller follows with *Iulye*. Both must have realized they were creating semantic nonsense, but could not get beyond the scrawl.

Other instances include the discrepant versions of Lapoole's exclamation in V.i.34: 'And yet, by all my fairest hopes, I swear...' Halliwell took the last two words to be 'of heauen' which—although the line is smudged and interlined, making the decode that much harder—vividly illustrates the challenges facing transcribers of the original.

Thirty years later Keller guessed right, but still felt so uncertain he omitted the phrase altogether, footnoting that what he thought might be 'I sweare' was written *'mit dunklerer Tinte.'*[12] It wasn't until Frijlinck's 1929 edition, checked by W.W. Greg, that the actual words in both these instances (*inly* and *I swear*) were definitively identified and restored.

Many inaccuracies, major and minor, have nonetheless survived. Thanks to modern computer technology they can now be resolved. Here are just two examples.[13]

Under the Blade
Halliwell and Frijlinck have the imprisoned Woodstock saying, just before his murder in V.i, that were he truly guilty of rebellion, he'd submit immediately to the angry king:

I'd lay my neck under the block before him
And willingly endure the stroke of death.

But Keller noticed that there was something wrong with this: heads about to be removed by the axe are normally laid 'upon' and not 'under' blocks. He thus suggested *upon the block* as a possible emendation.

Taking his cue, Rossiter opted for 'unto the block,' presumably to retain as much of *under* as possible. Editors since have either followed him or chosen some prepositional alternative.

---

[12] 'With darker ink.' (Keller, p. 106n.)
[13] For a complete list, please see my 'Text and Variorum Notes' in *The Tragedy of Richard II, Part One* (2006), Volume Two.

Computer magnification, however, suggests that what's been mistaken is not the preposition but the noun. *Blocke* is really *blade*. Kerning *cke* really tightly, like this, *de*, produces something easily mistaken for *de*, and of course vice versa. By imaginative extension, the *a* was read as *o*. My text thus gives *blade*, not *blocke*:

I'd lay my neck under the blade before him
And willingly endure the stroke of death.
—*1 Richard II,* V.i.180-1

We may note similar confusions in the manuscript of Peele's *Edward I*, where *blade* and *blode* (blood) are often mistaken for one another. Peele's editor, Frank S. Hook, notes that 'corruptions' of this sort 'are all of types likely to occur in reading secretary hand,'[14] the script used for *1 Richard II*.

Heaps
An even more striking instance is *heaps* at I.iii.261. Most editors, including Frijlinck, mistake the *p* for an *r*, incorrectly giving *here's*:

...the King, all careless.
Here's wrong on wrong, to stir more mutiny.

But Keller preferred '*heepes* wrong on wrong,' followed by a period. While he got the verb right, his stop for the MS's comma still leaves Woodstock nonsensically suggesting that it is he, and not the king, who is stirring up the rebellion:

The commons they rebell; and the king, all careless,
Heepes wrong on wrong. To stirr more mutiny,
Afore my God, I knowe not what to doe.

Carpenter finally got it right, as the degrained and magnified MS confirms. It is indeed the king who is to blame:

---

[14] Frank. S. Hook and John Yoklavich (eds.): *The Dramatic Works of George Peele,* 3 Vols. (Yale U.P. 1961), Vol. 2, pp. 42-3.

The Tragedy of King Richard II, Part One

The commons, they rebel, and the King, all careless,
Heaps wrong on wrong, to stir more mutiny.
Afore my God, I know not what to do!
—*1 Richard II*, I.iii.251-3

Hidden Iambics
The manuscript's poetically inexpert and perhaps bored copyist often ran lines together or displaced words and even phrases, destroying what were apparently intended to be iambic pentameters and even couplets. A frequent editorial conundrum is thus Steiner's 'fidelity' to a damaged but authentic text, or the guesstoration of what seems to have been the author's poetic purpose.

An example is III.i.61-65, where the original reads (spelling and punctuation modernized):

Queen: ... They are your noble kinsmen. To revoke the sentence were—
King: An act of folly, Nan. King's words are laws.

But editors Corbin and Sedge (COR) cleverly divide the last words of the queen's speech at *revoke*, revealing a hidden pentameter when *the sentence were* is taken with Richard's response:

Queen: ... They are your noble kinsmen, to revoke
The sentence were—
King: An act of folly, Nan!
Kings' words are laws: if we infringe our word,
We break our law. No more of them, sweet queen.
—*1 Richard II*, III.i.61-65

The realignment of the rest reveals additional fossilized iambics, confirming this inspired call.

In another example, this time my own, Richard opens a big speech with:

So, sir, the love of thee and these, my dearest Green [...]

190

It sounds and looks like prose, but simply resetting the first two words, 'So, sir,' one of Richard's habitual phrases, reveals an introductory iambic pentameter consistent with the rest of the speech.

So, sir:
The love of thee and these, my dearest Green,
Hath won King Richard to consent to that
For which all foreign kings will point at us, [...]
—*1 Richard II*, IV.i.143-5

Similarly, the farewell between the Duchess of Gloucester and Queen Anne in II.iii reveals a stepped pentameter of some complexity, since to make it work *desolation*, the final word, has to be syllabically sounded out, something no actor would of course really do. In a sense, the poet is writing for himself alone:

Duchess of Gloucester: Madam, ye hear I'm sent for.
Queen: Then begone:
Leave me alone in desolation.
—*1 Richard II*, II.iii.77-9

A redraft of IV.iii.162-3, which appears to have been incorrectly copied from the original, reveals two previously unsuspected iambic pentameters and a couplet. The MS and all prior editions give:

What loss can be compar'd to such a queen?
Down with this house of Sheen! Go, ruin all!

But 'Go, ruin all!' almost certainly should be at the start of the second line, thus recovering

What loss can be compar'd to such a queen?
Go, ruin all! Down with this house of Sheen!
—*1 Richard II*, iv.iii.162-3

At I.iii.32-3, the MS gives

But his maturity, I hope you'll find,

The Tragedy of King Richard II, Part One

True English-bred, a king loving and kind.

But transposing 'king' and 'loving' restores the iambic and adds perhaps Hamlet's sense of kinship to 'kind':[15]

But his maturity, I hope you'll find,
True English-bred, a loving king and kind.
—*1 Richard II*, 1.iii.32-3

Varieties of Language
Among *1 Richard II*'s remarkable accomplishments is a sweeping portrait of English society, literally from the masses to the monarch, excluding only the clergy. Its range of vivid speaking characters, each of whom possesses his/her own class, gender and regional registers, includes the king and his noble relatives, their household stewards with knighthoods, court dandies, the ambitious, landed bourgeoisie, well-off village merchants, corrupt local officials, devious lawyers, shrieves, servants, and soldiers, political prisoners, murderers, double-talking confidence tricksters, two ghosts and, yes, even a talking horse, about whom more in a moment.

All express themselves in their own distinctive ways, using accents, tones and vocabularies immaculately reproduced by a playwright with a sharp ear for speech rhythms and idiomatic differences. It's a theatrical *tour de force* that has unfortunately been overlooked these 150 years.

The mannered accent of the dandified Spruce Courtier, for instance, who rides onto the set demanding to see Woodstock, is deftly caught and mercilessly mocked, along with his equally ridiculous clothes, transparent social ambitions and stultifying arrogance. He unwittingly reveals himself not only in the way he speaks but—a very English critique—by his unkindness to horses and servants. Soon after arriving at Plashy House, the MS has him say of a groom too busy to help him:

---

[15] 'A little more than kin, and less than kind.' (*Hamlet*, I.ii.64-5).

A rud swayne by heauene, but stay heere walkes another. hearst ta. tho^u: fellowe, is this plasshy house

'Hearst ta. thou: fellowe,' with its odd pointing, has completely flummoxed the editors. Halliwell proposed 'hearst tro,' and Keller 'heer, sta thou,' or 'heerst ta thou, fellow,' without further explanation. After tepidly suggesting 'hearst tha,' Rossiter adopted Keller's second suggestion and quickly moved on.

My view however is that the *ta* after *hearst* is a successful attempt to phonetically render a faux upper-class accent. It tells the actor that the final 't' in 'hear'st' should be spoken with exaggerated emphasis, almost like a spit. It's funny but also not, like the twit himself. These are King Richard's new-moneyed idiots, the play suggests, who are now disastrously running and ruining the country after his successful palace revolution in II.ii.[16]

Woodstock: But this most fashionable chain, that links as it were the toe and knee together?
Courtier: In a most kind coherence, so it like your Grace, for these two parts, being in operation and quality different, as, for example, the toe a disdainer or spurner, the k-nee a dutiful and most humble orator, this chain doth, as it were, so toeify the k-nee, and so k-neeify the toe, that between both it makes a most methodical coherence, or coherent method.
—*1 Richard II*, III.ii.222-30

It's a caricature certainly, but a very good one. As we shall see, Shakespeare himself seems to have thought it so effective he borrowed the Courtier for Osric. More about this below, and what it may tell us about the play's composition date.

---

[16] Despite his tepid edit, Rossiter understands this. In his notes he brilliantly proposes, while not including them in his text, 'k-nee' and 'k-neeify' at III.ii.228-9. I gleefully accept this inspired suggestion, which not only gets audience laughs but is wholly consistent with the Courtier's witless self-satire.

The Tragedy of King Richard II, Part One

English of a sharply other sort may be heard in III.iii, when Nimble ruthlessly bullies a group of prosperous Dunstable merchants into signing away their lives and lands to the king and his money-hungry clique at court.

Farmers, butchers and graziers, the villagers are smart but uneducated, leery of the slick-talking government agent who is clearly up to something though they can't quite figure out what. The folk idioms fall thick and fast as they try to handle the future in the language of the past:

Nimble: Here, ye bacon-fed pudding-eaters! Are ye afraid of a sheepskin?
Grazier: Mass, 'tis somewhat darkly written.
Farmer: Ay, ay, 'twas done i' the night, sure.
Grazier: Mass, neighbors, here's nothing that I see.
Butcher: And can it be any harm, think ye, to set our hands to nothing? These Blank Charters are but little pieces of parchment. Let's set our marks to them, and be rid of a knave's company.
Nimble offers ink, pen and sealing wax. Butcher signs then hands pen to Farmer
Farmer: As good at first as last, we can be but undone. [*Signs*]
Grazier: Ay, and our own hands undoes us, that's the worst on't. Lend's your pen, sir. [*Signs*]
Butcher: We must all venture, neighbors, there's no remedy.
—*1 Richard II*, III.iii,118-130

Elsewhere in the same scene we meet the town's Bailiff, Master Simon Ignorance, whose rotund, oral pomposity contrasts sharply with the tight-lipped, muttered exchanges of the frightened villagers. Inwardly terrified himself, Ignorance tells Nimble:

Nay, look ye, sir, be not too pestiferous, I beseech ye! I have begun myself and seal'd one of your Blanks. I know my place and calling, my name is Ignorance and I am Bailey of Dunstable. I cannot write nor read, I confess it, no more could my father, nor his father, nor none of the Ignorance this hundred year, I assure ye.
—*1 Richard II*, III.iii.7-13

Like his brother, Master Ignoramus, who never appears, the Bailiff's catch-words are 'pestiferous' and 'pestiferously,' which he uses without comprehension variously to mean 'pressing' (III.iii.7), 'useful' (III.iii.36), 'serious' (III.iii.107), 'criminal' (III.iii.154, 210) 'assiduous' (III.iii. 160, 277), 'egregious' (III.iii.175), 'deceitful' (III.iii.216, 258) and 'rebellious' (III.iii.231).

In the same Dogberry-like fashion, Ignorance malapropriates 'examinations' for 'exclamations' (III.iii.217), 'strange' for 'effective' (III.iii.277), 'shameful' for 'serious' (III.iii.217) and 'reform' when he intends 'oppose' (III.iii.230). His linguistic universe, like his political standing, is distinct from the 'rich choughs,' all of whom he knows and all of whom he betrays.

To be clear, Simon Ignorance is not Dogberry, though he strongly evokes him, as all the play's editors since Rossiter have recognized. In other words, he is not a copy but a variation on a theme, recalling, or perhaps anticipating, Messina's constable in his mangling of the English tongue. Explicitly the embodiment of everything his name represents, Ignorance is also a politically more dangerous figure than Dogberry because *1 Richard II* is a politically more dangerous play than *Much Ado About Nothing*. The Bailiff of Dunstable is one of the *kapos* without which Richard's tyranny could not function.

As a last example of *1 Richard II*'s extraordinary linguistic variety, the nobility express themselves in an English different yet again. Never mocked or satirized, their speech is educated, literate and often soaringly poetic. For instance:

Queen: My sovereign lord, and you true English peers,
Your all-accomplish'd honors have so tied
My senses by a magical restraint
In the sweet spells of these, your fair demeanors,
That I am bound and charm'd from what I was.
My native country I no more remember
But as a tale told in my infancy,

> The greatest part forgot; and that which is,
> Appears to England's fair Elysium
> Like brambles to the cedars, coarse to fine,
> Or like the wild grape to the fruitful vine.
> And having left the earth where I was bred,
> And English made, let me be Englished.
> They best shall please me shall me English call.
> My heart, great King, to you; my love to all!
> —*1 Richard II*, I.iii.37-51

This is the young Queen on her wedding day, thanking the assembled lords and ladies for their warm welcome. But note how her pretty speech operates on an entirely different plane from the other examples we've looked at. Its theme is transformation, change and alteration, the 'golden metamorphosis' (I.iii.79) explored in almost every scene. This is a play about revolution, social and personal. As the shocked Woodstock says of Richard's historic palace coup in II.ii:

> What transformation do mine eyes behold,
> As if the world were topsy-turvy turn'd!
> —*1 Richard II*, II.ii.145-6

Queen Anne, who becomes the drama's moral center, is at once caught up in the 'sweet spells' of her hosts' warmth and kindness. They 'charm' her, a neat ambivalence—winning ways and necromancy—wiping away all memories of her former self and homeland, magically transforming her into an Englishwoman. But notice how at the same time her language performatively morphs—nouns become verbs (*English* to *Englished* in a single line), while the tales of her childhood evaporate in a trance-like oblivion.

Underpinning everything is the transformation of Nature itself, from uncultivated to cultivated—brambles to cedars, wild grape to fruitful vine, etc. Indeed, there's so much going on in these lines, including what seems to be a faint pre-echo of Macbeth's tale told by an idiot, that to suggest they were penned by some deservedly anonymous hack can hardly be maintained. This fifteen-line sonnet literally speaks for itself.

Dating the Play
The matter of when the play was written goes to the heart of its most intriguing mystery: who wrote it? Scholars routinely insist on a Jacobean date, contemporaneous with the manuscript, implying and often claiming that its numerous Shakespearean echoes are simply plagiarisms by a third-rater like Samuel Rowley, author of *When You See Me You Know Me* (1605). This is the position maintained by that formidable attributionist, Macdonald P. Jackson.

But Jackson's case is not supported by the play itself, whose features point again and again to 1592-3. The most revealing evidence, though by no means all, concerns the Spruce Courtier and what we might call his literary DNA.

As we've seen, the king's hat-flourishing messenger seems undeniably related to Osric. Everyone since Rossiter has recognized and acknowledged it. The question, however, like the egg and the chicken, is which came first? All the editors insist upon Osric, a figure of such distinctively Shakespearean originality that Anon must, of course, have stolen him. It follows then that *1 Richard II* was written after 1601, the earliest agreed date for *Hamlet*.

But the historical and literary evidence all go in the other direction. Anon got his Spruce Courtier not from *Hamlet* but from his own careful research—Rossiter calls it 'academic,' meaning thorough—into the history of Richard II. His sources demonstrably included contemporary documents, legal, historic and literary, many of which are unmistakably reflected in the play.

Among Anon's literary sources we find an untitled 1380s poem dubbed 'On the Times' by its modern editors.[17]

---

[17] Thomas Wright, (ed.): *Political Poems and Songs Relating to English History Composed During the Period from the Accession*

At 236 lines of alternating English and Latin verse ('macaronic'), it can't be quoted in full here, though I reproduce the key passages in my *Text and Variorum Notes* (2006), together with many of the documents referred to below.

'On the Times' (ca. 1400) is satirical folk poetry, among whose targets are precisely Richard II's so-called 'new men' (l. 133). They 'strut ridiculously' (l. 126), their shoulders puffed out to appear broader than they are (ll. 130-1) and—the detail seized upon by the author of *1 Richard II*—their slippers have long pointed toes or 'peaks' attached to their shins by chains of gold (ll. 141, 146). This absurd gear makes it impossible for them to kneel in church, upsetting others (ll. 145-155). Christ curses them, and their necks are ready for the sword (ll. 138, 159).

In the play, Cheney describes the 'strange fashions' of Richard's new courtiers, objective correlatives for the transformations everywhere. The details derive from 'On the Times':

They suit themselves in wild and antic habits
Such as this kingdom never yet beheld:
French hose, Italian cloaks, and Spanish hats,
Polonian shoes with peaks a handful long,
Tied to their knees with chains of pearl and gold.
Their plumed tops fly waving in the air
A cubit high above their wanton heads.
—*1 Richard II*, II.iii.95-106

It seems perverse to deny the literary DNA here. The bloodline clearly descends not from Osric but the 'new men' described in 'On the Times' and similar folk poems. These include 'Richard the Redeless' (1399-1400), and 'Mum and the Sothsegger' (1403-6), both of which harshly mock Richard II and his youthful councilors. The second explicitly urges the king to pay better attention to his 'sothseggers' or

---

of Edw. III. to that of Ric. II (London: Her Majesty's Stationery Office, 1859, Kraus Reprint Ltd., 2 Vols., 1965).

those who tell the truth, like Plain Thomas.[18] Osric is not the Courtier's ancestor but in fact his Danish cousin, summoned back to court when Shakespeare needed another ludicrous messenger from another murderous king to another doomed prince.

An even more influential document seems to have been John Gower's *Cronica Tripertita* (ca. 1400), a scathing indictment in Latin of Richard II's reign, still considered reliable by historians. It appears to have strongly affected Anon's overall historical analysis, and even contributed the unusual word 'pestiferous,' which is used repeatedly by Gower (Latin *pestifer*, pestilential) but by no other source.[19]

Another trace element may be Gower's unusual portrayal of the historically pugnacious Woodstock as both 'well-meaning' and 'honest.'[20] He also vividly describes the duke's kidnapping and murder using the same graphic imagery of a helpless creature hunted down and torn apart by savage wolves, *Plusque lupo saevit rex*, 'The king rages like a wolf.'[21]

Finally among Anon's probable sources we may note a popular contemporary ballad known by its first line, 'Ther is a Busche that is Foregrow.'[22] This satirical take-

---

[18] Helen Barr (ed.): *The Piers Plowman Tradition: A Critical Edition of Pierce the Ploughman's Crede, Richard the Redeless, Mum and the Sothsegger, and The Crowned King* (1993).

[19] Apparently Anon could read and translate scholarly Latin. This considerably narrows the field of possible authors.

[20] Eric W. Stockton: *The Major Latin Works of John Gower 'The Voice of One Crying' and 'The Tripartite Chronicle': An Annotated Translation into English With an Introductory Essay on the Author's Non-English Works* (Seattle: University of Washington Press, 1962), *Passus secunda*, 36.

[21] *Ibid.* For more on Gower, Anon and Shakespeare, see my General Introduction, *1 Richard II* (2006).

[22] William Hamper (ed.): 'Sarcastic Verses, Written by an Adherent to the House of Lancaster, in the last year of the reign of

down of Bushy, Green and Bagot may well have been the inspiration, not only of the Schoolmaster's 'treasonous ' song, 'Would ye buy any parchment knives?' (III.iii.199-207), but also for its strikingly similar puns:

A poison may be Green,
But Bushy can be no faggot:
God mend the King and bless the Queen
And 'tis no matter for Bagot.

Cuts, Deletions and Corrections
The case for an Elizabethan rather than a Jacobean *1 Richard II* is strengthened further by a close look at the manuscript's cuts, alterations and edits.

Building on Frijlinck's pioneering work, including a study of inks and letter formations, Rossiter identified nine scribal, interpolating, editing, and/or correcting hands in the MS. Apart from the copyist, Hand A, there are notes and reminders from stage managers, interventions by censors and, most interestingly, deletions and marginalia by the author himself.

Rossiter also shows that author and copyist worked closely together. The latter occasionally left spaces for illegible words, as we can still see, or made a mistake, such as an incorrect speech assignment or misplaced stage direction, which the playwright afterwards completed or corrected. At one point, for instance, the copyist called Sir Edward Bagot 'Thomas,' subsequently put right by the author.

These changes and other alterations are all part of the process A.C. Partridge, the MS's best and most careful scholar, called 'stratification'—editorial layers put in place at different times, including abbreviations and scribal habits typical

---

Richard the Second, A.D. 1399,' *Archaeologia 21* (1827), pp. 88-91; Thomas Wright, *ed. cit.*, and James Dean (ed.): *Medieval English Political Writings* (Kalamazoo: Western Michigan University, 1996), pp. 150-2. Also available on-line at http://www.ub.rug.nl/camelot/teams/tmsmenu.htm.

of their epochs. Partridge's conclusion is that while the MS itself is early Jacobean, the original play was made in the early to mid 1590s.[23]

Partridge's analysis is confirmed not only by the playwright's own cuts, interventions and alterations, but by the multiple 'unknown hand' edits we find throughout.

The systematic deletion of the text's frequent oaths and imprecations (*Zounds! Afore my God!* etc.), which all editors restore, also implies an original written some time before 1606, when the 'Act to Restrain Abuses of Players' prohibited actors from 'jestingly or profanely' invoking 'the holy Name of God or of Christ Jesus, or of the Holy Ghost or of the Trinity.'

The otherwise pointless deletion of a phrase describing the English monarch as 'Superior Lord of Scotland' (II.ii.111), sets the play's composition date even earlier, since it suggests sensitivity to James I's feelings following his accession in 1603. Patriotically appropriate during the 1590s, the title conferred on Richard at his coronation in the second act was tactfully omitted later.

Finally, the removal of the drama's climactic deposition scene strongly supports the likelihood that it was composed before such depictions were banned ca.1597, following the Q1 publication of *2 Richard II*. In its day Shakespeare's most popular work, *2 Richard II*'s deposition scene was strictly forbidden during the reigns of Elizabeth I and her successor. Its most famous performance, staged at the request of Essex and his supporters in 1601, specifically

---

[23] I studied with Partridge at Witwatersrand University when he was working on his influential *Orthography in Shakespeare and Elizabethan Drama; A Study of Colloquial Contractions, Elisions, Prosody and Punctuation* (University of Nebraska Press, 1964). On stratification, see also Rossiter, *Woodstock*, pp. 171-2.

included the illegal scene because it modeled the rebellion's intent, or so it was claimed at Essex's trial.

There is thus every reason to think that the censors simply removed the last page of the MS with its unacceptable conclusion. But it was of course there in the first place because when the play was originally written there were no injunctions against such portrayals. This gives us then a composition date no later than 1594, when *2 Richard II* was first performed.

Not all the text's deletions, however, reflect contemporary political or religious niceties. Many appear to be purely stylistic, providing us with a rare opportunity to observe an Elizabethan/Jacobean dramatist editorially at work—perhaps even Shakespeare himself, together with almost unique samples of his handwriting.

Among the most significant cuts are those carried out apparently because they echo—or pre-echo—*2 Richard II*. Like the deposition scene, they seem to have been deleted in hindsight.

This applies particularly to the MS's most famous passage and its eloquent removal. In IV.i, after leasing England to his court cronies for £7000 a month, Richard, who fully understands the revolutionary nature of what he has done, declares prophetically:

So, sir:
The love of thee and these, my dearest Green,
Hath won King Richard to consent to that
For which all foreign kings will point at us,
And of the meanest subject of our land
We shall be censur'd strongly, when they tell
How our great father toil'd his royal person
Spending his blood to purchase towns in France,
And we, his son, to ease our wanton youth,
Become a landlord to this warlike realm,
Rent out our kingdom like a pelting farm,

That erst was held, as far as Babylon,
The maiden conqueress to all the world.
—*1 Richard II*, IV.i.143-15

A pelting farm was an emblem of the nobility in decline, the word 'farm' as a verb meaning to exploit or turn something into ready cash. When strapped for money, aristocratic families would 'farm out,' as we still say, a village or an area to professional tax collectors. Their ruthless conduct, hinted at by Nimble in III.i.163ff., and graphically portrayed in the anonymous *Jacke Straw* (1594), is clearly identified in that drama as a major cause of the Peasants' Revolt (1381).

In Anon's hands, and of course Shakespeare's, the story is more about Richard II analogically putting his entire kingdom out to farm, reaping similar anger, revolt and finally deposition. The greedy minions laughingly describe their plans:

Scroop: There's no question on't. King Richard will betake himself to a yearly stipend, and we four by lease must rent the kingdom!
Bushy: Rent it, ay, and rack it too, ere we forfeit our leases, and we had them once!
Enter Bagot
How now, Bagot, what news?
Bagot: All rich and rare! The realm must be divided presently, and we four must farm it. The leases are a-making and for seven thousand pounds a month the kingdom is our own, boys!
Bushy: 'Sfoot, let's differ for no price! And it were seventy thousand pounds a month, we'll make somebody pay for't!
—*1 Richard II*, IV.i.52-64

The outrage is famously taken up by John of Gaunt in his 'sceptr'd isle' speech:

This land of such dear souls, this dear dear land,
Dear for her reputation through the world,
Is now leas'd out—I die pronouncing it—
Like to a tenement or pelting farm.
—*2 Richard II*, II.i.57-60

The relationship to Richard's statement is so close that everyone remarks on it. F.A. Marshall was the first, commenting that 'The similarity of expression is worth noticing.'[24] Frijlinck feels that 'the phrase in one play is copied from the other,'[25] Matthew W. Black records the echo,[26] while Kenneth Muir says that Shakespeare 'took several hints' from *1 Richard II*, including this passage.[27] Even Dover Wilson, who rejects *1 Richard II* as his *Ur*-Richard II source play, acknowledges that the second repeats the first 'almost word for word.'[28]

In Shakespeare's view, and by no coincidence Anon's, Richard has turned the whole country into a pelting farm, and himself into its landlord, a mere collector of rent—a humiliating descent into the mercantile class with its confusing new world of laws and contracts. As both *1* and *2 Richard II* see it, the king has criminally abandoned the nobility's traditional rights and privileges, demeaning 'this royal throne of kings.'

It may be noted too that when Richard was permanently deposed in 1399, the phrase 'pelting farm' was never used. Article One instead accused him of turning his kingdom over to 'men unworthie.' The pelting-farm analogy is unique to Shakespeare and Anon.

Yet even more striking than these connections is the fact that Richard's original 'pelting farm' speech was deleted from the MS of *1 Richard II*. Given the authority and precision of

---

[24] Irving and Marshall (eds.): *The Works of William Shakespeare*, Vol. II, p. 463 n.
[25] Frijlinck, p xxvi.
[26] Black, *Richard the Second*, (1955) p. 104.
[27] 'From *Woodstock* Shakespeare took several hints—the attack on foreign fashions, the phrase "pelting farm", and the idea of the King as landlord.' Kenneth Muir: 'Shakespeare Among the Commonplaces' (*The Review of English Studies*, NS, Vol. X, No, 39, August 1959) p. 286.
[28] Dover Wilson, *op. cit.*, p. lvii.

The Tragedy of King Richard II, Part One

the surgery, the remover was almost certainly the dramatist himself.

One asks why, and the answer seems to lie in the speech's key phrase, 'pelting farm,' which was repeatedly altered and replaced. Among its interlined alternatives we find *petty*, *peltry* or *paltry*, and perhaps *plteg*. When none of these proved satisfactory, the author drew a canceling line through the entire speech and for good measure wrote the word *Out* in the margin.

It had to be 'pelting farm' or nothing, because the term had a specific legal meaning, lost if *pelting* were replaced with *petty* or *paltry* or even nothing at all.

We're thus looking at part of the creative process and not, as Rossiter dismissively suggests, a word choice anyone might have made. Anyone hasn't. Other than these two obviously related theatrical moments, there are no others in all English and indeed world literature.

Ian Robinson, the critic and editor who published the first serious investigation into the authorship of *Woodstock*, as he called it, accepts the scholarly consensus that the author of *2 Richard II* must have had access to the manuscript in Egerton 1994:

There are of course various ways in which Shakespeare might have come to read it; the simplest possibility is that the manuscript was made from his own papers and revised by him. He then realized he needed the 'pelting farm' image for [*2 Richard II*], and excised it from *Woodstock*.[29]

Other stylistic cuts tend to confirm this. For example, the author deleted a key line from the farewell scene between Woodstock and his brothers:

---

[29] Ian Robinson: *'Richard II' and 'Woodstock'* (Brynmill Press) 1988, p. 46.

On earth, I fear, we never more shall meet.
—*1 Richard II*, III.ii.107

perhaps because it too strongly recalls a similar parting of three in the later play:

Bagot: If heart's presages be not vain.
We three here part that ne'er shall meet again
—*2 Richard II*, II.ii.142-3

Similar deletes include references to the bearing and career of the Black Prince in *1 Richard II*, I.i.34-40, closely followed in *2 Richard II*, II.i.171ff. [30] All the evidence bears in the same direction.

A Touring Play

Among *1 Richard II*'s most remarkable moments is a sequence dominated by a real horse in conversation with a human, a *coup de théâtre* almost unique in Elizabethan drama. The nearest thing to it, perhaps unsurprisingly, is Launce and his expressive dog Crab in *Two Gentlemen of Verona*.

In *1 Richard II* the horse is ridden onto the set by the Spruce Courtier, his florid hat decorated by a feather 'waving in the air a cubit high' above his head.

However one defines a cubit, the hat and its feather would add considerably to the overall height of even a modest horse and rider, conservatively estimated at around eight or nine feet. This is much higher than the typical Elizabe-

---

[30] The complex matter of the relationship between *1* and *2 Richard II* unfortunately cannot be explored here. Please see the introduction to my *1 Richard II* (2006) under *2 Richard II*. In summary, Part One, not originally conceived as such, was written as a self-standing play, radically advocating what we now call constitutional monarchy. Shakespeare returned to its ideas, characters, themes and, concepts when he set out to dramatize the king's final year, 1399, which begins immediately after Part One.

than stage entrance of about seven feet, confirmed by recent excavations and beautifully visualized by Walter Hodges in his conjectural illustrations of the Swan and other theatres.[31]

The point is that the Spruce Courtier's mounted entrance could never have been intended for any known London stage. Coaxing a horse up a flight of wooden stairs and then, plus rider, onto a small stage, obviously presents major problems. There are also the complications and costs of stabling, feeding, transporting to and from the theatre, saddling and mounting the beast quietly backstage, and finally splashing its sides with a little water as it clatters on, since Woodstock remarks that it's sweating.

All this too before the critter decides to relieve itself mid-scene, which in the grand tradition of the theater it surely would, and at the wrong time and place and in the most awkward way possible. Obviously an in-house horse is an on-stage nightmare (no pun intended).

Outdoors it's an entirely different matter. Space is no longer a problem, there are no steps to mount or descend, and the more unpredictable the horse's behavior, the funnier things get.

A lot of the humor depends on the stand-up skills of the actor playing Woodstock, who is given a series of comments rather than a speech. Their sequence can be varied according to anything the horse might do, including neighs, headshakes and assorted digestive processes. Imagine the delight of a rural audience when Tom Pierce's grey mare, hired for the occasion, suddenly drops a load and Woodstock smirks, about the citified Courtier, 'I think you have as much wit as he, i' faith!'

The dramatist even provides for a completely unresponsive

---

[31] C. Walter Hodges: *Enter the Whole Army: A Pictorial Study of Shakespearean Staging 1576-1616* (Cambridge U.P. 2000), p. 192.

animal. Woodstock's options include, 'Ah, your silence gives consent, I see!'

It's a brilliant comedic episode, perhaps the best in a very funny play, leading to my suggestion that *1 Richard II* may have been originally conceived for the provincial tour and thus consciously designed for performance in market places, fields, tavern yards or other open spaces. This would also explain the stage directions in V.iii, providing for not one but two whole armies simultaneously on stage in full armor with drums and colors flying. They then both 'march about' before engaging in shouted insults and a lengthy battle. Given an open space it could all be quite spectacular, something villagers from miles around would flock to see.

Performance Anxieties
Under open-air conditions then the horse, far from being a complication, becomes a triumph—a scene-stealer, the star of the show, who always gets the biggest cheer at the end.

Absent an outdoors venue, however, and access to a suitable horse (as in a 1999 production in Northampton, MA, which absolutely worked), modern directors will be challenged.

Michael Hammond's 2002 Emerson College production ingeniously resolved the difficulty by having a talented actor play the part, not in pantomime, but barefoot and with long tousled hair, which he tossed from time to time like a mane. Inspired perhaps by Peter Shaffer's *Equus*, this device worked surprisingly well.

Another solution might be to imply the horse by using sound recordings of hoof beats, neighs, clanging gates, etc. Enter and exit the Spruce Courtier. Woodstock holds the reins and talks to the animal just off stage or behind a bulging curtain. This would also provide plenty of opportunities for vulgar horsey noises in the right places, with Woodstock pointing them by his reactions.

Another of the play's most difficult scenes, theatrically

speaking, dramatizes Richard II's historic attempt to break the power of the old nobility through the redivision of his kingdom. His new class allies, the emerging rural bourgeoisie represented by Bushy, Bagot, Green and Scroop, reappear in Part Two. Richard's notorious invocation of the law on their behalf was a direct challenge to the established aristocracy, helped along by bitter family hatreds and ancient rivalries. At several points the author suggests that the great civil war between York and Lancaster began with the murder of Woodstock, a judgment supported by modern historians.

The critical scene, however, in which Richard parcels out England—the constitutional question being whether he has in fact the legal right to do so[32]—is excruciatingly specific, listing each of the 39 shires allotted and spelling out their lessees' responsibilities, including when and how to pay their rent. Before that, Tresilian reads aloud the particular terms and conditions of the agreement, phrased in perfect legalese (another of the play's many linguistic styles).

The directorial temptation is to cut, and frankly little seems lost, theatrically speaking, if 'fifteens, imposts, foreign customs, staples for wool, tin, lead, and cloth; all forfeitures of

---

[32] See Ernst H. Kantorowicz: *The King's Two Bodies: A Study in Medieval Political Theology* (1957). The two bodies are the institution of the monarchy itself, eternal and incorruptible, and the king *in propria persona*. The first, or Body Politic, in the words of Edmund Plowden, the Elizabethan jurist of whom more below, 'cannot be seen or handled, consisting of Policy and Government, and constituted for the Direction of the People, and management of the Public Weal.' The second is the monarch's Body Natural, 'subject to all the infirmities that come by Nature or Accident, to the imbecility of Infancy or Old Age and to the like Defects that happen to the natural Bodies of other people.' As Schell notes, the foregoing is cited by Kantorowicz (*op. cit.*, p. 7) from Plowden's *Commentaries*, a text referred to in *1 Richard II*, V.vi.33. Kantorowicz argues that *2 Richard II* is an exploration of the tension between these two bodies. Without making any connection between the plays or their author(s), Schell shows that the same may be said of *1 Richard II*.

goods or lands confiscate' (IV.i.94-5) is dropped from Tresilian's recitation.

But the rest of this critical scene needs to be given its full dramatic weight. As Rossiter points out, the historic document that emerges is the very one which

> Shakespeare's Gaunt must be supposed to have in mind when he speaks of England 'bound in...with inky blots and rotten parchment bonds' [*2 Richard II*, II.i.64-5]. Indeed the accusation, 'Thy state of law is bond-slave to the law' [*2 Richard II*, II.i.113-14], is nearly unintelligible without what we see here.[33]

The implications of this are considerable, especially if we continue to insist, as Rossiter does, that *1 Richard II* comes from a hand other than Shakespeare's. It means either that the best mind of his generation plagiarized his analysis of the Wars of the Roses from a long-forgotten, anonymous drama, or—even more remarkably—that some long-forgotten, anonymous drama provided Shakespeare with his fundamental understanding of Elizabethan England's most important historical episode.

Theatrically, the challenge is communicating to a modern audience what will have been experienced as shock and outrage by the play's contemporaries. London—given away! Shropshire in the greedy hands of an upstart commoner! The analogy is perhaps with Trump's horrific presidency, unearned but technically legal, and the shock felt when he won and took office.

In my view, the most useful theatrical analogy is *King Lear*, I.i, which also involves the dramatic division of the kingdom, pointed by the gasps and other reactions among the assembled courtiers.

In the same way, the extent of Richard's revolution might be dramatized by the ad-libbed applause, congratulations,

---

[33] Rossiter, *Woodstock*, p. 227.

etc., of the assembled court and the king's praetorian guard of archers, who after II.ii accompany him and his minions everywhere.

Also among the drama's difficult moments is the king's exclamation at MS II.i.112: 'Thirteen sixty-five? What year is this?'

It's almost impossible to deliver this line without sounding like a complete idiot, though that cannot be the dramatist's intent. Richard is many things, but not unintelligent. His question, skillfully provoked by the scheming minions, prepares the way for his famous palace revolution against his uncles, dramatized in the next scene.

So again directorial deletion is not an option. Richard's exasperated query is dramatically rhetorical—of course he already knows the answer and may, as I imagine it, flourish a calendar as he speaks. Including this as a stage direction, however, goes beyond my brief. Instead, I edit the line and Bushy's response to bring out Richard's exasperation and even annoyance:

King: Thirteen sixty-five! [And] what year [then] is this?
Bushy: 'Tis now, my lord, 1387!
—*1 Richard II*, II.i.112-13

Sir Pierce of Exton

Among the surprising but forgotten facts about *1 Richard II* is that it includes Sir Pierce of Exton among its characters. Exton of course is historically famous as Richard II's assassin, suggesting that his inclusion is not fortuitous. Even more interesting, he is specifically identified and pointed out on stage although given no lines. The dramatist wanted him to be noticed.

The detail is so significant that Rossiter, who denies Shakespeare's hand in the play, not only questions whether Exton is even there, but 'proves' it by deleting him.

In the MS, Woodstock enters in I.i with an entourage including London's 'Lord Mayor' and another man called 'Exton.' But Rossiter conflates the two into a single figure, 'the Lord Mayor Exton,' whom he literally conjures out of thin air. Rossiter supports this by deciding that the author simply didn't know what he was doing, but that he, Rossiter, does. He explains:

The MS reads, *Enter the Lord Mayre & Exton*, but I take it that only one person is meant, on Holinshed's authority and the single exit at [l. 130].[34]

But there is no authority for this in Holinshed or anywhere else and, as Sir John Dover Wilson points out, obvious stage exits, such as 'Hie thee, good Exton!' and many a concluding *Exeunt*, were not always written in. Exiting actors, he notes, could be trusted to find their way off stage.

Rossiter's fabrication unfortunately scrubs out one of the play's subtler ironies: Sir Pierce of Exton, Richard II's future murderer, glimpsed briefly at an early point in his career as a minor court functionary on the Lancastrian side. The next time we meet him he's still a minor court functionary, now working for Richard's usurper and willing to do whatever he wants. Sir Pierce's two appearances are subtle bookends to Richard's full story.

Rossiter's previously unrecognized intervention has had scholarly consequences, since all succeeding editors, intimidated by that vague reference to Holinshed, have followed him. The most recent casualty is Charles Forker, whose Arden edition of *2 Richard II* falsely claims that 'A Lord Mayor Exton appears as a character in *Woodstock*.'[35]

Thirteen Editions
A comparative chronological review of the play's previous editions follows, indicating each one's role in the evolution

---

[34] Rossiter, p. 182.
[35] Charles R. Forker (ed.): *King Richard II* (2002) p. 178 n.

of the text. The process offers an instructive and perhaps unique account of a significant Elizabethan drama, evolving from its original script to the modern stage.

1 *A Tragedy of King Richard the Second*, ed. J.O. Halliwell (1870)

As noted, the manuscript was recovered ca.1868 by the Victorian scholar J.O. Halliwell, also known as J.O. Halliwell-Phillipps, who found Egerton 1994 in a dusty box among the stacks of the old British Museum. It's a testament not only to Halliwell's industry but his literary acumen that he quickly recognized *1 Richard II*'s superior artistic qualities and—the heart of the play's continuing mystery—its tantalizing pertinence to Shakespeare.

Intrigued by all the possibilities, Halliwell published a clean, scholarly transcription in 1870, featuring a mock-Elizabethan title in a Gothic font. Only eleven copies were made available, however, with Halliwell at first declining even to identify himself as editor:

A Tragedy
of
King Richard the Second
Concluding with
the Murder of the Duke of
Gloucester at Calais.
A Composition Anterior to Shakespeare's Tragedy
on the same Reign, now first printed from
a Contemporary Manuscript

Later, however, Halliwell semi-changed his mind, autographing, dating and numbering each copy, and noting on the flyleaf of the eleventh, which he donated to the BM on 18 March, 1871, that the text had been 'Prepared from a MS in the British Museum — Eg. 1994.'

Sometime afterwards he added: 'See also *The Athenaeum*,

April, 1871,' referring to a letter he had published in that distinguished Victorian journal describing his edition as

a curious and altogether unknown early drama of Richard the Second, composed, I should say, judging from internal evidence, previously to the appearance of Shakspeare's [sic] play on other events of the same reign, and written with no small ability.[36]

Halliwell went on to hope that 'competent judges of old handwriting' might 'give an opinion respecting its date, and introduce to the further notice of the public a volume which well deserves to be better known.'[37]

Halliwell's Text

Halliwell's edition is a neatly printed and readable version that sticks closely to the original. A modest but quite successful effort is made to clean up the manuscript without altering it too substantially: capitals are inserted at line-starts and most of the text clearly set out as verse.

The spelling and design generally follow the MS, with some occasional carelessness, e.g., I.i.69 gives *then* for MS *them*, I.iii.283 *brotheer* for *brother* and III.iii.118 *punding-eaters* for *pudding-eaters*.

Less forgivably, Halliwell characteristically renders *your* as *youre* (e.g., III.ii.191, III.ii.193 and III.iii.36), and at I.ii.47 gives *alittle* for *a little*, at III.ii.216 *apolonian* for *a Polonian*

---

[36] *The Athenaeum*, April, 1871, pp. 401-2. A copy of Halliwell's letter appears in *1 Richard II* (2006), Vol. III.

[37] References to Halliwell's edition include Henry Paine Stokes: *An Attempt to Determine the Chronological Order of Shakespeare's Plays. The Harness Essay, 1877* (London: Macmillan & Co., 1878) p. 44; Adolphus William Ward: *A History of English Dramatic Literature to the Death of Queen Anne* (rev. edition, 3 vols., London: Macmillan & Co., 1899) Vol. II, p. 103; and Frederick Gard Fleay: *A Biographical Chronicle of the English Drama, 1559-1642* (London: Reeves and Turner, 1891) Vol. II, p. 320.

and at III.ii.222 *lickes* for *links*.

Lines are sparsely and inconsistently punctuated—sometimes he pops in a final period, though he usually follows the MS by omitting them. Where Halliwell perceives the need, he modestly emends, but without explanatory notes or editorial comment.

These are, however, minor cavils. Many of Halliwell's silent emendations are obviously correct and have been incorporated by almost all subsequent editors, including myself.

The most important occurs at II.iii.58-73, all of which was cut at some point and their speech-heads lost. Halliwell restores the text, identifies the missing speakers (Queen Anne, the Duchesses of Gloucester and Ireland) and assigns a short speech (ll. 59-60) to a (perhaps) previously silent Maid.

All editors except William A. Armstrong (1965) and E.B. Everitt (1965), who allocate these words to the Duchess of Ireland, accept Halliwell's introduction of the Maid. Others have built on his emendations and given three further lines that he assigned to the Duchess of Gloucester to the Duchess of Ireland (ll. 43-5).

At IV.iii.47-62 there are no visible speech-heads. Following Halliwell, editors now conventionally assign these lines to Tresilian and Nimble.

While these edits are not particularly difficult, given the context, later at IV.iii.112 the MS shows only *h* for a speech-head. Halliwell clearly guessed right when he gave these important lines, announcing Queen Anne's death, to Bushy.

Other Emendations
Halliwell was also a sharp-eyed editor of individual words. It was he who first noticed the absurdity of Richard's comment at III.i.95: 'or lett o^r predissessors yett to come' [...].

The Tragedy of King Richard II, Part One

He declined to emend, but inserted a cautionary '(*sic*)' after 'predissessors.' Keller took the hint and supplied 'successors,' reinstating the meaning but losing a beat. Rossiter emended further, 'Or *let* all our successors yet to come,' finally restoring the pentameter. The work, however, was really begun by Halliwell.

Nimble's important lines at MS III.iii.248-254 are severely damaged, thanks to a torn right edge where several words are lost. The recreation below, in a reduced font to fit my margins, employs the symbol < to indicate page damage:

that's all one if any man whissells treason tis as Ill as speakeing <
marke me m^r bayle. the bird whissels, that cannot speake, & <
ther be birds in a manner that can speake too: your Rauen will call ye<
yor crow will call ye knaue m^r Bayle ergoe he that can whisse<
can speake, & therfore this fellowe hath both spooke & whissled treaso<
how say yo^u bayley Ignorance

Halliwell partially restores and emends this speech but doesn't quite get it right. 'Whissel' and 'treasone' are easily completed, but the rest is harder, as his still-mutilated version shows:

Thats all one if any man whissells treason tis as ill as speaking [it] marke me master bayle. the bird whissells that cannot speake, and ther be birds in a manner that can speake too; your rauen will your crow will call ye knaue master Bayle ergoe he that can whissell can speake, and therfore this fellowe hath both spooke and whissled of treason how say you bayley Ignorance

To achieve coherence, Halliwell added 'it' to the end of the first line, and dropped 'call' from the third, perhaps intending that Nimble should appear to be correcting or supplementing himself: 'Your raven will—your crow will—call ye knave,' etc. Halliwell also added 'whissled of treason' toward the end, perhaps in error.

While Halliwell's rendition did not prove entirely successful, subsequent editors certainly built on it. Keller brilliantly contributed 'Your raven will call ye [rascal],' clarifying the overall sense, and Frijlinck perhaps supplied (or read—it defeats me, despite Photoshop) the word 'yet' in the second line.

Rossiter pulled it even further together, cleaning up Keller's version slightly and repunctuating the whole speech for greater clarity.

My edition draws on all these improvements, but supplies 'black' in place of Keller's 'rascal,' since it refers to a popular Elizabethan idiom, 'The raven chides blackness,' a meaning similar to 'the pot calls the kettle black.'[38]

The finished version now reads:

That's all one. If any man whistles treason, 'tis as ill as speaking it. Mark me, Master Bailey: the bird whistles that cannot speak, and yet there be birds in a manner that can speak too. Your raven will call ye black, your crow will call ye knave, Master Bailey, *ergo* he that can whistle can speak, and therefore this fellow hath both spoke and whistl'd treason. How say you, Bailey Ignorance?
—*1 Richard II*, III.iii.248-254

Nimble's lines at V.v.2-6 are similarly damaged but more successfully restored by Halliwell. Again using < to indicate damage, the MS gives:

as light as a fether my lord. I haue putt off my shoo<e
that I might Rune lustely, the battailles lost & t<h
prisoners, what shall we doe my lord. yonders a<
we may Rune alonge that. & nere be sene I warra<

Halliwell emends this to

As light as a fether my lord. I haue putt of my sho[oes] that
I might rune lustely, the battailles lost and [all are] prisoners,
what shall we doe my lord. yonders a [ditch] we may rune
alonge that and nere be sene I warrant.

---

[38] Also used in *Troilus and Cressida*, II.iii.211

Aside from *of* for *off* in the first line, which is probably just a typo, this is almost the version now generally accepted. Keller extended the final line to read 'I warrant ye,' and Rossiter even further to 'I warrant you, sir.'

But these edits are too gratuitously conjectural, in my opinion. 'Warrant' *tout court* does the job, while for lengthy reasons outlined in my *Text and Variorum Notes* (2006), I supply 'the young lords are prisoners' and 'stream.'

The reconstructed text reads:

As light as a feather, my lord. I have put off my [shoes] that I might run lustily. The battle's lost and [the young lords] prisoners. What shall we do, my lord? Yonder's a [stream.] We may run along that and ne'er be seen, I warra[nt.]
—*1 Richard II*, V.v.2-6

Drums sound within at V.iii.37 is a composited stage direction first assembled by Halliwell and accepted by all subsequent editors except Everitt and Armstrong. From a confusion of additions, corrections and deletes, Halliwell took 'how now what dromes are these,' which he assigned to Arundel, relocated a stage-manager's reminder, *Dromes*, and combined them all with the s.d. fragment *s sounds in*, to create a coherent direction that clarifies the action and moves the scene along.

A related and even more important reconstruction is the stage direction inserted at V.iv.20, *They fight and Green is slain*. The badly damaged MS shows only '& ne'. Halliwell brilliantly supplied the missing letters, permanently restoring a crucial moment. Again, almost all later editors have followed him.

Omissions and Limitations

The discussion so far should give a clear sense of Halliwell's indispensable contribution to the history of *1 Richard II*. That said, it is also necessary to call attention to his lapses, a few of which are quite serious. For example, a mistranscription of *paleing* for MS *pooleing*, i.e., polling, contributed this non-existent word to the OED whose editors, as Frijlinck points out, accepted it entirely on the strength of Halliwell's scholarly authority.[39]

Also notable are Halliwell's inexplicable omissions of entire lines and, in one case, of a reasonably significant speech. In Act III.iii the Bailiff of Dunstable says to Nimble:

You shall find me most pestiferous to assist ye; and so I pray ye, commend my service to your good lord and master. Come, sir, stand close.
—*1 Richard II*, III.iii.160-2

But Halliwell inexplicably leaves it all out. Similarly, he omits 'By wolves and lions now must Woodstock bleed,' (IV.iii.215), and Lapoole's important verbal stage direction 'The time serves fitly, I'll call the murderers in.' (V.i.52-4.)

Halliwell enigmatically assigns the Bailiff's speech at III.iii.202-4 to Nimble, but then omits his last four words. At II.ii.190 he inserts the stage direction *Exitt B[aggott]*, though there seems to be no dramatic or textual justification for it.

After York and Lancaster leave Plashy in III.ii. Woodstock says:

I have a sad presage comes suddenly
That I shall never see these brothers more.
On earth, I fear, we never more shall meet.
—*1 Richard II*, III.ii.105-7

The MS deletes the whole of the third line, but Halliwell's response seems confused. He restores 'I fear, we never more shall meet,' a reasonable editorial decision, but then omits 'on earth,' truncating the pentameter. Whether this is an error or a conscious emendation (though why?) is again

---

[39] Frijlinck, *Introduction*, p. xxxxiii. The word was subsequently withdrawn.

unclear.

At III.ii.129 a servant describes the Spruce Courtier as 'Some fine fool: he's attir'd very fantastically, and talks as foolishly.'

But Halliwell omits 'and talks as foolishly,' although the Courtier's affected speech is a big part of the scene's humor. While it's true that there is partial damage to the line—as Keller notes, 'the last part of [fantastically] is smeared and the *T* obliterated'[40]—all subsequent editors, including myself, have had no difficulty reading and publishing 'and talks as foolishly.'

Finally, Halliwell includes some highly questionable transcriptions.

Apart from the meaningless 'The Julye passions boiling in my breast' (I.iii.230), at V.vi.36-7, where the MS breaks off, he gives the equally nonsensical 'for I haue plodded in ployden and can beard no lawe...'

As Frijlinck later clarified, however, Woodstock's 'Julye passions' are his 'inlye passions,' and the play's last surviving line is 'I have plodded in Plowden (an anachronistic reference to a famous Elizabethan legal authority) and can find no law...'

These corrections do not seem difficult and might have suggested themselves to an editor of Halliwell's ability. That they did not is puzzling and, together with other avoidable errors, tend to confirm some of the doubts about his scholarship that have been raised.[41]

---

[40] Keller, p 79.
[41] Akrigg for example describes Halliwell's two-volume *Letters of the Kings of England* (1848) as 'completely unreliable, being one of the horrors of Victorian "scholarship."' (G.V.P. Akrigg: *Letters of King James VI & I* (1984) pp. 33-4.)

2 *A Collection of Old English Plays*, Vol. I, ed. A.H. Bullen (1882-89)

Not surprisingly, Halliwell's eleven anonymous copies went virtually unnoticed. About 12 years later, however, A.H. Bullen, in his compendious four-volume anthology of forgotten English dramas, cited a few edited lines together with a dismissive and misleading characterization that suggests he barely skimmed Halliwell's text:

Much of the play is taken up with *Greene* and *Baggott*; but the play-wright has chiefly exerted himself in representing the murder of *Woodstock* at Calais.[42]

Bullen's notice is nevertheless of historical significance, not least because it caught the eye of the play's next important editor, Wolfgang Keller, whose notes and introduction both refer to it.

3 *Richard II. Erster Teil. Ein Drama Aus Shake-speares Zeit*, ed. W. Keller (1899)

Wolfgang Keller was a German academic whose landmark edition of *1 Richard II* appeared in *Jahrbuch der Deutschen Shakespeare-Gessellshaft XXXV*, ed. Alois Brandl and Wolfgang Keller (Berlin, 1899).[43]

A long, untitled introduction not only intelligently and appreciatively discussed the play, but also outlined Keller's main editorial objectives.[44] These were in some measure a

---

[42] Bullen, I, Appendix 1, pp. 427-8. His light edits are recorded in my *Text and Variorum Notes* (2006).

[43] Founded in 1865, renamed *Shakespeare Jahrbuch* in 1925.

[44] Keller's fine critical analysis has not received the recognition it deserves, perhaps because it is in German. F.S. Boas for example drew heavily upon it for his *Woodstock* chapter in *Shakespeare and the Universities*, as did A.P. Rossiter, both without acknowledg-

response to Halliwell's edition which, as Keller observed,

> was published without introduction, notes, or even preface, and—although the play deserves it—made no attempt to update the punctuation or orthography.[45]

Keller undertook to remedy all of the above and thereby bring the play to a wider public. He largely succeeded. Without his edition we might still be waiting to hear of this remarkable and perhaps epochal drama.

Macro and Micro
Keller's important contributions are both particular and universal. Like most early Elizabethan plays, the MS lacks act and scene divisions. Keller introduced clearly numbered scenes and lines, though not the ones that prevail today, corrected words and phrases, supplied enduring emendations, and provided a quantity of informative and descriptive footnotes.

While retaining most of the MS's antique spellings, he freely punctuated the text, conferring upon it an indispensable coherence. In Woodstock's speech at I.i.130-144, for example, Keller's deft punctuations bring lucidity and movement to what in its raw Halliwell version seems a rather dull and uninspired declaration.

Keller's interventions also highlit many of Woodstock's subtler complexities as a dramatic and historical figure. Far from Halliwell's saintly political martyr, he emerges under Keller as a dithering if good-hearted court advisor not dissimilar to Polonius, sustained by his personal integrity and sense of responsibility to England. At the same time, like Lear's Gloucester, whose title of course he shares, Woodstock can often be short-tempered and tactless. His confrontation with Richard in the wedding scene, I.iii, ineluctably

---

ment. My translation of Keller's introduction appears in the *Commentary* section, *1 Richard II*, Vol. III (2006).
[45] Keller, p. 5, *1 Richard II*, Vol. III (2006).

recalls the row between Kent and Lear in *Lear*, I.i

As noted, Keller was the first to recognize the play's well-organized scenic structure. An Aristotelian at heart, he held that a 'scene' must be a unified action in one place involving the same group of characters. His *1 Richard II* thus comprises five acts of three scenes apiece, though to make this work he was forced to introduce the concept of *Nebenscenen*, side- or sub-scenes, contained within the larger moments. Thus in his version of V.ii-V.vi, the climactic final battle, V.ii, (Nimble and Tresilian planning to run away), and V.iv, (the death of Green), are merely *Nebenscenen*, prologue and epilogue.

All editors since Rossiter, however, have recognized that these arrangements are too mechanical. The fifth act actually comprises six rapid-fire battle sequences, comparable to the climactic montage in *Anthony and Cleopatra*, hurrying the narrative towards its exciting dénouement—the defeat, deposition and restoration of the king.

Keller's organizational efforts nevertheless helped to understand the play more fully as a cohesive unit. He also provided quality emendations, words and repointings that sharpened up a speech here, battened down a moment there, collectively bringing everything into a clearer focus. There are few readers, I think, including my younger self, who fully appreciate the impact of editing on comprehensibility.

Two of Keller's edits in particular deserve to be noticed. The first, touched on earlier, is his reorganization and clarification of Nimble's lines at III.iii.250-4:

Your raven will call ye [rascal,] your crow will call ye knave, Master Bailey: ergo, he that can [whistle treason] can speak, and therefore this fellow hath both spoke and whistl'd [treason].

It is only one speech, but a key one. Keller's conjectural emendations, especially *rascal* in the first line, helped pull both it and thus the whole scene together.

The Tragedy of King Richard II, Part One

The second notable edit is more important, indeed so much so that at least three subsequent editors (Rossiter, Parfitt and Shepherd) brazenly stole it and passed it off as their own. Among scholars, plagiarism is the sincerest form of flattery.

At V.i.263-74 Woodstock has just been murdered. While his assassins drag his body off to be arranged neatly on his bed, so that he appears to have died naturally, Lapoole calls in his troops to kill his killers and so cover up the crime.[46]

The MS is so damaged at this point, however, with missing speech-heads and stage directions, not to mention the copyist's faded scrawl, that it's hard to figure out exactly what's supposed to be going on.

Keller brought order to this confusion by assigning the correct lines to their speakers, directing the entrance of a couple of soldiers and assigning to them a short verbal response. It's well rendered and obviously right. All subsequent editions have followed Keller, whose version is reproduced below. The square-bracketed speech-heads and stage directions represent his emendations:

[*Lapoole*] Take it up gently, lay him in his bed;
Then shut the door, as if he there had died.
[*1st Murderer*] It cannot be perceived otherwise, my lord. Never was murder done with such rare skill. At our return we shall expect reward, my lord.
[*Lapoole*] 'Tis ready told. Bear in the body, then return and take it.
[*Exeunt Murderers with the body*] Within there, ho!
[*Enter Soldiers*]
[*Soldiers*] My lord?
—*1 Richard II*, V.i.256-64

Keller also corrected many of Halliwell's mistranscriptions,

---

[46] The analogies with *Macbeth* are striking, as is Lapoole's conscience-stricken speech before Woodstock's murder. The tension between the two killers, one reluctant, the other greedy and ambitious, also hints at Macbeth and Lady Macbeth.

restored the Bailiff's speech at III.iii.131-3, Woodstock's 'By wolves and lions now must Woodstock [bleed.]' (IV.iii. 225), and Lapoole's 'The time serves fitly, / I'll call the murderers in.' (V.i.51-2.)

Some Inaccuracies
On the other hand, Keller—harshly reprimanded for it later by both Rossiter and Frijlinck—did bow a little too easily to Halliwell's authority, mechanically reproducing some of his more questionable readings. Perhaps the German scholar felt a little insecure as a non-native speaker. He certainly did get confused about his English grammar at one point, discussed below.

A list of Keller's significant followings appears in my review of Frijlinck's edition, and more fully in my *Text and Variorum Notes* (2006).

Among them is his repeating Halliwell's absurd, 'Julye passions boiling in my breast' (I.iii.221), pointlessly replacing the *J* with an *I*. He also reprints Halliwell's careless substitution of 'sweete Richard' for MS 'sweete king' in II.ii.211.

At II.iii.32 Keller follows Halliwell's 'resent' where 'repent' is the actual word ('Nor now repent with peevish frowardness'). He also accepts Halliwell's emendation 'be off' at III.iii.103 where the MS gives 'begone.'

The censored play's incomplete concluding phrase, 'I have plodded in Plowden and can find no law...' is reproduced in Halliwell's meaningless version with only 'playden' for 'ployden' as a minor variant.

A little more seriously, at II.iii.43 Keller copies Halliwell in ignoring or overlooking a speech-rule,[47] thus assigning a

---

[47] As was common in Elizabethan and Jacobean prompt-books, the MS separates speeches by free-hand lines known as speech rules.

small but important declaration to the Duchess of Gloucester (rather than to the Duchess of Ireland, as do all other editors).

At III.iii.210 he appears to have again accepted Halliwell's authority in unwarrantedly transferring one of the Bailiff's speeches to Nimble.

While both these emendations could be defended on editorial grounds, there seems to be no explanation other than scholarly deference to explain Keller's omission of 'a day' from

> How like you that, Green? Believe me, if you fail, I'll not favor ye a day.
> —*1 Richard II*, IV.i.202-3

and the final 'well' in

> Would he were come! His counsel would direct you well.
> —*1 Richard II*, II.ii.196

Keller also followed Halliwell in placing a pointless *Exitt B[aggott]* after this line.

Not all of Keller's faults can be laid at Halliwell's door, however. At I.iii.170 and IV.ii.181 he unprecedentedly inserts an anachronistic and comic-like interrobang to express what he took to be combined surprise and indignation: 'Cankors?!' (I.iii.170) and 'Am I betrayd?!' (IV.ii.181).

Unfortunately this odd and very un-Elizabethan pointing has been repeatedly copied by other editors, including Rossiter and, through him, ARM and OXF. Yet both instances are wildly out of place and confer a sort of Bugs Bunny effect that may have encouraged some readers—most of whom won't know that they are not in the original—to feel that the play probably is some kind of scholarly hoax.

A second important editing mistake occurs in III.ii at the

conclusion of Woodstock's Launce-and-Crab dialogue with the Spruce Courtier's horse:

> Say a man should steal ye and feed ye fatter, could ye run away with him lustily? Ah, your silence argues a consent, I see! By the Mass, here comes company. We had been both taken if we had, I see.
>
> —*1 Richard II*, III.ii.178-9

Keller introduces a *not* into the last line, 'We had been both taken if we had not, I see.' commenting in a footnote that 'not is missing in MS. Without it the line makes no sense.'

But it is of course Keller who renders the line nonsensical. This is the little error we referred to earlier. As both Carpenter and Rossiter observe, the context makes it plain that Woodstock means, 'I see that we should both have been caught even if we *had* run away.'

Keller's edition nevertheless was a decisive step forward, and especially historic because he recognized the play's outstanding quality. He took seriously an obscure and almost forgotten drama where Halliwell had equivocated and Bullen merely sneered—'I will not inflict more of this stuff on the reader,' etc.[48]

Keller perceived that *1 Richard II* was well worth his time, attention and scholarly energy, and in so doing laid the groundwork, not only for the play's next two great editors, W.P. Frijlinck and A. P. Rossiter, but for its acceptance as a serious literary work and perhaps forgotten Shakespeare play (though he declined to make the call himself).

I don't think it's an exaggeration to say that Keller put *1 Richard II* on the map, albeit in an obscure corner. Nonetheless he successfuly called attention to what may yet prove to be an historic and transformative drama.

---

[48] Bullen, *op. cit.*, p 428.

4 'Notes on the Anonymous *Richard II*' by F.I. Carpenter (1900)

Carpenter's 'Notes' are not an edition but a five-page article in *The Journal of Germanic Philology,* Vol. III (1900), presented as a kind of extended commentary on Keller.

One gets the impression that the publication of *Richard II. Erster Teil* took Carpenter by surprise. A professor at the University of Chicago, he was evidently preparing an edition himself, noting in a brief introduction that his comments and suggestions were based on a transcription of the play, now lost, 'corrected from the original MS.'[49]

Nevertheless Carpenter acknowledged generously, if perhaps a little wryly, that Keller's text was 'an excellent piece of work,' which made available

an interesting and significant drama of Shakespeare's time, hitherto practically inaccessible, although previously printed by Halliwell in an edition of eleven copies.[50]

While fate may have been a little unkind to Frederic Ives Carpenter, he deserves honorable mention here because many of his proposed edits have in fact passed into general acceptance.

I especially welcome the opportunity to recognize emendations not always acknowledged as his by later editors, some of whom were nonetheless willing to let it be understood that his clever suggestions were their own.

Carpenter's most useful clarification concerns the play's closing fragment (V.vi.36-7). Nimble enters the lords' camp leading the bound Tresilian, and Arundel asks him: 'What moved thee, being his man, to apprehend him?'

---

[49] Carpenter, p. 139.
[50] Carpenter, p. 138.

As we've noted, Keller and Halliwell give Nimble the following incomprehensible response:

Partly for thes causses, first the feare of the proclematione for
I haue plodded in playden and can beard no lawe

But Carpenter recognized that the reference was anachronistically to the distinguished Elizabethan jurist Edmund Plowden (1518-85), and that the mysterious 'beard' was really 'fynd' (find), which again tells us how hard it is to accurately read the MS.[51]

Carpenter's two emendations cleared up everything, allowing subsequent editors to intelligibly read the final existing line:

Partly for these causes: first, the fear of the proclamation,
for I have plodded in Plowden and can find no law ...
—*1 Richard II*, V.vi.35-6

Rossiter and his successors have outrageously taken credit for this useful insight, and not only this one. At 1.ii.129 and V.vi.29 they give *Certiorari* for MS *surssararys*, usually with a scholarly explanation of the difference.[52] But these edits were originally Carpenter's.

Another of his skilled repairs occurs just before the big battle in Act V. John of Gaunt challenges the king:

And dost thou now plead doltish ignorance
Why we are landed thus in our defence?
—*1 Richard II*, V.iii.70-1

The word *landed* has created some debate. First, it does not accurately describe the occasion, and second, it appears to confuse John of Gaunt with his son, Henry Bullingbrook, also Duke of Lancaster, who more famously did land on the

---

[51] Carpenter, p. 142.
[52] Rossiter, p. 208.

coast at the start of his insurrection against Richard II. Carpenter resolved the issue, however, by proposing *banded* for *landed*, which may indeed have been the mistranscribed original. All editors since have copied him, though again without acknowledgment.

The following emendations, originating from Carpenter, have also been silently incorporated by his successors:

I.i.104 Let others *jet* in silk and gold, says he (*jet* for Halliwell's and Keller's *set*).

I.i.123 Alack the day, the night is made *a veil* (*a veil* for MS *auayle*).

I.i.130 Thanks from my heart. I swear afore my God (for MS 'Thankes from my harte I sweare: afore my god,')

II.i.134-5 Methinks 'tis strange, my good and reverend uncle, You and the rest should thus malign against us (*maligne* for MS *malinge*).

Carpenter made many other suggestions later editors quietly accepted, although most are too trivial to warrant discussion here—e.g., *handful* for *hand full* at II.iii.98, etc. He also proposed a few changes that never caught on, such as *shilling* for *pressing* at V.ii.9.

5 *The first part of the reign of King Richard the Second; or, Thomas of Woodstock*, ed. W.P. Frijlinck (1929)

The single most important edition of the play, Frijlinck's text is a 'type facsimile' in the Malone Society Reprint series, recreating the MS using print conventions. The copyist's handwriting is given in ordinary Times Roman, additions or comments by other hands in **Times Roman Bold**, and stage directions in *italics*. Deletions appear in [square brackets] and MS damage indicated by left and right carets, < >.

Frijlinck's edition also has a useful introduction describing the manuscript, its various hands and inks, and speculating about dates of composition. Her text, checked for accuracy by W.W. Greg, includes brief but descriptive footnotes of Halliwell's, Keller's and Carpenter's edits and/or errors.

Frijlinck's literary judgment is that *1 Richard II* 'marks a great advance towards historical tragedy after the chronicle plays,' and that 'the lively exposition has special merit.' It is successfully humorous where it needs to be, delineates and differentiates character well, and is unquestionably 'a forerunner to Shakespeare's *Richard II.*' Many of its speeches possess 'some poetic power.'[53]

Among Frijlinck's important textual clarifications are:

I.ii.137: 'I thanke your lordshipp, and a figg for the Roope then.' (For *Roope* (rope), Halliwell gives *Raxe*, Keller *raixe* and Carpenter *raxe*.)

I.iii.217: 'Shall we, that were great Edward's princely sons.' (For *sons* (MS *Sonnes*), Halliwell, Keller and Carpenter give *fame*.[54])

I.iii.230: 'The inly passions boiling in my breast.' (For *inly*, Halliwell gives *Julye*, and Keller *Iulye*.)

II.iii.25: 'That dost allow thy polling flatterers.' (For *polling*, MS *pooleing*, Halliwell and Keller give *paleing* which, as we have noted, led to an erroneous but temporary addition to the OED.)

II.iii.30: 'The sighs I vent are not mine own, dear aunt.' (For *vent*, Halliwell and Keller give *sent*.)

---

[53] Frijlinck, pp. xxiv-xxv.
[54] Carpenter compounds the misreading by going on to suggest *wear* for *were*—a classic instance where one editor's mistake (Halliwell, followed by Keller) leads to another's false emendation and the complete dist\ortion of the original.

II.iii.32: 'Nor now repent with peevish frowardness.' (For repent, Halliwell and Keller give *resent*.)

III.ii.57-8: 'Thou mak'st me blank at very sight of them! / What must these...?' ('What myscheefes' (Halliwell) and 'what mischeef...?' (Keller).[55])

III.ii.66: 'And then the bond must afterwards be paid.' (For *paid*, Halliwell and Keller give *seald*.[56])

III.ii.198: 'Go, sirrah, take you his horse.' (For *sirrah*, Halliwell and Keller give *for-[ward]*.) [57]

III.iii.6: '...be ready to assist us.' (Halliwell and Keller give *...be ready to [fill them vpp]*.[58]

III.iii.113: 'I'm e'en stroke to at heart too.' (For *stroke*, Halliwell gives *sticket*, and Keller *stirne*. But Frijlinck correctly notes that '*stroke to*...is the original reading, which has been obscurely altered, *ro* to *ic* and *ke* to something illegible, while the final *o* has been deleted all in darker ink.'[59])

IV.i.96-7: 'some near-adjoining friends.' (For *near-adjoining*, Halliwell and Keller give *of his*.)

IV.i.202-3: 'How like you that, Green? Believe me, if you fail, I'll not favor ye a day.' (WPF restores the last two words, inexplicably omitted by Halliwell and Keller.)

---

[55] Keller notes that he follows Halliwell here because again he was unable to make out a rapidly degrading text.
[56] Keller follows Halliwell because, as he again notes, 'The word is almost completely lost.'
[57] Keller: '*For[ward]* obliterated.'
[58] Keller follows Halliwell because '*Fill them vpp* illegible in the MS.'
[59] Frijlinck, III.iii.113n.

IV.i.226: 'Thou [may'st] now live at ease.' (For *[mayst]*, Halliwell and Keller give *[shalt]*.)

V.i.34: 'And yet, by all my fairest hopes, I swear.' (For *I swear*, Halliwell gives *of heauen*. Keller gives nothing while footnoting: '*hopes: I sweare* written behind it in darker ink.')

IV.iii.10: 'come off lustily.' (For *lustily*, Halliwell and Keller give *lusely*, and Carpenter suggests *easely*.)

V.iii.137: 'With much ado we got her leave the presence.' (For *presence*, MS gives *psence*, Keller gives *presence*, Halliwell *palace* and Carpenter *place*.)

IV.iii.172: 'Oh, dear my liege, all tears for her are vain oblations.' (For *oblations* Halliwell gives *illutions*.[60] Keller gives *oblations*.)

6 *Woodstock, a Moral History*, ed. with a preface by A.P. Rossiter (1946)

This is the play's best-known and most influential edition. Louis Ule drew upon it to work out his own version and concordance,[61] Armstrong (1965) reproduced it with only minor changes, and Parfitt/Shepherd (1977, 1988) accepted its scholarly authority virtually without argument—indeed suggesting, in the play's great editorial tradition, that many of Rossiter's most successful insights and emendations were really their own.

A plain-text version (without stage directions or notes) is available on-line at the Oxford Text Archives Internet site

---

[60] Perhaps an emendation rather than a misreading.
[61] Ule's *Concordance* is a stylometrically tallied list of words and their occurrence in the play. I am grateful to the late Eric Sams for sending me a copy. Ule's Oxford Text Archives (OTA) edition is reviewed below.

(http://ota.ahds.ac.uk/), replacing the Ule/Smith edition.[62]

Woodstock, a Moral History[63] is a large, thorough and compendious editing job based on a close re-reading of the original MS. It is equipped with a 76-page preface dealing with the most important aspects of the play, including the authorship question, dating, influences upon and of, and more.

It also has 26 pages of small-print text notes, 29 pages of general notes, and a lengthy appendix of source materials citing Holinshed, Stow, and Grafton, and an extended glossary of Elizabethan word usage. If you want to argue with Rossiter, you had better do your homework.

This wealth of research and information accounts to some extent for the edition's influence. Unless you're willing to match Rossiter's diligence and capacity for detail, you're obliged to accept his scholarship, which was considerable, his rendition of the text, which is actually quite shaky, and finally his critical judgments, which are by no means always reliable.

But getting to this point requires a level of energy and concentration most—I would say all—of the play's post-Rossiterian editors have been unwilling to exert, most likely because of his emphatic conclusion that the play is not by

---

[62] OTA provides the following bibliographical information: '*Woodstock: a moral history* / edited with a preface by A. P. Rossiter ... — London: Chatto and Windus, 1946. — 3 p., 255, [1] p.: p.; 23 cm. — Edited, and presented in a modernized text, from the Egerton MS 1994 in the British Library. — An anonymous play of doubtful date, probably about 1590 or later, generally regarded as preceding Shakespeare's play on the same subject; known variously by the titles *Richard II, Thomas of Woodstock,* and *Woodstock*.'

[63] In the *Times Literary Supplement*, 23 November 1946, the anonymous reviewer thought Rossiter's title 'not very happily chosen' because of its association with the novels of Scott.

Shakespeare. So for the greater part of the last century and most of this, Rossiter pretty much has had it his way, with even assiduous scholars tending to gesture vaguely in his direction when referencing the play and its details.

To put the matter concisely, Rossiter created *Woodstock* even as he consigned Halliwell's and Keller's *1 Richard II* to the ash-heaps of literary history. His famous conclusion—

There is not the smallest chance [the author] was Shakespeare... I must leave him, as I found him, a quiet ghost among that great majority who must for all the troublings of their lives and labours rest ANON.[64]

—continues to prevail, despite the fact that he repeatedly contradicts himself and ends up in an almost Freudian way confirming Shakespeare's presence everywhere in the play.

As an editor, I am as much in his debt as any of his successors, not least because his text was the one I dutifully read as an undergraduate at Cambridge, where he had been a Lecturer in English. More than a decade after his premature death in 1957 his presence was still strongly felt.

Rossiter's scholarship was indeed prodigious and indispensable, his sense of the play's theatrical possibilities finer than any of his predecessors, his willingness to rethink and reinvestigate an inspiration, and his historical conclusions generally well supported and seldom arbitrary.

He was also quite funny and endearingly unable to resist risqué and, by modern standards, completely inappropriate academic jokes. I learned much from Rossiter and unhesitatingly incorporated many of his readings and suggestions.

Act and Scene
In addition to providing *Woodstock* with its modern identity, Rossiter successfully laid bare the play's inner structure—

[64] Rossiter, p. 76.

that is, he correctly identified and numbered its acts and scenes, though not their location.[65]

As we've noted, Keller had made a start, but was unable to get beyond his Aristotelian *ideé fixe* that each act, including the fifth, was organized into three scenes held together by the unities of time, place and action.

Frijlinck understood the drama's looser organization but, given her brief, confined her comments to often cryptic footnotes. Rossiter took her cue and clarified everything, including the six scenes in Act V, and has been followed in this respect by all subsequent editors.

With a sure hand and keen theatrical intelligence, Rossiter also cleaned up several murky stage directions, many of which I also follow.

As a representative instance, consider his s.dd. at III.i.108, which pull together the ragged manuscript's

{*sound*} se it be done: com Anne to our great hall
wher Richard keepes his gorgious ffeastiuall — *Exeunt*
Manett Trisillian

and replaces it with the coherent and functional

Trumpets sound. Exeunt all but Tresilian.

Likewise at III.i.116 s.d., where the MS gives only *Enter Nimble*, APR supplies

Enter NIMBLE, in peaked shoes with knee-chains.

---

[65] Only one location is specified in MS, Woodstock's estate at Plashy. It is an indication of Rossiter's influence that his vagueness carried over into subsequent editions. Even Corbin and Sedge (2002) leave the question untouched. I have tried to remedy these uncertainties by emending conjecturally, based on what the text and actual history suggest.

The Tragedy of King Richard II, Part One

Rossiter notes: 'I fill in details from text,' a manoeuvre successfully carried out more than once and often followed by later editors.

At the end of II.i and the beginning of II.ii, Rossiter brilliantly resolves the long-standing puzzle of some apparently irrelevant stage directions by noticing that they have been displaced from II.iii. He restored them and made the moment whole.

Later in the same scene, II.ii.25, the right edge of the MS is damaged, leaving only the fragments *Ex, ff, s, he*, and some ambiguous marginal reminders, *florish* and (*sound*). Using Malone Society conventions, the MS looks approximately like this:

Queen: May heaven direct your wisdoms to provide
florish   for englands honno^r, & king Richards good — <
          yorke: beleeue no less sweete queene attend hir highnes
       Arond: the king is come my lords
————*wood*: stand from the doore then, make way Cheney./ <
Ex < ff   s> he/
(*sound*) ————————
Enter King. Richard, Baggott Busshey Greene & Scroope, & others

Rossiter clears it all up by compositing a whole new set of stage directions, indicated below by my square brackets:

Queen: May heaven direct your wisdoms to provide
For England's honor and King Richard's good.
York: Believe no less, sweet queen. Attend her Highness.
[*Exeunt Queen Anne and the Duchesses of Gloucester and Ireland*]
Arundel: The King is come, my lords.
Woodstock: Stand from the door, then. Make way, Cheney.
Sound [*a flourish.*] *Enter King Richard, Bagot, Bushy, Green, Scroop and others.*

Lines and Words
Other emendations by Rossiter that have been generally

accepted go to the level of lines and words. Among the most important is II.ii.205-7, where the damaged MS gives:

an excellent deuice, the commons has murmord a g <
a great while, and thers no such meanes as meate to stopp <

Halliwell and Keller conjecturally emended this to

An excellent deuice, the commons has murmord a[ngrily]
a great while, and thers no such meanes as meate to stopp [them].

But Rossiter came up with the much improved

An excellent device: the commons have murmured against us
a great while, and there's no such means as meat to stop [their mouths].
                                                                    —*1 Richard II*, II.ii.205-7

Another small but extremely important emendation, touched on earlier, concerns the much-disputed III.i.95, which the historically-challenged copyist, if indeed the error was his, gave nonsensically as 'or lett o[r] predissessors yett to come.'

The solecism was later corrected by Halliwell to a stuttering 'or lett o[r] successessors yett to come,' and then improved further by Keller's lame-footed 'Or lett our successors yett to come.' It took Rossiter to supply the rhythmic patch: 'Or let *all* our successors yet to come,' the iambic pentameter now universally accepted.[66]

A further nice touch occurs at III.ii.119-21, where Rossiter introduces the word *so* in order to clarify an otherwise impossibly prescient remark by Woodstock. The Spruce Courtier has just arrived at Plashy, Woodstock's Essex estate, and the duke tells his servant to bid the man enter:

---

[66] The italicized *all* is Rossiter's, the same treatment he gives all his edits.

to see me saist tho[u], agodsname lett hime com,
he brings no blancke charters wth hime
prethee bid hime light & enter

Rossiter suggests rendering this as prose, which I accept, despite the MS. His addition of the logical conjunction *So* markedly improves intelligibility:

To see me, say'st thou? A' God's name, let him come, [so] he brings no Blank Charters with him! Prithee, bid him 'light and enter.
—*1 Richard II*, III.ii.119-21

MS II.ii.201-3 breaks off at the right edge, calling for some kind of editorial prosthesis:

Sblud & I were not a counsello[r]. I could fynd in <
to dyne at a Tauerne to day

Rossiter supplies, 'I could *find in myself* to dine at a tavern today,' overlooking the familiar Elizabethan expression 'I could find in my heart,' etc., which I supply instead.

This has the double merit of colloquialism and consistency with the likelihood that Shakespeare is our author—he used the phrase 'find in my heart' seven times: *Much Ado About Nothing*, I.i.126, III.v.19-22, *The Comedy of Errors*, IV.iv.155-6, *As You Like It*, II.iv.5, *All's Well That Ends Well*, II.v.12, *1 Henry IV*, II.iv.50, and *The Tempest*, II.ii.156.

Problems and Omissions

Rossiter's skills as a scholar and critic were unfortunately offset by some limitations. Among the gravest is that he was often tempted to editorial over-ingenuity, resulting in distortions of some scholarly consequence.

Examples include unjustified deletions, among them the character of Sir Pierce of Exton, discussed earlier. A second over-ingenious edit occurs at IV.iii.143ff. with the excision of Sir Henry Green, the king's favorite favorite, together with Bagot's line, 'Here comes King Richard, all go comfort him.'

In both cases Rossiter weakly justifies his edits on the grounds that the characters have no spoken lines, though elsewhere he leaves other non-speakers in place. We may note too that eloquently silent on-stage presences were of course quite common in Elizabethan and Jacobean drama.[67]

Plagiarisms

Rossiter also often unsettlingly suggests that Keller's edits are actually his own. It's quite gratuitous, since his personal scholarship hardly comes into question; yet that he did it remains indisputable.

We have discussed the worst instance already, his appropriation of Keller's decisive reorganization of V.i. 256-64 (the killing of Woodstock's murderers). It cannot be supposed that Rossiter merely overlooked this pillage, since he mendaciously notes, 'I supply *Enter Souldiers.*'

Another important theft occurs at III.ii.138-9, 'Hear'st-ta, thou, fellow...?' Rossiter's commentary references only one of Keller's two suggestions about the problematic suffix *–ta*, while brazenly adopting the second as his own.[68]

What these remarks and judgments reveal is that like a good scholar Rossiter minutely examined Keller's text, but like a bad one he stole many of its most important editorial contributions.

Indeed, one almost gets the impression of a kind of scholarly kleptomania, extending even to the tiniest objects, like the clarifying dashes inserted at I.ii.27-8. Such small potatoes would hardly be worth commenting upon, except that Ros-

---

[67] See Chambers, *William Shakespeare* I, p. 231; Albert Feuillerat: *The Composition of Shakespeare's Plays* (1953) pp. 56-7.
[67] Rossiter, pp. 194n.,135
[68] Rossiter, p. 184.

siter goes out of his way to note, 'my dashes.' The fact is, they appeared in Keller's text first.

The Attack on Keller

Rossiter's commentary also includes a sustained critique of Keller's scholarship—legitimate enough among editors, though in this case too often crossing the boundaries of honesty and fair debate.

Clearly the practice becomes even more questionable when the attacker ruthlessly plunders the work of the attackee and, moreover, grossly misrepresents his faults. In a note to II.i. 151-2, for example, Rossiter blatantly ignores Keller's recognition of a reference and then blames him for its omission.[69]

It's possible that Rossiter's harsh critique of the German scholar was affected by the wartime conditions under which he worked. At III.ii.79 he perhaps unconsciously rendered the MS phrase, 'God and country,' as 'king and country,' because of the times. Certainly he was a ζωον πολιτικον who emphasized the play's political dimension and willingly drew analogies between it and current events.[70] Keller however was not Rossiter's only victim—he stole liberally from everyone.

Some of his embezzlements are quite substantial, such as Halliwell's brilliant emendation at V.iv.18.s.d., *They fight and Green is slain*, which he silently assimilates.

Rossiter also credits himself for Halliwell's important speech head *Maid* at II.iii.59-60, noting, 'No speech-heading in MS but the *sir* makes the guess easy.'[71] Perhaps, but he does not add that the easy guess was not his.

---

[69] Rossiter, p. 215, Keller, p. 30.
[70] Rossiter, p. 193.
[71] Rossiter, p. 192.

Indeed, many of Rossiter's apparently sharp-eyed observations are actually taken unacknowledged from elsewhere, especially Carpenter's obscure and hard-to-access article. They include *banded* for *landed* (V.iii.71), *Certiorari* for *Surssarari*s (I.ii.29, V.vi.29), the s.d. *Paper* (II.ii.66) together with its explanatory note, *whiles* for *wilse* (III.ii.209) and Carpenter's replacement of Keller's *care all for* with *are all for* (III.i.41).

He also feasted on Keller and Frijlinck. For instance, Rossiter twice perceptively notes that Tresilian and York never appear on stage together, speculating that one actor doubled both roles.[72]

This is quite ingenious, but in fact the original observation was Keller's, who remarks on the doubling possibility in his introduction.[73] It is Rossiter however who has received whatever *kudos* derives from this insight. Crime often pays, at least in the groves of academe.[74]

Grammatical Changes
These petty thefts are reprehensible, but in my view a more serious offense is the unreliability of Rossiter's much-read text.

Its main deficiencies are inaccuracy and the imposition of unacknowledged grammatical preferences, including suppressing the writer's use of the Elizabethan noun-verb discord, as in

...and if any disturb ye, we four comes presently
—*1 Richard II*, IV.i.156-7

a stylistic marker often used to identify Shakespeare. These

---

[72] Rossiter, p. 215.
[73] Keller, p. 38.
[74] In *Shakespeare & the Universities* F.S. Boas also draws heavily on Keller without acknowledgment.

false data are then cited to bolster Rossiter's conclusion that the author could not possibly be he.

A second red-alert concerns Rossiter's practice of almost never distinguishing between the MS's enunciated and un-enunciated past and present tenses, e.g., *readst* vs. *readest*. This is a problem because obviously there's a significant rhythmic (and often rhyming) distinction between single-, double- and multi-syllabic verbs.

Rossiter's punctuation too is idiosyncratic, with often irrelevant or arbitrary dashes, brackets and multi-dot ellipses, two, three, four and, in one case, seven in a row......!

These intrusions and eccentricities alter the rhythm, emphases and feel of the text so that it hardly resembles a Shakespeare drama in any familiar way. Rossiter's motives, conscious and unconscious, may only be surmised.

Oversights and Errors
Some of Rossiter's misrepresentations seem merely to be oversights. Among them: 1.ii.67, *stubborn law* for *subtle law*; II.ii.1, *How now* for *Now*; II.iii.109, *starv'st* for *starvest*; III.i.30, *our* for *out*; III.ii.79, *king and country* for *God and country*; III.ii.102-3, *adieu* for *farewell*; III.ii.193-4, *If you so please* (twice) for *If so you please*; III.ii.222, *as twere* for *as it were*; III.iii.92-3, *There's* for *There is*; III.iii.247, *if a man whistles treason* for *if any man whistles treason*; IV.i.189-90, *ever* for *never*; IV.ii.58, *the* for *her*; V.i.203-6, *breathest* for *breath'st*.[75]

A handful of the above are obviously trivial, though still unacceptable by scholarly standards.[76] Others, such as *king and country* for *God and country*, and *if a man whistles*

---

[75] Additional examples are cited below when discussing Armstrong's 1965 edition, which is a plagiarized copy of *Woodstock, a Moral History*, including its mistakes.
[76] See Harold Jenkins' critical assessment in *Review of English Studies*, Vol. 24, No. 93, (January, 1948) p. 67.

treason for *if any man whistles treason,* have had exegetical consequences. Like lexicographers, scholars may be harmless drudges, but their mistakes have repercussions.

Despite the foregoing, Rossiter's achievement remains overwhelmingly positive. Frijlinck's hard-to-read edition is for specialists, and by 1946 Keller's *Jahrbuch* was all but unavailable, and Carpenter's commentary long forgotten. APR reintroduced the play to a new generation largely unaware of it, and did so in a popular edition that was well received and widely read among Shakespeare scholars.

7 From *Thomas of Woodstock*, ed. Geoffrey Bullough (1960)

Thanks in part to the success of Rossiter's edition, Geoffrey Bullough included a severely abridged version entitled *Thomas of Woodstock* in his *Narrative and Dramatic Sources of Shakespeare,* Vol. III (1960).

Bullough derives his text chiefly from Frijlinck, though he edits and emends irresponsibly at will, perhaps hoping to make his version look 'authentic.'

He also includes brief and often deliberately misleading summaries of most, though not all, of the omitted material.

In at least two glaring instances—the Spruce Courtier and Osric, and Edward III's ghost and King Hamlet—Bullough ignores his own brief of exploring possible sources.

An editorial footnote on the first page claims that the punctuation has been modernized, though in fact it's a hit-and-miss affair. Some but not all lower-case line-starts are given capitals, a few medial *u*'s and initial *v*'s are replaced (e.g., *heavey* for MS *heauey* and *uncles* for *vncles,* etc.), while here and there consonantal *i*'s are altered to *j*'s.

These difficulties extend even to the layout. Bullough renders every court scene in full verse, a complete misrepresentation of the MS.

Nimble's declaration at I.ii.112-115, for example, is clearly not verse, though Bullough prints it as such, and in the same cumbersome versiform he imposes throughout:

I, saveing your honnors speech, your worshippfull tayle was whipt
For stealeing my dinner out of my Satchell: you were ever
So craftye in your childhood, that I knewe your worshipp would
Prove a good lawyer.

Bullough's free hand with the text nevertheless leads to some minor but important emendations.

The most significant occurs at III.i.36, the entry of Queen Anne. As she and her entourage sweep in, the MS gives a short speech to a character identified only as 'g':

g be yor leaue ther. giue way to'the queene.

Because of the 'g' most editors reflexively assign this line to Green. Bullough, with perhaps greater theatrical awareness, gives it to [*a*] g[*uard*], which he reasonably imagines posted at the door. I accept this emendation, further editing and re-punctuating the speech to

[*A Guard*:] By your leave there, give way to the Queen!
—*1 Richard II*, III.i.36

An Abridgment Too Far

The most notable aspect of Bullough's edition is its savage abridging of the play by some 1880 lines, or approximately two-thirds.

Tallying only the spoken text, BUL deletes I.i—80 lines; I.ii —36 lines; all of I.iii and II.i; II.ii—142 lines; II.iii—all but three lines; III.i—80 lines (about half the scene); III.ii—126 lines; III.iii—140 lines; IV.i—105 lines; IV.ii—118 lines; IV.iii—all but 13 lines; V.i—205; V.ii—the whole scene;

V.iii—all but the first 26 lines; V.iv—all but 29 lines; V.v—the whole scene; V.vi—18 lines.

Most of these omissions are replaced by summaries. The following substantial cuts are indicated only by ellipses and are not summarized: I.i.31-40, 71-98, 110-130, 198-222; III.i.83-163; IV.i 1-61, 151-163, 196-228; IV.ii.197-215; V.iii.27-128.

In addition, the whole of V.v is omitted without comment or explanation.

Worse still, Bullough's so-called summaries seriously distort the play. For example, the wonderfully comic scene with the Spruce Courtier, arguably the original for Osric, becomes this:

'A spruce courtier on horsebacke' enters to bid Woodstock back to Court. Mistaking the Duke for a groom he asks him to mind his horse. The Duke does so, and when the mistake is revealed, demands the tip promised him.[77]

But the business with the tip is trivial compared to the theatrically bold and inventive portrait of court dandyism, the imaginative dialogue between Woodstock and the horse, and the subtle, satirically sketched class dynamics of the encounter between a gracious old-style nobleman and one of Richard II's brash 'new men.' In Bullough, the scene is politically, socially and even theatrically sterilized.

Another big cut, V.i.59-207, is misrepresented thus:

The Ghosts of the Black Prince and Edward III appear to Woodstock in a vision and he awakes in terror. Lapoole urges him to write & submit to King Richard. Woodstock agrees to write, not to submit, but to admonish the King.[78]

---

[77] Bullough, p. 473.
[78] Bullough, p. 487.

Lost however are Lapoole's Macbethian psychomachia over murdering Woodstock, the deep connections between the spooky appearance of the prince's kingly father and *Hamlet*, and, almost word-for-word, the parallels with Richmond's ghostly visitors the night before Bosworth. This, in a book on Shakespeare's sources.

Bullough's summary of III.iii completely overlooks its menacing portrait of the Elizabethan police state and the satirical pre-echoes of Dogberry and Verges.

At V.vi.6 he omits, 'Who is't can tell us which way Bagot fled?' making complete nonsense of what little is quoted of the rest of the scene.

Finally, Bullough incorrectly gives *Lights, light* for *Lights, lights* at I.i.1; *kindsmen* for *kinsmen* at I.i.138; *well not* for *not well* at II.ii.149; *for all whisperers* instead of *all for whisperers* at III.iii.60, *Their* for *There* at III.iii.115; and *dist* for *didst* at IV.i.225.

8 *Thomas of Woodstock or 1 Richard II*, ed. E.B. Everitt in (1965)

E.B. Everitt (*The Young Shakespeare*, 1954), is one of the unsung heroes of early-Shakespeare studies. It was thus quite appropriate that he should edit, together with Ray L. Armstrong, *Six Early Plays Related to the Shakespeare Canon* (*Anglicistica*, Vol. XIV, 1965), including *Thomas of Woodstock*.[79]

Everitt's title page notes that his text is 'From MS Egerton 1994 in the British Museum.' He later adds that it represents a 'literal transcription...collated with all earlier editions but

---

[79] The others plays were John Bale: *King John*; Anonymous: *Edward the Third;* John Ford: *Perkin Warbeck*; Robert Davenport: *King John and Matilda*. Armstrong edited only *Edward III*.

stayed with the most conservative reading of the verbal text.'[80]

Since I generally admire Everitt's work, I would very much like to report that his edition is a good one. Unfortunately, this is not the case. His *Woodstock* is among the most error-prone and execrably proof-read of all, with one textual pratfall after another.

The most unforgivable occurs at II.i.86, where Bushy gravely informs the King:

This was called the Battle of Poitiers, and was fought on Monday the nineteenth of September, 1963, my lord.

After absorbing this future shock, Richard wisely if inaccurately commands, 'Shut up thy book, good Busby!' (II.i120). Similarly, and even funnier, Woodstock's gracious wife is later referred to as the 'Duckess.'[81]

More serious mistakes include mislabeling V.ii as V.iii, and Nimble's 'Good bless my lord Tresilian!' at V.v.40-1 (for 'God bless,' etc.). The phrase is one of the drama's grimmest running jokes, and Nimble's use of it at this moment is the ultimate punch line. Everitt's most casual check would have revealed that wooden O.

Additional careless misprints include *loyal* for *royal* at I.i. 45; *subject* for *a subject* at II.i.36; *fashion* for *fashions* at II.ii.214; *forwardness* for *frowardness* at II.iii.32; *King's* for *Kings'* at III.i.64; *on ill word* for *an ill word* at III.i.146; *villany* for *villainy* at III.ii.77; *have him' light* for *had have him' light* at III.ii.123; *the king Richard's Council* at III.ii. 206; *turk cock* for *turkey-cock* at IV.i.141; omission of the word *lands* from IV.i.199; *Thou issue of King Edward's*

---

[80] Everitt, *Text Notes*, p. 7
[81] Everitt, p. 290. This one really quacked me up.

loins for *Thou royal issue of King Edward's loins* at V.i.66; *Pole* for *Poole* at V.i.159; *I'l* for *I'd* at V.i.180; *baron's* for *barons'* at V.i.296; *demurrer* for *demur* at V.ii.32; and *tender dare* for *tender care* at V.vi.1.

The poor proofing extends to the punctuation: *Yes, Who storms at it?* at I.iii.167; a period after *Scroop* (instead of a comma) at II.i.3; a solecistic period after *Ireland* at II.ii.87; the incomplete question *What must these?* at III.ii.59; and an incorrectly inserted period at III.ii.186, giving the tautological, *The error was in the mistake,*

Like Rossiter, Everitt is ambiguous about the status of *-ed* and *-est*. For example, he gives I.i.136 as: 'Th'art vexed I know. Thou greiv'st, kind Edmund York'

But the juxtaposition of *vexed* and *greiv'st* suggests *vexèd*, which is clearly not the intent of MS *vext*. Even more bewildering, at IV.iii.159 he gives the past-tense of *drown* as *drownd*, a literal but (for his edition) unique reproduction of the MS.

Everitt carelessly gives, 'Or let our predecessors yet to come,' at III.i.95, unpersuasively claiming in an afternote that he retains the original because 'it is probably the correct sense.'[82] Whatever that means, it seems likelier that Everitt was simply unaware of the textual debate until too late.

Also unique among editors, Everitt accepts Carpenter's highly doubtful emendation, 'shilling,' in Nimble's speech at V.ii.11-12, though Keller's superior 'pressing' is now generally followed.[83] Everitt compounds his poor judgment by mistakenly setting these lines as verse.

Despite these shortcomings, a few of Everitt's emendations

---

[82] Everitt, Textual Notes, *ed. cit.*, p. 307.
[83] The *OED* gives 1707 as the earliest use of the phrase 'to take the king's shilling.'

The Tragedy of King Richard II, Part One

have survived. The most important is at MS I.ii.99-101, where Nimble tells Tresilian:

yes any thing. so yor honno^r. pray not for me. I care not for now you're lord chiefe Iustice: if euer ye cry, lord haue marcy vppon me, I shall hange fort Shure

Thanks to the commas after *cry* and *me*, most editors insert quote marks around 'Lord have mercy upon me.' But Everitt more intelligently gives

... if ever ye cry 'Lord have mercy' upon me, I shall hang for't, sure!

Everitt also neatly repunctuates MS II.ii.193, 'seeke hime, hang him, he lurkes not farr off I war^{r}ant,' so that it reads more clearly:

Seek him? Hang him! He lurks not far off, I warrant.

There are other minor edits where I either accept Everitt or am influenced by his reading—for example, 'the young lords' at V.v.4, which builds on his emendation, 'the lords.'

9 *Woodstock*, ed. William A. Armstrong (1965)

In the same year of Everitt's edition, William A. Armstrong, not be confused with Everitt's colleague Ray L. Armstrong, produced *Elizabethan History Plays* for OUP, including among his selections the anonymous *Woodstock*.

Armstrong's version need not detain us long; as we've noted, it is little more than a superficially edited xerox of *Woodstock, a Moral History*, omitting Rossiter's commentary and notes. All of Rossiter's innovations, good and evil, are photographically repeated, including the unjustified removal of Exton from the first scene, Green from IV.iii, and the deletion of Bagot's supporting line, 'Here comes King Richard, all go comfort him,' at IV.iii.143.

Armstrong also witlessly follows Rossiter's doubtful re-assignment of the Second Murderer's speech and action to the First Murderer, 'Not too fast for falling! (*Strikes him*)' (V.i.232).

He likewise carelessly reproduces all Rossiter's sleepy-eyed repetitions, including *king and country* for *God and country* (III.ii.79); *adieu* for *farewell* (III.ii.102-3); *the* for *her* (IV.ii.58); and *if a man whistles treason* for *if any man whistles treason* (III.iii.247).

At V.i.59 Rossiter emends MS 'Night horror' to 'Night-horror.' Although there is no justification for creating this strange compound, Armstrong goes along.

Armstrong also fails to proof-read carefully. I.iii.56 appears as 'Shall sing in raise of this your memory,' (instead of *praise*); III.i.151-2 as 'I will treat this paper,' (instead of *tear*); IV.i.247 as 'Westmorland' (instead of APR *Westmoreland* or even MS *westmerland*); V.ii.24 as 'but the sword and lance' (instead of *by the sword and lance*); and IV.iii.95 as 'Well, then: I see my whistle must be whipped...' (instead of *whistler*).

Sir Pierce of Exton Redux
One of Armstrong's few independent edits throws an interesting light on the textual debate concerning the presence of Sir Pierce of Exton in I.i.

As we've seen, Rossiter deletes this historically and Shakespeareanly significant character by claiming that the dramatist somehow didn't really mean to include him. Rossiter thus kindly helps out by creating an entirely new figure, 'The Lord Mayor Exton.'

Armstrong makes his unconscious contribution to the debate by mechanically reprinting Rossiter's emended stage direction sans Exton but with the new Lord Mayor:

Enter THOMAS OF WOODSTOCK *in frieze. The Mace [afore]*

him. The LORD MAYOR EXTON, *and others with lights afore them.*

Soon afterwards, however, the grammatically literate Armstrong spots an apparent contradiction in Rossiter's version, and reflexively repunctuates the dialogue by inserting a semicolon after 'Exton':

Woodstock: ... Hie thee, good Exton;
Good Lord Mayor, I do beseech ye prosecute
With your best care a means for all our safeties.
—*1 Richard II*, I.i.117-20

Armstrong's pointing properly separates 'Hie thee, good Exton,' who then exits, from the 'Good Lord Mayor' who remains on stage in further conversation about the security of the Lancastrian party in his city.

At II.iii.59 Armstrong declines to follow Rossiter's emendation, taken from Halliwell, assigning a short speech to a 'Maid.' He gives the lines instead to the Duchess of Ireland, as does Everitt.

10, 11   *Thomas of Woodstock*, ed. George Parfitt and Simon Shepherd (1977, 1988)

These two texts are virtually identical and therefore may be safely treated as one, although the 1988 edition inexplicably fails to reprint pp. 3 (I.i.1-34) and 66 (V.i.146-199), some 87 lines.

The first edition of NOT was prepared for the *Nottingham Drama Texts* series, published by Nottingham University. The second, commissioned by Brynmill Press eleven years later, accompanied Ian Robinson's groundbreaking 1988 essay, '*Richard II*' & '*Woodstock*', the first extended attempt to make the case for Shakespeare as the play's author.

A relic from the pre-computer age, NOT appears to have been typed on an IBM Selectric and then photocopied. It is staple-bound in dingy cartridge-paper, its textual layout marred by gaping white spaces, varying page lengths and erratically set footnotes full of typographical redundancies and inconsistent abbreviations.

The editors provide a short introduction and an incomplete list of earlier editions. Frijlinck is dismissed as offering a 'detailed but unscientific account of the state of the ms and its hands and inks, but a less thorough critical appraisal,' while Rossiter published 'much the most useful edition, although [he] imposes on the text his own notions of dramatic speech,' with notes that are 'thorough and helpful, although the viewpoint is often perverse.' Everitt's text 'is highly dubious,' without 'worth-while commentary' except for 'postulated relationships which teeter on the incredible.'

Parfitt/Shepherd also repeatedly claim or imply that they consulted the MS, but tell-tale errors show that at best they glanced occasionally at Frijlinck's literal transcription while deriving most of their editorial material from the perverse Rossiter and the highly dubious Everitt.

Minor unacknowledged borrowings from APR include the emendation *Accomp'nied* for MS *accompined* (II.iii.86), *peers* for *peere* (III.i.44), parentheses and an exclamation point for *I sir, would yo^u & they were sodden for my swyne* (III.iii.133-4); and *the* for *they* (IV.ii.13).

Everitt's contributions include the incomplete sentence, *What must these?* (III.ii.59); the omission of *had* from *have had him light* (III.ii.121-3); and the unacknowledged adoption of his successful repointing of *'Lord have mercy' upon me* (1.ii.100-1).

Fake Scholarship
A feature of NOT is the editors' claim to have worked from the original. They refer confidently to the MS which 'shows

evidence of political intervention...[and] deletions seemingly made by the scribe.' Its pages are 'damaged' or 'damaged here,' and they repeatedly observe that a particular ink or hand has been used. [84]

But if Parfitt and Shepherd really did check the MS for its inks and edits, it was extremely cursory and, as I know from personal experience, almost impossible to accomplish without serious laboratory backup. Their prevarications may be inferred from the descriptive errors they claim proudly for themselves, and the fact that almost all their scholarly observations are transparent paraphrases from other editors.

For example, at V.i.188 the MS reads:

& such liues heere: though death King Richard s <

Parfitt and Shepherd conjecturally emend the last word to *send*, explaining in a footnote that in the MS the 'S is damaged.' [85]

But no, it is not—in fact, the *S* is the only part of the word that survives. The editors have simply mistaken Rossiter's note, 'All but the *s* of *send* is gone,'[86] reading it as 'The *s* of *send* is gone.' A similar blunder occurs at III.iii.193.

At II.ii.185 the MS is obscured. All we get is the half-verb *sha* followed by *country*. The topic is beards and shaving, and Rossiter once again provides the most successful conjectural emendation, shown here in square brackets:

Pox on't, we'll not have a beard amongst us. We'll [shave the] country and the city too, shall we not, Richard?

NOT copies Rossiter without acknowledgment, brazenly

---

[84] Parfitt and Shepherd (1988) p. vii.
[85] Parfitt and Shepherd, (1977) p. 66 n. As noted, p. 66 is missing from NOT 1988 edition.
[86] Rossiter, p. 204.

adding in a note: 'for *shave*, MS 'sha'; we add *the* before *country*'.[87]

MS II.ii.198 is another damaged line:

Troth, I think I shall trouble myself but with a few <

Halliwell originally supplied the missing final word, *counselors*, followed by all subsequent editors, excepting Everitt, who mysteriously leaves the line incomplete.

Unsurprisingly, Parfitt and Shepherd also give *counsellors*, which they found in Rossiter—HAL and KEL spell the word with one *l*—and then, in a sort of what-the-hell spirit, award themselves all the credit anyway:

counsellors: MS damaged after 'few'—we supply on basis of probable play on king's 'counsel' [l. 190].[88]

Green's speech at II.ii.205-7, as we have already noticed, contains one of Rossiter's most successful emendations. The damaged MS reads:

an excellent deuice, the commons has murmord a g a great while, and thers no such meanes as meate to stopp

Halliwell and Keller tried 'angrily,' and 'stopp them,' and Frijlinck suggested 'against you.' But Rossiter supplied the most widely accepted conjecture:

An excellent device: the commons have murmured [against us] a great while, and there's no such means as meat to stop [their mouths.]

You wouldn't know any of this from NOT's footnote, however, which proudly announces:

---

[87] Parfitt and Shepherd, p. 26 n.
[88] Parfitt and Shepherd, p. 26 n.

[ll.197-8] damaged MS; we supply 'a [gainst us]' (G would probably identify with the king), and 'their mouths'.[89]

Halliwell's superb emendation assigning a small but clarifying speech to 'A Maid' at II.iii.59 was, it turns out, actually first made by Parfitt and Shepherd a hundred years later, as they straight-facedly explain:

We give [these lines] to one of the maids on stage since she seems respectful. [90]

In the same back-to-the future way, Parfitt/Shepherd post-anticipate Keller's 'Your raven will call ye [rascal]' at III.iii. 250, patting themselves on the back for it and all the other long-established edits in Nimble's speech, ll. 247-54):

MS damaged; 'yet', 'whistle' completed, 'rascal' supplied as alliteration.[91]

This account of the editors' cynical malfeasance could be extended, but there seems little point. A full report appears in my *Text and Variorum Notes* (2006).

12 *Thomas of Woodstock*, compiled by Louis Ule, reviewed by M.W.A. Smith (Oxford Text Archives)

This edition was published online ca. 1998-2001 by Oxford Text Archives (http://ota.ahds.ac.uk). As noted, it has since been repealed and replaced by a battered version of Rossiter. Compiled originally by Ule for his concordance of the play's word frequencies,[92] the text passed ultimately to Oxford,

---

[89] Parfitt and Shepherd, p. 27 n.
[90] Parfitt and Shepherd, p. 29 n. Cf. Rossiter, p. 192
[91] Parfitt and Shepherd, p. 45 n. The 'alliteration' is unclear.
[92] Louis Ule was a Marlowe scholar who developed his own text-analysis program 1960-80 for numbering word occurrences in Elizabethan plays, which he published as a *Concordance*. I am grateful to the late Eric Sams for sending me a copy. Ule took

who published it online as an OTA resource 'reviewed' by M.W.A. Smith. The site gave the following bibliographical information, possibly by Ule himself:

Woodstock, key-punched in 1968 from the 1946 edition of the manuscript by A. P. Rossiter. Modern American spelling. Proofread by Freda Dusnic, 1977. Collated with text by Wilhelmina Frijlinck (1929 ed.) to minimize Rossiter's emendations, Jan. 1978 by Louis Ule. Converted to upper/ lower case, December 1983 by Louis Ule.

As this indicates, OXF is a genuine edition, albeit the most intrusive of all. The MS is so mauled and mangled as to be hardly recognizable, and so sloppily presented that one can hardly credit a university of Oxford's reputation publishing such a travesty.

On the other hand, it was also OUP which published Armstrong's plagiarized edition. Like ARM, Ule worked principally from *Woodstock, a Moral History*, although his text is not an uncritical reprint, overruling many of Rossiter's edits, including his deletion of Bagot's 'Here comes King Richard, all go comfort him' (IV.iii.133).

This is not to say that OXF is more accurate than APR —far from it. The text's worst feature is its systematic expansion of all colloquial contractions, e.g., *I'm, 'tis, for't, you'll, we're*, etc., rewriting each in full—*I am, it is, for it, you will, we are*, and so forth.

Every apostrophe *s* has been replaced (*king's* becomes *king is*, etc.), every *'gainst* rendered *against*, every *'fore* expanded into *afore* (or sometimes *before*), and all past- and present-tense endings given their full weight as *-ed* and *-est*.

---

pride in his editing, and bequeathed many of his texts, including *Thomas of Woodstock*, to Oxford. Donald W. Foster finds Ule's Marlowe *Concordance* to be 'inaccurate.' (*Elegy by W.S.* (1989) p. 250 n.)

The Tragedy of King Richard II, Part One

The result is an ugly and pedestrian effort, unfortunately quite influential during its time online. Indeed, it does almost sound like imitation Shakespeare, which is exactly how some of its readers took it.

A single instance will have to stand for many others. At MS II.ii.176-7 Scroop says to the King:

old dooteing gray beards, fore god my lord had they not bene yor vncles, Ile brooke my counsell staffe about their heads

But Ule/Smith gives:

old doting graybeard!
before god, my lord, had they not been your uncles
I had broke my council staff about their heads.

This is obviously different from the MS in important and distorting ways. Throughout, Ule's version capriciously inserts meaningless and insensitive line breaks of this sort. First-word capitalizations are used throughout Act I, but thereafter lazily abandoned.

Inconsistencies like these lead to wholesale confusion. MS III.i.28-31, e.g., appears ambiguously as—

not if his beard were off, prethee Tressillian, off wth itt.
sfoote tho^u seest we haue not a beard amongst vs
tho^u sendst out barbars ther to poole the whole country
sfoote lett some Shaue thee

—which some editors render as verse, others as prose. Because of OXF's variable and uncertain practice, however, it's impossible to tell what its editors' intentions are:

not if his beard were off! prethee Tresilian,
off with it. sfoot, thou seest we have not a beard
amongst us! thou sendest our barbers there to poll
the whole country. sfoot, let some shave thee!

Another egregious example occurs at III.iii.183-5, where the editing completely destroys the rhythm and impact of the dangerous political ballad created and sung by a provincial schoolmaster. In MS, the verse reads:

Will ye buy any Parchment kniues
We sell for little gayne
who ere are weary of ther liues
Theyle rid them of ther payne

But OXF mechanically changes the two last lines to:

whoever are weary of their lives
they will rid them of their pain.

Additional difficulties stem from an apparently careless use of word-processors. Having rendered Ule's text into digital code, the Oxford editors made certain decisions, among them instructing their program to 'Change All' instances of a particular usage, including a capitalized *King* for *king*. This is a perfectly defensible edit, but unhappily they did not bother to check the outcome closely enough. OXF thus includes such absurdities as *bucKinghamshire* (IV.i.262) and *bucKingham* (IV.ii.185), *Kingly bones*, *Kingly spirit* and *Kingly deed* (I.iii.214, IV.i.122, IV.i.224), *speaKing* (III.iii.247), and the sudden appearance of *Kingdom* (IV.i.158) in an otherwise entirely lower-case line.

In the same bludgeoning way, the editors capitalized all instances of *grace* to read *Grace*, resulting in the obviously incorrect 'now we are all so / Brave to Grace Queen Anne,' at I.iii.139-41.

They also ordered *Anne* throughout, failing to notice that their literal-minded software obediently generated the bizarre *mAnner* at III.iii.250.

The editors apparently ran their spellcheck too with unintentionally hilarious consequences. After Queen Anne's pretty thank-you speech at their wedding, Richard tells her gallantly, according to OXF: 'Gramercy, man, thou highly honourest me!' (I.iii.36-52.)

Probably *nan* showed up in the spell-check dialogue box, with a recommendation to change to *man*, and someone thoughtlessly clicked *OK*.

It's an easy mistake, but what it indicates, of course, is that the text was never taken seriously enough to be properly proof-read. Readers interested in all OXF's minor errors, such as *mound* for *mount* (I.iii.95) and *baron's* for *barons'* (V.i.296), etc., will find them in my *Text and Variorum Notes* (2006).

At some point in the MS's history, II.iii.58-73 was deleted (a sequence including the entrance of Sir Thomas Cheney, come to summon Woodstock's duchess, who is attending the Queen). In its place Cheney is directed to enter and simply say, 'Health to your majesty!' followed by a resumption of the original text.

Most editors, including myself, reprint the deleted passage, ignoring the obviously non-authorial cut and 'Health to your majesty!' Ule/Smith, however, hamfistedly supplies both: 'but to my message: health to your majesty! my lord the Duke,' etc.

It's hard to know what to make of this, since OXF's text as it stands suggests incorrectly that it is the Queen and not the Duchess who is being summoned. The editors compound their inaccuracy by omitting the word *Madam* from the resumed lines, 'Madam, my lord the Duke / Entreats your Grace prepare with him to horse.'

There are further tell-tale indications of a generally slapdash approach.

In II.ii, just before Richard pulls off his spectacular palace revolution, two speeches, ll.20-2, 23-4, are mistakenly run together. In the same inattentive way the king's declaration at IV.i.206-8 is ludicrously assigned to Bushy:

'Tis very good. Set to your hands and seals. Tresilian we make you our deputy to receive this money. Look strictly to them, I charge ye.

As noted, the Ule/Smith edition has been removed from the OTA site, though the unreadable version of Rossiter that has replaced it is not much of an improvement.

13 Thomas *of Woodstock or Richard the Second Part One* (2002) ed. Peter Corbin and Douglas Sedge

Early in the new millennium the established team of Peter Corbin and Douglas Sedge produced a fresh edition for Manchester University Press in its well-known *Revels Plays* series.

Corbin and Sedge had worked together on similar projects for over 20 years, and *Thomas of Woodstock* displays all the hallmarks of their long collaboration, good and bad.

A workmanlike introduction reviews the main editorial issues without coming to any fresh conclusions: the MS is 'probably' a Jacobean transcription of a 1590s text, its author 'of considerable range and competence' capable of 'singular dramatic skill in providing [his] audience with a variety of dramatic tone and linguistic register.' [93] Despite this, they hastily add,

any ascription of the play to Shakespeare or any other dramatist must, however, remain highly speculative.[94]

It seems indisputable, the editors note, that the play influenced *2 Richard II*, especially in the 'telling phrases' about

---

[93] Corbin and Sedge, pp. 3, 4, 33.
[94] Corbin and Sedge, p. 4.

England becoming a 'pelting farm' and Richard its 'landlord.' Shakespeare's portrayal of John of Gaunt too, they say, 'appears to be modelled on Woodstock.'[95]

As this suggests, Corbin and Sedge evince an unusually high opinion of the work—a sign perhaps of the respect it was finally being accorded.[96] *1 Richard II* 'presents a significant democratisation of the drama' by speaking to the political concerns of its audience, and thus constitutes 'a significant advance' in opening up the processes of government to scrutiny and judgment.[97]

This is a remarkable claim for such an obscure work, and should encourage the editors of the latest *Oxford Shakespeare* to take a second and less dismissive look at it. COR approvingly references Stavropoulos's view of the masque's theatrical originality, noting that it

> does not follow the elaborate patterning of the Jacobean masque but is closer to the 'disguising' in which Henry VIII courts Anne Boleyn in [*Henry VIII*, I.iv.64-86].[98]

These observations, together with some fine critical insights in their textual notes, add weight to the case for an early composition date and the possibility of Shakespeare's hand in the play. A further mark of the editors' enthusiasm is the fact that they successfully persuaded the RSC to give a 're-

---

[95] Corbin and Sedge, p. 7.
[96] See for example Edgar Schell: *Strangers and Pilgrims: From The Castle of Perseverance to King Lear* (University of Chicago Press, 1983) pp. 77-112; Charles R. Forker (ed.): *King Richard II* (London: Arden Shakespeare, 2002), pp. 144-152; Janet C. Stavropoulos: ' "A masque is treason's license": the Design of *Woodstock*,' *Journal of the South Central Modern Language Association* (Summer, 1988) pp. 1-12; Alzada J. Tipton: ' "The Meanest Man...shall be permitted freely to accuse": The Commoners in *Woodstock*,' (*Comparative Drama*, Vol. 32, 1998), pp. 117-145).
[97] Corbin and Sedge, p. 14.
[98] Corbin and Sedge, p. 36.

hearsed reading' of their text in August, 2002 at The Swan Theatre, Stratford-on-Avon. Unfortunately, there was no follow up, so once again *1 Richard II* faded from view.

Revisions
COR's text is firmly though capriciously managed. The editors do not hesitate to intervene decisively, adding to or altering the MS as judgment and experience dictate.

By far their most successful edit, acknowledged earlier, is a redrafting of an exchange between the king and queen, revealing a series of hidden iambic pentameters:

Queen: ... They are your noble kinsmen, to revoke
The sentence were—
King: An act of folly, Nan!
Kings' words are laws: if we infringe our word,
We break our law. No more of them, sweet queen.
—*1 Richard II*, III.i.65-9

Another thoughtful redrafting occurs at III.ii.66-7,

And then the bond must afterwards be paid
That shall confirm a due debt to the king.

Corbin and Sedge notice that these lines are apparently reversed, 'since it is the blanks which confirm the debt, the bonds being paid subsequently.'[99] The editors set matters right, and again I follow.

A less visible but equally valuable rereading occurs at IV.iii.178, when Richard exits lamenting the sudden death of Queen Anne: 'My wounds are inward. Inward burn my woe!'

Rossiter, Armstrong and Parfitt/Shepherd all emend the verb to *burns*—'Inward burns my woe.' But COR retains the original, persuasively noting that the emendation 'weakens the

---

[99] Corbin and Sedge, p. 111 n.

sense of Richard's guilt which is suggested by the subjunctive mood of the MS reading.'[100]

Another useful feature of COR's edition is its routine substitution of characters' names for the generic titles given in the MS's speech-headings—*Queen*, *Bayle*, etc. The editors retrieve the full forms from the text and insert them. While harmlessly redundant in most cases (e.g., *King Richard* for *King*) these edits pay off handsomely among the smaller roles, particularly in the Dunstable scene where Cowtail, identified by name at III.iii.62, suddenly emerges as an individual from the group.

Among the MS's speech-heads he is vaguely 'Grazier,' just another face in the rustic crowd, but as Cowtail, the only named speaker, he becomes a distinct and interesting personality—the articulate one, the leader, the explainer of the Blank Charters, the mutterer of curses, and the one whose name is menacingly noted down by Nimble.

Insights and Corrections
A mark of good criticism is that it sends the reader back to the text with fresh or refreshed eyes. Several of COR's footnotes are of this quality.

At III.ii.41, for example, Lancaster bitterly complains about the minions having become 'four kings' themselves. Corbin and Sedge perceptively note that this is 'an ironic inversion of Edward III's triumph through London,'[101] recalled when his ghost laments that his grandson

Rents out my crown's revenues, racks my subjects
That spent their bloods with me in conquering France,
Beheld me ride in state through London streets,
And at my stirrup lowly footing by
Four captive kings to grace my victory.
—*1 Richard II*, V.i.93-7

[100] Corbin and Sedge, p. 159 n.
[101] Corbin and Sedge, p. 110 n.

COR's observation turns out to be extraordinarily fruitful, allowing us to trace lines of authorial and narrative development between three acknowledged Shakespeare plays—*Henry V*, *2 Richard II* and *Edward III*—and their anonymous contemporary, *1 Richard II*. These include repeated references to Edward III's famous victory parade, the legitimacy of England's lineal claim to France, followed up of course in *Henry V*, and the dire moment at Crecy Field when Edward III famously refused to send help to the Black Prince.

Earlier, in IV.i, Richard determines to abduct Woodstock, ship him secretly to the English fortress at Calais and there have him murdered. He concludes his speech with,

Beware, Plain Thomas, for King Richard comes
Resolv'd with blood to wash all former wrongs!
—*1 Richard II*, IV.i 281-2

Corbin and Sedge comment:

Whilst at the simplest level this is a statement of straightforward revenge for Woodstock's past treatment of Richard's former supporters, at another level the language suggests a striking blasphemy in its recollection of the Christian sacrifice.[102]

Again, yes. This fine critical insight comments implicitly not only upon Woodstock's murder and its narrative dynamics but, looking ahead to *2 Richard II*, reflects upon the King's own final sacrificial death. The parallels between the two are quite striking and are important intertextual references suggesting a common authorial hand.

Finally, Corbin and Sedge resolve a couple of minor textual debates and inaccuracies, among them the identity of the town of Hockley (III.iii.58), which Keller believed to be Hackley or Hacklay, and Rossiter Hockliffe in Essex. COR persuasively identifies it as Hockley-in-the-Hole, 'a village between Dunstable and Fenny Stratford which had a reputa-

---

[102] Corbin and Sedge, p. 141 n.

tion for highway robbery.'[103]

Stage Directions
Four of COR's emended stage directions are functional and/or clarifying. They include *Woodstock walks the horse* at III.ii.162, the Duchess of Gloucester *weeping* at the start of V.iii, and *Manet the King [with Greene's corpse]* at IV.iv.23. The addition at II.iii.80, noting that the Duchess of Ireland addresses her aunt, the Duchess of Gloucester, and not the Queen, may also prove helpful to readers and perhaps directors.

The rest of COR's conjectural emendations are not so useful. At IV.ii.106, the masquers' entrance, the editors vastly complicate a relatively simple matter which, in the MS, looks approximately like this (font reduced):

Enter Cheney thare com my lord
Anticke they all are wellcome Cheney: sett me a **fflorish Cornetts**
Chayre : **Dance**
we will behould ther sports in spight of care **& musique:**
cornetts. /
sound a florish, then a great shout & winding a hornes, Then Enters Cinthia

The marginal addenda, set in bold to indicate a hand other than the MS writer's, are evidently reminders by some forgotten stage manager or director to prepare these elements for the upcoming masque. COR however gives the following unhappy composite, my square brackets indicating their emendations:

Enter Cheney
Cheney. They're come, my lord.
Woodstock. They all are welcome, Cheney. Set me a chair:
We will behold their sports in spite of care.
Sound a flourish of cornets. [Enter Masquers *conducted by Cheney who exits.] Antic dance and music; then a great shout and winding o' horns. [Exeunt* Masquers.]
Then enters *Cynthia*.

[103] Corbin and Sedge, p. 120 n..

The constant entering and exiting renders this orchestration theatrically impractical. First Cheney comes on, announces the players and sets Woodstock's chair, then he leaves only to return redundantly at the head of at least eight disguised masquers (the King, three minions and four other knights 'in green, with horns about their necks and boar spears in their hands').

Cheney once more exits. The masquers shout, dance, etc., after which they too depart. Finally Cynthia comes on and delivers her prologue, which of course it no longer is because the same group of masquers then re-enter.

It's the academic version, by which I mean hopelessly impractical, justified only by the opportunity to provide scholarly notation. No company of actors in its right mind would run it in performance, especially when the original is so usably straightforward.

COR does not do much better at II.i.121ff., which in MS is without stage directions, though clearly something is required. Richard and his new councilors are in informal session when his uncle, Edmund of York, arrives to 'invite' the King to meet with Parliament—a highly political act. The theatrical task is to get him on and move the scene along. Rossiter simply and elegantly solves the problem by directing a knock at the door answered by Bagot, followed by the duke's entrance.

COR however replaces Rossiter's directions with another unclear and logistically complicated set of moves requiring the entrance and exit of a new character, a messenger, who hands a note to Bagot, who then tells the King that his uncle craves admittance.

After thinking about it, Richard says, 'go admit him,' suggesting that Bagot should exit and return with the duke, though COR provides no directions at this point. Finally they give '*Enter York*' followed by Bagot's now supererogatory,

'He comes, my lord.'[104]

Again, it's much too convoluted and certainly not better than Rossiter's solution. I see no reason to abandon a well-established and more practical approach.

On three occasions, however, Corbin and Sedge do follow Rossiter's stage directions, though unwisely.

The first is Rossiter's poorly defended excision of Green at IV.iii.142. COR's editors ignorantly believe the cut is in the original, and thus revealingly puzzle over Green's absence which, as they say, is 'odd, as he is the favourite whom one would expect to be most prominent in comforting Richard.'[105]

The second instance—their reassigning of V.i.232, 'Not too fast for falling! [*Strikes him*]' to the First Murderer, plus similar explanatory notes—is a conscious plagiarism of Rossiter. COR claims that

it is clear that it is the First Murderer who has the hammer, and that it is he, not the Second Murderer, who strikes Woodstock with it.'[106]

But this is just a thin paraphrase of Rossiter's:

MS gives this to 2 *m.*: but it is clear that No.1 has the hammer.[107]

Corbin and Sedge are thus not only wrong—the whole point is that there are no marks on Woodstock's corpse, notoriously allowing Richard to later claim that he died a natural death—but they fail to acknowledge their faulty source.

As the foregoing suggests, COR's scholarship and textual

---

[104] Corbin and Sedge, p. 83.
[105] Corbin and Sedge, p. 157 n. Exactly.
[106] Corbin and Sedge, p. 169 n.
[107] Rossiter, p. 205 n.

The Tragedy of King Richard II, Part One

readings are often poorly supported or, even worse, second-hand. These are serious charges, so I need to back them up.

At II.i.14, 'As if the sun were forced to decline,' COR footnotes:

[*decline*] *declyne* Keller (not as emendation); *delyne* MS.[108]

But this simply reproduces Rossiter's note,

MS *delyne*: Keller *declyne* (not as emendation).[109]

At III.i.95, 'Or let all our successors yet to come,' a line with a long and interesting history, COR overlooks Rossiter's successful emendation, *all*, completing the pentameter, and simply transcribes Frijlinck's superseded scholarship.

Here's COR:

[*successors*] *successessors* MS (owing to faulty correction—*succe* being interlined by another hand in darker ink above *predi* which is deleted.[110]

and here is Frijlinck:

successesso^{r}s] *sic*, owing to faulty correction: *succe* being interlined by another hand in darker ink above *predi* deleted.[111]

This is not only the crudest plagiarism, but it allows the editors to bolster their dubious claim that their observations are based on a close examination of the actual MS.

At II.i.75-88, a long reading by Bushy from a chronicle of English history, COR's explanatory footnote is a virtual

---

[108] Corbin and Sedge, p. 78 n.
[109] Rossiter, p. 187.
[110] Corbin and Sedge, 105 n.
[111] Frijlinck, p. 43 n.

transcription of the Nottingham edition's.[112]

Elsewhere, the editors fiddle gratuitously with the text. The most intrusive is the substitution at III.i.179 of *God buy ye* for MS *god boy* (*good-bye*), prompting the note,

> Either *Good-bye* or perhaps, ironically, given Tresilian's schemes, *God redeem you.*[113]

But this is mere editorial preening—an unjustifiable change permitting a smart academic comment. It is indulged in again when the editors insist on *gape* for *gate* at II.ii.208, 'make their gate wider,' followed by a footnote 'assuming' that an earlier conjecture by Rossiter is correct, which by definition cannot be certain, and then, without further evidence, since the MS is quite unambiguous, the unjustified claim that 'the scribe has misread his copy here.'[114] The scribe often misreads his copy, but not here.

COR later unwarrantedly replaces MS *stroke* (*struck*) with the obscure word *stern* (III.iii.113), despite acknowledging ultimately that 'I'm e'en struck at heart too' is probably the better version, as Frijlinck long ago pointed out.[115]

At I.i.42 the editors give *he'd've done* for MS *he'd 'a done*, altering the line's colloquial ring. In the same self-indulgent spirit they change *now* to *new* at III.i.71.

In a note to IV.i.231ff. they incorrectly take the dramatist to task for miscounting the number of territories Richard disburses among his cronies. At IV.ii.85 they give 'I'm glad to hear your grace addicted so,' instead of MS, 'I'm glad to see,' etc.

---

[112] Corbin and Sedge, p. 80 n., Parfitt and Shepherd, p. 20 n.
[113] Corbin and Sedge, p. 108 n.
[114] Corbin and Sedge, p. 93 n.
[115] Corbin and Sedge, p. 123 n.

COR's carelessness becomes increasingly marked in the later acts: either the editors' interest flagged, or they divided the work between themselves and whoever had responsibility for the latter half felt less committed than his partner. I found only one minor error in Act I (*nourishèd* at I.iii.169, where MS gives *norisht*), but five in Acts III-V: *yet* for *ye* at III.i.13; solecestic commas after *Let* (III.i.5), *we'll* for *we* at IV.iii.8; *owest* for *ow'st* at V.i.155; and a full stop in the middle of a sentence at V.vi.13-14 ('Our proclamations soon shall find him forth. The root and ground of all these vile abuses.')

The edition's references also contain minor errors following the same pattern. The most revealing is a footnote to V.i.34, which claims that *I protest* replaces MS *I swear*. In fact, wisely it does not. Perhaps at one point the editors intended the substitution, then changed their minds, later proofreading so sloppily that the old note was left in place.[116]

A Note on the Final Scene
The present edition of *1 Richard II* contains what may be the longest conjectural emendation in Elizabethan dramatic literature—V.vi.37-159 or 122 lines.

I am of course very conscious of my limitations, especially as I think the play is by the world's greatest playwright and poet, justifying my efforts on the grounds that half a loaf is better than none. A finish tying up at least some of plot's loose ends may mean more frequent performances, leading to the play's acceptance as the forgotten masterpiece it is.

It's also not strictly true that I wrote the scene's conclusion without help. Because I believe *1 Richard II* to be Shakespeare's, I took as much as possible from his own treatment of Woodstock's death, a theme running all the way from the opening of *2 Richard II* through *Henry V* and the night before Agincourt.

---

[116] Corbin and Sedge, p. 161 n.

I also used, or transfused, lines and phrases from earlier moments in *1 Richard II*, together with appropriate references to *Macbeth, Hamlet*, and other works. My joke is that I am Shakespeare's most recent collaborator.[117]

Finally, the really fun part, I adjusted my conclusion in the light of requests from the director and actors at Emerson College, Boston, who performed an earlier version of my text and conclusion in March-April 2002.[118]

Among other opportunities, this gave me a first-hand sense of how Elizabethan dramatists probably worked. Speeches I'd originally assigned to John of Gaunt, for example, were transferred during rehearsal to his gentler brother, Edmund of York, and I unhesitatingly accepted these judgments. I was also asked to 'toughen up' Richard's handling of his uncles, and complied.

Some time later I incorporated Corbin and Sedge's suggestion that the Duke of York, who is puzzlingly absent from the final scene's opening stage directions, subsequently enters as the captive king's escort.[119]

Bold Speculations
Editors and literary commentators have often speculated about the drama's resolution and Richard's fate. All the elements appear to be given by the play itself, the historical record, and *2 Richard II*, which of course begins almost immediately afterwards with Bullingbrook demanding Richard's accountability for their sainted uncle's murder.

Keller, whose introduction was the play's first critical

---

[117] A full list of my borrowings appears in *1 Richard II*, Vol. I, *Background and Synopsis* (2006).
[118] http://www.theatermirror.com/towecr.htm
[119] Corbin and Sedge, pp. 38, 185 n. The editors also include an interesting Appendix suggesting possible doubled roles, pp. 219-20.

appraisal, noted about the missing conclusion that unless

the king appears once more to confront the Lords…the
piece suffers both literary-historical and aesthetic loss. [120]

Similarly, Corbin and Sedge comment that in IV.iv.49-56, Richard's remorse and 'recognition of his crimes,'

may perhaps prepare the way for the play's resolution in terms of repentance and uneasy truce between the king and his nobles, but since the text is incomplete this must remain speculative.[121]

The critic Michael Mannheim hypothesizes with greater imagination and historical awareness:

The lost ending of the play certainly involves reconciliation of some kind between Richard and his rebellious uncles, but any treatment of Richard's reign also assumes audience knowledge that he would one day be deposed, and the possibility of deposition hardly seems unwelcome in *Woodstock*.[122]

This too seems reasonable, since Richard II's deposition and the Wars of the Roses were among the most famous historical narratives in Elizabethan England. The Roses were their civil war, Henry VII their Lincoln, and its constitutional issues continued to dominate his granddaughter's political life. 'I am Richard II. Know yet not that?' she once famously said.

David Bevington also observes:

Although Woodstock goes to his death still wishing Richard's safety, his brothers evidently (although the manuscript is imperfect) extort from Richard some of the conditions for which they

---

[120] Keller, p. 121
[121] Corbin and Sedge, p. 4.
[122] Michael Mannheim: 'The Weak King History Play of the Early 1590s' (*Renaissance Drama* n.s. Vol. II, 1969) p. 253.

have fought.[123]

As elsewhere, Edgar Schell intelligently explores the play's dramatic and political issues, implicitly tying *1 Richard II* to its great successor:

It is unlikely that Richard himself is either deposed or killed at the end of *Woodstock*. The well-known facts of his deposition by Henry Bullingbrook and subsequent death, argue against that. And while there is some ambiguity about the intention of Lancaster and York (it is not clear how far they mean to go to avenge Woodstock's murder) on the whole their aims seem to be as limited as they were in act 1. What they seem to seek is the restoration of the King's body politic: the purgation of its wanton humors and the return of mature wisdom to the council. Those, at least, are the demands they make on Richard when they confront him just before the battle in act 5, scene 3. It seems likely, then, that the play ended as generations of morality plays had ended, with Richard passing back under the control of his uncles, who have expelled from the Body Politic those who urged him towards vanity. If it did, the playwright deftly negotiated a passage between the claims of historical truth and the political dangers of seeming to advocate the deposition even of a tyrant; for he has dramatized the logic by which Richard historically deposed himself without ever showing him deposed. But if Richard did come to rest under the guidance of his uncles at the end of the play, it is difficult o believe that he did so willingly. He is more likely to have been a prisoner than a penitent. [124]

Most of these speculations are persuasive and moreover broadly consistent with the contemporary sources which almost certainly shaped the play's ending. Contrary to its current reputation among academics, *1 Richard II* is a very well-researched and historically accurate drama, consistent

---

[123] David Bevington: *Tudor Drama and Politics* (1965) p. 253.
[124] Edgar Schell: *Strangers and Pilgrims*, pp. 104-5. Schell later notes: 'Historically, [the Lords'] victory meant a return to the Good Parliament of 1387.' (*Ibid.*, p. 204.)

with what we know about Shakespeare, and drawing on all the same rare sources he consulted for *2 Richard II*.[125]

Analyzing the insurrection of 1387-8 and exploring its consequences were Anon's principal objectives, accomplished with an unusually high level of scholarly inquiry. *1 and 2 Richard II* are perhaps the most thoroughly researched history plays in the entire corpus of the Elizabethan theatre. Their authors read the same books and came to the same conclusions, including the importance of understanding the first part of Richard II's reign in order to appreciate the catastrophe of the second.

It must be added that the second drama depends in almost all essential matters of early fact upon the historical analysis (right or wrong) of the first. These include Woodstock's plain and simple personality, his faux 'confession' put out by Richard after his death, and the transparent lie that he died of natural causes after being kidnapped and imprisoned in Calais.

Also carefully researched is the depiction of Richard II's flamboyant sadomasochism, his bisexuality and favoritism, the outrage of the Blank Charters, his self-subjection to the law, his criminal leasing out of the kingdom like to a tenement or pelting farm, his notorious bodyguard of archers, his destruction of Sheen in a fit of grief over Anne's death and, above all, his deadly political rivalry with Woodstock and its historic outcome. The nobility did rise up in 1387, the king was defeated at Radcot Bridge, his closest associates were executed by the Merciless Parliament and, after a brief deposition, he was restored as (in effect) England's first constitutional monarch. In history's long view, and Shakespeare/

---

[125] Documenting this is a lengthy matter not appropriate here, but please see 'The Dramatist as Historian' in the introduction to my *1 Richard II* (2006). Independent studies showing the depth and breadth of Shakespeare's scholarship in *2 Richard II* include Matthew W. Black: 'Sources of Shakespeare *Richard II*' (1948) pp. 199-216, and Dover Wilson, *ed. cit.*, pp. lxi, xxxviii-lxiv.

Anon's, Woodstock was the first Lancastrian casualty in the Wars of the Roses.

Nigel Saul summarizes the historical situation after Radcot Bridge in 1387:

When the King was suitably chastened [the Lords] made a number of demands on him. Knighton reports their insistence on the arrest and imprisonment of the five appellees. Walsingham, offering a different view, says that they required him to attend a council meeting at Westminster the next day; Richard, lachrymose and confused, initially agreed but then changed his mind and in the end only submitted under threat of deposition. The suggestion of deposition is picked up by the Westminster writer, who gives us a picture of difficult and prolonged crisis. The Lords, the writer says, rebuked Richard for his duplicity and misgovernance, and gave a clear warning that he must correct his mistakes and rule better in the future. The chronicle of Whalley Abbey, Lancashire, suggests that for a brief while Richard actually ceased to reign. On entering the Tower, the chronicler says, the Lords deposed Richard and for some three days he was deprived of his crown. Gloucester and his nephew Derby [i.e., Bullingbrook] could not agree on which of them was to take his place and in the end he was restored to his title.[126]

Based on the foregoing, our play's internal dynamics, and the requirements of *2 Richard II*, the necessary elements for a strong, theatrical conclusion are that (i) Tresilian must be hanged, (ii) Woodstock's murder publicly revealed and at least partly avenged, and (iii) the arrested king forcefully reprimanded but restored. This sequence also makes dramatic sense.

1. Tresilian

As the story's chief villain, architect of the despised Blank Charters scam, and the man responsible for 'more wrangling i' the land than all the wars has done these seven years' (V. ii.37-8), Tresilian must clearly be arraigned and dispatched.

---

[126] Saul, *Richard II*, p. 189.

Everything in history and the play's foreshadowings require it. When Woodstock first hears of the Blank Charters, he wishes that 'he were hang'd that first devis'd them,' (III.ii. 242). Even the harmless Schoolmaster sings:

Blank Charters they are call'd—
A vengeance on the villain!
—1 *Richard II*, III.iii.186-7

Finally, just before Nimble drags him on stage, perhaps with a Godot-style rope around his neck, Lancaster says, in the play's characteristically back-to-the-future way:

Had we Tresilian hang'd, then all were sure!
—1 *Richard II*, V.vi.10.

And in historic fact, Tresilian was captured, tried and executed by the Merciless Parliament of 1388.

There are so many ironies at this point in the play (justice judged, the accuser accused, the silencer silenced, the master mastered, etc.) that I cannot imagine any dramatist not cashing in at least a few.

At all events, I couldn't resist. Tresilian is sent whimpering to his fate, damned both by poetic and military justice and with the play's grimmest running joke—'God Bless my Lord Tresilian!'—ringing in his ears.

2. Woodstock's Murder

As we have noted, Richard's troublesome uncle died under highly suspicious circumstances while in the monarch's custody after being kidnapped and transported to France. His relatives maintained that he'd been killed in such a way as to make his death appear natural. The play agrees. 'Never was murder done with such rare skill' (V.i.258-9), his assassins gloat.

Since *1 Richard II* is loyal to the Lancastrian cause, it is thus likely that the final scene included some kind of evidence to support their claim of a politically motivated murder. This appears in the form of Tresilian's warrant commanding that 'no marks nor violence show upon him, that we may say he naturally died' (V.vi.44-5).

Tresilian's written orders provide a number of theatrical opportunities.

First, it seems appropriate and in keeping with the play's spirit that a lawyer and a man who lived by crafting crafty documents—among them the Blank Charters and the contract turning England into a 'pelting farm'—should die by one ironically bearing his own signature.

Secondly, his warrant effortlessly reopens and makes historic the matter of Gloucester's assassination, giving the audience clear proof of Tresilian's guilt, and so cleaning the Lords' hands of his and Lapoole's executions.

I assume Bushy, Scroop and Lapoole are on stage for a purpose, and that there is also a reason why we've been told, 'King Richard's been taken prisoner by the peers' (V.v.9).

As Woodstock's proximate assassin, Lapoole must be present to be tried and condemned along with Tresilian. Both he and the king have already unwittingly forecast his fate— Richard threatens his execution should he allow Woodstock to be killed (IV.iii.175-6), while Lapoole himself says, 'The black reward of death is traitor's pay!' (V.i.285). And so he goes.

This gives us two executions for Woodstock's death—a satisfactory but not gratuitously bloody ratio. Scroop and Bushy are relatively guiltless, but they must be present for the interrogation—in effect, Richard's trial—helping both to implicate and excuse him. It is after all to Bushy that Richard says

Send post to Calais and bid Lapoole forbear
On pain of life to act our sad decree.

For heaven's love, go prevent the tragedy!
—*1 Richard II*, IV.iii.175-7

Bushy testifies to this and thus gets Richard partly off the hook, preparing the way for the drama's dénouement—the fate of the king and his kingdom.

3. Deposition and Restoration

When Richard's minions are questioned, they first turn on one another and then, self-seeking cowards that they are, lay all the blame upon him, fulfilling York's prophetic 'Thou lean'st on staves that will at length deceive thee' (II.ii.137).

This allows us to bring Richard back on stage—the moment, of course, that everyone has been waiting for.

The King's trial and reconciliation with the Lords has to be the climax of the play, since it is the event about which the whole of the action and the beginning of *2 Richard II* revolves. Accompanied by the Duke of York, he is led on stage in chains and forced to account for Woodstock's death, together with his general mismanagement of the kingdom. This is something the uncles have repeatedly threatened direly, and so must be honored:

If he [Woodstock] be dead, by good King Edward's soul,
We'll call King Richard to a strict account
For that, and for his realm's misgovernment.
—*1 Richard II*, V.iii.19-21

Yet Richard's guilt is ambiguous, as the play suggests, so he is allowed ambiguously to excuse himself and ambiguously to be forgiven (V.vi.90-5). In keeping with this and other outcomes also promised earlier—

Let him revoke the proclamations,
Clear us of all supposed crimes of treason,
Reveal where our good brother Gloucester keeps,
And grant that these pernicious flatterers

May by the law be tried...
—*1 Richard II*, V.iii.114-118

and

[Richard must] learn to govern like a virtuous prince,
Call home his wise and reverend councilors and
Thrust from his court those cursed flatterers
That hourly works this realm's confusion.
—*1 Richard II*, V.i.193-6

—he is forced to dismiss his minions, repeal the charges of treason against the old nobility, and admit them back into the country's governing council.

A passage from Holinshed is relevant here. It describes the negotiations between the King and Gloucester's brothers after his death, the dukes having 'assembled their powers to resist the king's dealings.' The historian continues:

There went messengers betwixt him [Richard] and the dukes, which being men of honour did their indeavour to appease both parties. The King discharged himself of blame for the duke of Glocester's death, considering that he had gone about to breake the truce, which he had taken with France, and also stirred the people of the realme to rebellion, and further had sought the destruction and loss of his life, that was his souereign and lawfull King. Contrarilie, the dukes affirmed, that their brother was wrong-fullie put to death, hauing done nothing worthie of death. At length, by the intercession and meanses of those noble men that went to and fro betwixt them, they were accorded, & the King promised from thenceforth to do nothing but by the assent of the dukes, but he kept small promise in this behalfe, as after well appeared.[127]

Corbin and Sedge also refer to this passage, observing that there must obviously be some sort of political reconciliation and restoration of the *status quo ante*:

---

[127] Holinshed, *Chronicles* II, pp. 838-9

The Tragedy of King Richard II, Part One

It seems unlikely, however, that the lost ending of the play could actually have involved the deposition of Richard, since his successor, Bullingbrook, is not active in the drama (or even mentioned) so no preparation for a change of monarch has been established. The most likely scenario is that Nimble's comic interlude with which the manuscript breaks off would have been followed by York's entry with the defeated King. York is a much more conciliatory character than his brothers, regarded by Richard as 'gentle, mild and generous' [II.i.125], and he has already interceded between Richard and Woodstock. It is fitting, therefore, that he should perform the delicate business of leading in the 'captive' Richard and effect a general reconciliation with the King.[128]

Richard is thus ambiguously restored to the throne we find him precariously occupying at the start of *2 Richard II*.

In Act II the entire movement of the play is summed up by the King himself in an unconscious prophesy:

Here, uncles, take the crown from Richard's hand
And once more place it on our kingly head.
—*1 Richard II*, II.ii.113-14

The drama ends with a weakened monarch apprehensively facing an uncertain future, which the historical record bears out. May McKissak notes:

On 31 May [1388] Richard entertained the parliament at his manor of Kennington; and on 3 June there was an impressive ceremony at Westminster Abbey when, after mass, lords and commons renewed their oaths of allegiance and Richard promised to be 'a good King and lord,' for the future…In June 1388 many must have hoped, and some may even have believed, that the worst troubles of the reign were over.[129]

---

[128] Corbin and Sedge, p. 38
[129] May McKisssak, *The Fourteenth Century 1307-1399*, pp. 459, 461.

Index

Act to Restrain Abuses of
Players 201
Anthony and Cleopatra 223
Armstrong, Ray 247
Armstrong, William A 182,
215, 218, 233, 243, 250,
251, 252, 257, 263
Bevington, David 273, 274
Black, Matthew W 204
Boas, F.S. 180, 181, 221, 242
British Library 7, 180, 185, 234
Bullen, A.H 182, 221, 227
Bullough, Geoffrey 182, 244,
245, 246, 247
Carpenter, Frederick I 169, 182,
185, 189, 227, 228, 229,
230, 231, 233, 242, 244, 249
Cartwright, William 180
Chambers, E.K. 180, 181, 240
Charlemont, Lord 180
Corbin, Peter 168, 170, 182,
184, 190, 236, 261, 262,
263, 264, 265, 266, 268,
269, 270, 271, 272, 273,
280, 281
See also Sedge
Cronica Tripertita, 199
Dean, James 200
Dogberry 170, 171, 195, 247
Dulwich College 180
Edmund Ironside 180
Egan, Michael 7, 183, 184
Egerton 1994 7, 180, 181, 205,
213, 247
Elizabeth I 174, 201
Equus 208
Essex, Earl of 35, 52, 56, 68,
105, 106, 162, 164, 201,
238, 265
Everitt, E.B 178, 181, 182, 184,
187, 215, 218, 247, 248,
249, 250, 252, 253, 255
Frijlinck, Wilhelmina P 168,
181, 183, 184, 185, 186,
188, 189, 200, 204, 217,
219, 220, 225, 227, 230,
231, 232, 236, 242, 244,
253, 255, 257, 269, 270
Gower, John 199
Greg, W.W 188, 231
Halliwell, J.O 168, 171, 181,
182, 183, 184, 185, 186,
187, 188, 193, 213, 214,
215, 216, 217, 218, 219,
220, 221, 222, 224, 225,
226, 227, 228, 229, 231,
232, 233, 235, 238, 241,
252, 255, 256
Hamlet 170, 179, 181, 192, 197,
244, 247, 272
Hammond, Michael 208
Hamper, William 199
Hodges, C. Walter 207
Holinshed, 163, 175, 212, 234,
280
Hook, Frank S 189
Jacke Straw 167, 203
Jackson, Macdonald P 197
James I, 201
Kantorowicz, Ernst H 209
Keller, Wolfgang 168, 180, 181,
183, 184, 185, 186, 187,
188, 189, 193, 216, 217,
218, 220, 221, 222, 223,
224, 225, 226, 227, 228,
229, 230, 231, 232, 233,
235, 236, 238, 240, 241,
242, 244, 249, 255, 256,
265, 269, 272, 273
King Lear 181, 210, 222, 262
Macaronic 198
Macbeth 196, 224, 272
Malone Society 181, 183, 184,
230, 237
Mannheim, Michael 273
Marshall, F.A 204
Merciless Parliament 275, 277
McKissak, May 159, 281
Much Ado About Nothing 195,
239
Muir, Kenneth 204
Mum and the Sothsegger 198
On the Times 197, 198

Osric, 169, 197, 198, 244, 246
Parfitt, George 183, 224, 233, 252, 253, 254, 255, 256, 263, 270
See also Shepherd
Partridge, A.C. 200, 201
Peele, George 189
Plowden, Edmund 151, 179, 209, 220, 225, 229
Polonius, 222
Ribner, Irving 181
Richard the Redeless, 198, 199
Robinson, Ian 205
Rossiter, A.P. 163, 168, 170, 181, 182, 184, 185, 186, 188, 193, 195, 197, 200, 201, 205, 210, 211, 212, 216, 217, 218, 221, 223, 224, 225, 226, 227, 229, 233, 234, 235, 236, 237, 238, 239, 240, 241, 242, 243, 244, 249, 250, 251, 252, 253, 254, 255, 256, 257, 261, 263, 265, 267, 268, 269, 270
Rowley, Samuel 197
Sams, Eric 180, 233, 256
Saul, Nigel 159, 276
Schell, Edgar 209, 262, 274
Sedge, Douglas 168, 170, 182, 184, 190, 236, 261, 262, 263, 264, 265, 266, 268, 269, 270, 271, 272, 273, 280, 281
See also Corbin
Shaffer, Peter 208
Shakespeare 168, 180, 181, 182, 183, 193, 199, 201, 202, 203, 204, 205, 206, 210, 211, 213, 214, 221, 227, 228, 231, 234, 235, 239, 240, 242, 243, 244, 247, 252, 258, 261, 262, 265, 271, 272, 275, 276
Shepherd Simon 183, 224, 233, 252, 253, 254, 255, 256, 263, 270
See also Parfitt
Steiner, George 180, 190
Swan Theatre, 207, 263
The King's Two Bodies 209
Ther is a Busche that is Foregrow 199
Trump, Donald 210
Two Gentlemen of Verona 206
Ule, Louis 183, 233, 234, 256, 257, 258, 259, 260, 261
Verges, 247
Wilson, J Dover 177, 204, 212, 275
Wright, William 197, 200